# Design and
# National Identity

# Design and National Identity

Javier Gimeno-Martínez

**Bloomsbury Academic**
An imprint of Bloomsbury Publishing Plc

B L O O M S B U R Y
LONDON · OXFORD · NEW YORK · NEW DELHI · SYDNEY

**Bloomsbury Academic**

An imprint of Bloomsbury Publishing Plc

| 50 Bedford Square | 1385 Broadway |
| London | New York |
| WC1B 3DP | NY 10018 |
| UK | USA |

**www.bloomsbury.com**

**BLOOMSBURY and the Diana logo are trademarks of Bloomsbury Publishing Plc**

First published 2016

© Javier Gimeno-Martínez, 2016

Javier Gimeno-Martínez has asserted his right under the Copyright, Designs and Patents Act, 1988, to be identified as Author of this work.

**British Library Cataloguing-in-Publication Data**

A catalogue record for this book is available from the British Library.

| ISBN | HB: | 978-1-4725-9104-3 |
| | PB: | 978-1-4725-9103-6 |
| | ePDF: | 978-1-4725-9105-0 |
| | epub: | 978-1-4725-9106-7 |

**Library of Congress Cataloging-in-Publication Data**

A catalog record for this book is available from the Library of Congress.

Cover design by Louise Dugdale
Cover image © Kimberley Coole/Getty images

Typeset by RefineCatch Limited, Bungay, Suffolk
Printed and bound in Great Britain

# Contents

# List of Illustrations

# Acknowledgements

This book has gradually taken shape over several years of reading and teaching, and has been encouraged by the influences and support of many people. Special thanks must go to my colleagues at the Vrije University Amsterdam for their support and to Bert Watteeuw who shared with me the seventeenth-century pictures shown in Chapter 1. In preparing the book itself, I have benefitted enormously from the criticism and advice of my PhD students Joana Ozorio de Almeida Meroz and Katarina Serulus. The reading group sessions at the University of Hertfordshire with Steven Adams, Grace Lees-Maffei, Pat Simpson and Barbara Brownie were extremely helpful. The book would have not been possible without the contributions of the many students from the MA-programme Design Cultures at the Vrije University Amsterdam whom I have taught over the past few years. Special thanks go to the students that have worked on themes related to national identity, especially to Laurens van den Broek, Janna van der Linden, Federica Mantoan, Georgie Sinclair and Shanna Soh. The book owes a great deal to them. As always, however, the responsibility for the views expressed herein and for the text's deficiencies is all mine. I should perhaps add that my research has explored design in Belgium, the Netherlands and Spain. This admission may help to explain some of the book's biases and choices of examples.

# Introduction

This book examines the literature on national identity in the humanities and social sciences, and elaborates an analytical framework for the relation between design and national identity. The structure is based on three theoretical approaches to the study of national identity. These theories are illustrated with examples from the history of design, with a focus on the period from the early nineteenth century to the present day. The book thereby explores the role of design from the formation of the modern idea of the nation to its intertwinement with forms of subnationalism and globalization. Although one might expect the emergence of global culture to lead to an erosion of national identity, on the contrary, new national cultures have continued to appear over the last three decades. Historians and social scientists have explored the mechanisms that forge a given national identity and the role that the creative industries play in this process. For example, authors have focused on factors such as money and other symbols of the state (e.g. Gilbert 1999; Unwin & Hewitt 2001; Raento et al. 2004; Raento & Brunn 2005); but also on the more mundane practices associated with nationalism (e.g. Edensor 2002; Jones & Desforges 2003; Haldrup et al. 2006; Jones & Merriman 2009, pp. 165–6).

Since the publication of the social psychologist Michael Billig's *Banal Nationalism* (1995), theorists of nationalism and national identity have turned their attention to the study of everyday life and popular culture (Palmer 1998; Skey 2009). Billig proposed that the field of enquiry be expanded beyond high culture to incorporate the everyday symbols that lay at the centre of modernist theorists. Later, the geographer Tim Edensor (2002) sought to link nationalism to everyday life. He advocates an analysis of nationalism from below, in which the citizen is the focus of analysis. The specific nature of design is very much connected to everyday life, but there is an attempt to reach beyond this framework to connect design with processes of nation-building and state-related initiatives. The role of design in theories of nationalism and national identity is not merely relegated to 'banal nationalism' and 'nationalism from below'. On the contrary, design plays a role in top-down processes of nation-building, to which modernist theories of national identity are still applicable and valid. The same is true of primordialist or essentialist theories of nationalism, which help us to understand how design might be perceived as related to national identity. The three theoretical approaches presented in this book do not exclude one another, but are complementary approaches that allow us to form a proper understanding of the manifold connections between design and national identity.

Studies of the relation between national identity and design have been carried out by both design historians (e.g. Crowley 1992; Goodrum 2005; Narotzky 2007; Yagou 2007; Kikuchi & Lee 2014) and more generalist historians (Jones & Merriman 2009; Penrose 2011). Since historians without a background in design have contributed to studies of design, one might wonder how the history of design could contribute to understandings of nationalism. The political scientist Benedict Anderson wrote in his book *Imagined Communities* that '[c]ommunities are to be distinguished, not by their falsity/genuineness, but by the style in which they are imagined' (Anderson 1991[1983]: 6). In turn, Billig has stated that 'more detailed, empirical investigation will still be required, in order to show the operations of banal nationalism in their detail' (Billig 1995: 9). These two authors argue for more interpretation of national symbols and analysis of their circulation. Design historians are well equipped to do this, as their methodologies include the interpretation of symbols and their circulation. Design history examines the life-cycle of objects from their production to their consumption, and the changes in meaning experienced in each phase. Moreover, the focus of design history ranges from 'high design' to everyday objects, which seems a good foundation on which to expand our knowledge of the mechanisms of banal nationalism.

# National histories of design

National histories of design have been a common format to reflect on design history. There are a myriad of examples related to diverse countries and any attempt to enumerate them would imply to forget many others. If examples are numerous, reflections on their underlying mechanisms and theoretical foundations are less abundant. One of them is John A. Walker's *Design History and the History of Design* (1989). In its chapter entitled 'Varieties of Design History', different methodologies and approaches are discussed, ranging from social history to structuralism. National origin has been a recurrent method to group objects in exhibitions and publications. Nevertheless, the multiple nationalities of products – designed, produced and consumed in different countries – have challenged narrow pigeonholing of products in national categories. Whatever the criterion chosen, reality seems to be difficult for strict categorization. Walker pinpoints the nationality of designers as a common criterion to classify objects within national categories, only to later acknowledge that, for example, British designers working in Italy would actually contribute to define Italian design, and not British design (Walker 1989: 122). It is, therefore, that the concept of nationality as related to design needs to be revised and updated constantly to avoid oversimplifications.

Walker acknowledges how national design has been reduced to stereotypes. Examples of these are Nikolaus Pevsner's *The Englishness of English Art* (1956) or Jonathan Glancey's exhibition catalogue *National Characteristics in Design* (1985, see Chapter 3). These works reduce national design to a bunch of national characteristics related to apparently ahistorical and essential traits of the nation such as climate, geography, ethnicity or character. Even when this categorization is often contested, it is still a recurrent aspect in national histories of design. Walker concludes that in many cases alleged national peculiarities, such as German efficiency, are the result of pointing to the 'worldview of the dominant group in a particular society' (Walker 1989: 123). Needless to say, the consolidation of a dominant group is not necessarily representative of the whole nation. As soon as the multi-layered character of nations becomes recognized, the more stereotypes fall short in crystallizing a nation.

National histories of design have been seen as reproducing dominant visions of the nation but also as an antidote against reductive histories of design. Similarly to Walker, Gregory Votolato reflected on various approaches within design history in his book *American Design in the Twentieth Century* (1998). He acknowledges that national minorities have contributed to evidence the mythical nature of the nation. He opposes studies of Adirondak and Pueblo traditions as opposed to dominant, homogeneous narratives of American design. Their traditions do not fit in with general narratives of American design, yet are constitutive of it. His conclusion is that 'any serious analysis of nationalism must take account of a range of attitudes, from national flag-waving and regional "boosterism" to subcultural and minority values' (Votolato 1998: 268). On the other hand, Tony Fry wrote his *Design History Australia* (1988) to contest design historical accounts in which only a few countries were represented, what he called 'a single global history with a few dominant powers at its centre' (Fry 1988: 14). This claim referred to a Pevsnerian historiographic tradition in which some countries such as Britain, Italy, Germany and the United States seemed to guide the developments of design history; meanwhile many others remained unmentioned. If the former position contested national histories of design as reductive visions of the nation, the latter defended their capacity in expanding the geographies of design history. This double nature, both conformist and revisionist, has marked the further development of national histories of design.

A debate on a proper globalization of design history emerged in the late 1990s with the ICDHS conferences, starting in Barcelona in 1999 and the Globalising

Art, Architecture and Design History (GLAADH) at the University of Sussex, the Open University and Middlesex University (2001–2003). Both projects sought to expand the geographical framework in which design history had developed until then. The former organized conferences in countries in which design history had been less developed. The latter sought to encourage and embed cultural diversity in the design history curriculum (Gieben-Gamal 2005). Their reflection on the global has touched upon the national, too. If to some extent national histories of design have expanded the geography of design, their validity to reflect global dynamics has been put into question. For example, Jonathan Woodham suggests looking at world design organizations such as the International Council of Societies of Industrial Design (ICSID) and the International Council of Graphic Design Associations (ICOGRADA) in order to research 'a more comprehensive and inclusive geographical and cultural spread of design activity' (Woodham 2005: 263). He argues that these organizations supersede the limits of national units and reveal otherwise undisclosed interconnections. Similarly, Jilly Traganou proposes to abandon an orthodox focus on the nation-state to acknowledge conditions of internal diversity and transnational networks that constitute the national (Traganou 2011b: 166). She argues that internal diversity of the nation is often downplayed. Furthermore, international dynamics are necessary to understand the national and therefore a revision of this format needs to be undertaken.

National histories of design have not ceased to appear in recent years, both regarding countries that have been previously included in general design histories such as Germany and Britain (Buckley 2007; Aynsley 2009), and also regarding countries that had been traditionally excluded, such as Argentina, Colombia or Croatia (Devalle 2009; Buitrago Trujillo 2012; Vukić 2015). The first group might be characterized by a rather revisionist and higher self-reflexive character. Not only the national but also the regional has been revised in Kjetil Fallan's *Scandinavian Design. Alternative Histories* (2012). His book was not looking for common traits to define 'Scandinavian-ness' but to revise a generated mythology about design from the region. To achieve this goal, he offered 'alternative histories' to a widely researched topic (Fallan 2012: 5). Nevertheless, this book defended regions and nations as an analytical unit because of being valid categories for 'demarcation and identity' (Fallan 2012: 5). Indeed, if the world is organized in nations, then this might still be a defining issue for design, too. The same author, along with Grace Lees-Maffei, defended again the nation as a 'tried-and-tested unit of analysis' (Fallan & Lees-Maffei 2013: 2). Paradoxically, its apparent invariability has been the major critique towards the nation. A deep analysis of the nation and national design as a unit of analysis can actually reconsider their validity as an analytical unit and reveal a diversity of conceptualizations.

The very formulation of what is understood as 'design' has had an impact on what nations to include in general narratives. As D.J. Huppatz explains, there has been a shift from 'artefacts conceived by professional designers and produced by mechanized mass production' towards design as 'the creation of useful artefacts in general' (Huppatz 2015: 188). Consequently, narratives of industrialization and post-industrialization are less relevant when deciding what nations have been more design-intensive. This is manifest in Pat Kirkham and Susan Weber's book, *History of Design. Decorative Arts and Material Culture, 1400–2000* (2013), whose chronological and geographical coverage includes fields that previously belonged to the decorative arts and ethnology. The chronological framework of Victor Margolin's *World History of Design* (2015) stretches back even further to pre-history. As far as sub-fields of design are concerned, Kirkham and Weber's book mainly covers furniture, product design, graphic design, dress and crafts. Margolin's account covers most of these areas too, but includes technological devices and excludes dress. The geographical scope of both books is inclusive, although Kirkham and Weber do not cover Oceania.

When discussing national histories of design, Walker referred to the theories formulated by Benedict Anderson and Ernest Gellner (Walker 1989: 119–20). The interconnection between design history and the scholarship about nationalism seems necessary when conceptualizing national design properly. Likewise, the present book builds bridges between theories of nationalism and design history and theory. Theories of national identity are illustrated with examples from design history in an attempt to reconsider what is national design. These examples are intended to be as global as possible and are always illustrative of these theoretical approaches. Following Kirkham and Weber, the disciplines covered in the book include furniture, product design, graphic design, dress and crafts. The ultimate goal of this book is to rethink what is national design and accordingly what is the object of study of national histories of design.

# Thinking about nationalism

Primordialist theories of nationalism derive from the work of the pre-Romantic philosopher Johan Gottfried von Herder (1744–1803). Herder presented the nation as the 'Volksgeist'; a natural, organic being that had always existed, but that had only recently become an object of study. For Herder, the essence of the nation was embodied in its language: 'nun wird die Sprache schon Stamm' (for an analysis of Herder, see Smith 1993: 64). This was the beginning of a historical tradition whose defenders were themselves nationalists, who sought the objective 'roots' of the nation (read, their 'own' nation). As Billig has noted, this identification between the nation and language becomes problematic when analysing the incongruity between national boundaries and philological divisions, since perfectly comprehensible languages are considered different according to political divisions (Danish, Norwegian and Swedish), and incomprehensible dialects become derivations of the same language as a result of political unification (for example, the Gegh and Tosk dialects of Albanian) (Billig 1995: 32). Consequently, language seems to be one of the pretexts that underpins a nation, rather than being its crucial cause.

During the 1960s, authors from the post-colonial school began to study the configuration of nations in former colonies, since territories in which nations had not previously existed were reproducing nation-states in the process of gaining independence. Paradoxically, instead of going back to a pre-colonial division of territory and political authority, post-colonial countries embraced the legacy of the colonial powers; that is, the political structure of the nation-state. The imposition of the nation-state as a political organization provided a broad range of material for analysing the nation as a 'cultural' convention, rather than as a 'natural' fact. Several authors, such as Frantz Fanon (1961), Albert Memmi (1957) and Kwame Nkrumah (1964), published work on the effects of colonization in Algeria, Tunisia and Ghana. With them came the first constructionist approaches to nationalism. For example, Elie Kedourie (1926–1992) wrote in 1960:

> . . . nationalism is a doctrine invented in Europe at the beginning of the nineteenth century . . . Briefly, the doctrine holds that humanity is naturally divided into nations, that nations are known by certain characteristics which can be ascertained, and that the only legitimate type of government is national self-government.
>
> Kedouri quoted in ÖZKIRIMLI 2000: 52

Edward Said (1978) later became the best-known exponent of this constructionist approach. Said analysed colonization as a cultural process and explored the new geo-cultural relationships that were established between the ex-colonized and the ex-colonizers.

During the early 1980s, the study of nationalism gained important contributions in the works of Benedict Anderson (*Imagined Communities*, 1983), Ernst Gellner (*Nations and Nationalism*, 1983), Eric J. Hobsbawm and Terence Ranger (*The Invention of Tradition*, 1983) and Anthony D. Smith (*The Ethnic Origins of Nations*, 1986). These authors established the modernist approach to nationalism and extended the analysis of nations as cultural constructions to European nations, demonstrating that, despite their self-professed antiquity, nations were a modern phenomenon. Though previous nationalist theories had presented the nation and nationhood as 'inevitable', this explanation proved to be insufficient (Özkirimli 2000: 64–74). On the contrary, constructivist approaches showed that nationalism was something that was created externally by the state and the elites and later adopted by the citizenry.

Constructivist theories are deeply critical of the primordialist approach. Nevertheless, some authors argue that primordialism does reflect how national feeling is created and experienced. In this sense, Rogers Brubaker has written that:

> No serious scholar today holds the view that is routinely attributed to primordialists in straw-man setups, namely that nations or ethnic groups are primordial, unchanging entities. Everyone agrees that nations are historically formed constructs, although there is disagreement about the relative weight of pre-modern traditions and modern transformations, of ancient memories and recent transformations, of ancient memories and recent mobilizations, of 'authentic' and 'artificial' group feeling.
>
> BRUBAKER 1996: 15

Contemporary theories of nationalism began to consider new factors as central components of new nationalism, such as the mobilization of symbols of the past and economic rationales. Constructivist approaches were consequently taken, approaches that revealed the 'cultural' assumptions underlying so-called 'natural' facts. The first myth to be debunked was that of the determining role played by language in the formation of society. The logic behind the creation of a nation cannot be reduced to a single criterion, and neither can we generalize about why a nation is formed on the basis of geographic, religious, linguistic or historical factors alone. While the religious rationale was strong enough to make a nation out of Belgium in 1830, for example, conversely, in 1993 Belgium became a federal state on linguistic grounds. What is more, multilingual, multiracial and multireligious states can still be found, while at the same time, language, race and religion have also caused the fragmentation of states. This proves that none of these factors necessarily creates a nation in itself, even though they are sometimes flagged as the ultimate reason.

In the mid-1990s, new theories focused on the marginal issues that had been briefly introduced in the theories of the 1980s (Billig 1995; Brubaker 1996). Billig introduced the concept of 'banal nationalism', which referred to the unnoticed nationalism of everyday life (Billig 1995). Certain elements, such as flags, institutional propaganda and even the lay-out of newspapers, remind the citizenry that they belong to a nation and make this a natural fact. Billig's main goal was to eliminate the distinction between peripheral nationalism and patriotism and to present the two as different types of nationalism. This perception had in fact already been present in previous accounts on nationalism, such as Anthony D. Smith's *National Identity* (1991), though admittedly, the idea had not drawn significant attention until Billig brought it to the foreground. According to these authors, nationalism does exist in Canada and Spain, as it exists in Quebec and Catalonia. Any example in which communal elements are mobilized to create links between the citizens and the territory in which they live – whatever its political status – can be studied as a nation, even though these cases may be better known as federations, autonomous communities, countries, regions or transnational units. This approach will form the cornerstone of the methodological framework used in this book.

Billig's work forms an outstanding complement to that of Smith, not so much because Billig contradicts Smith, but rather because he goes more deeply into some of the relevant aspects that Smith addresses only in outline. Indeed, according to the political scientist Umut Özkirimli, Billig opened up a series of new approaches to nationalism during the 1990s. These new approaches were not revolutionary in the sense that they invalidated the previous approaches of the 1980s – actually they were 'generally sympathetic to modernist arguments' (Özkirimli 2000: 190). As mentioned above, Billig considers patriotism and nationalism to be two words for the same concept, depending on whether or not the territory in which they are produced belongs to the category of the nation-state (Billig 1995). He wonders what happens to nationalist actions once a territory has managed to become a nation-state. In his opinion, these actions continue to be manifest, even though from this point onwards they are practised in an official – and, for him, more subtle – way, as a result of what is called 'patriotism' or 'chauvinism'. These manifestations might appear to be more progressive or more reactionary, depending on the group to which they are addressed. The way in which nationalism is expressed in daily life can be very subtle, but in any case, it links citizens to their surroundings as well as to administrative bodies. Billig explores the mechanisms through which established nations remind their citizens that they belong to the nation, calling this 'banal nationalism'; a term that includes 'the ideological habits which enable the established nations of the West to be reproduced [. . .] Daily, the nation is indicated, or "flagged", in the lives of its citizenry. Nationalism, far from being an intermittent mood in established nations, is the endemic condition' (Billig 1995: 6). We might describe 'banal nationalism' as a recurrent reference to the idea of a country that is present in numerous everyday activities; a reference that, despite going unnoticed, reminds the citizen that she or he belongs to the group.

One of the authors to have followed Billig to a certain extent, but who offers new points of view, is the geographer Tim Edensor (2002). He has developed Billig's account of the presence of national reminders in everyday life. To be sure, Billig does analyse certain cases in which national identity is disseminated through textual discourse, particularly newspaper language, but he does not pay sufficient attention to non-verbal communication as a transmitter of nationalist messages. By contrast, Edensor focuses on everyday locations (e.g. Times Square in New York), experiences (e.g. attending a football match) and material culture (e.g. local crafts), which can be read as texts. In this vein, Edensor explores everyday actions as deeply embedded in a national context, meaning that every ordinary element can be analysed as a component of national identity.

The importance of the consumer in the process of infusing objects with a national character is further explored by authors such as the historians Maarten Van Ginderachter and Marnix Beyen (2011) and the sociologist Michael Skey (2011). Their main contribution is to focus on ordinary people in the study of the formation and dissemination of nationalism. Studies of the nation had long been dominated by the dichotomy of primordialism/modernism that prioritized top-down articulations of national identity, mainly in the hands of the state and elites. These authors recognize the merit of Michael Billig's work, in that it opens up the debate on nationalism to encompass the everyday. However, their accounts depart from the top-down character of Billig's banal nationalism, to later build it up further in exploring proper bottom-up formations of nationalism.

In short, over time the focus has shifted from a militant, exalted vision of nationalism in primordialist – also called essentialist – theories, to the analytical, dispassionate approach of modernist – also called constructivist – theories of nationalism. Accordingly, the methodological tools have also changed, as has the position of the researcher. The scholar has ceased to be someone who has to condemn or defend the nationalist cause, and has become someone who has to discern the causes that led to the configuration of a given national identity. The reactions to Billig's book opened up the debate to include a 'bottom-up' understanding of nationalism.

# National identity and design

Some theories show more potential than others when it comes to applying this literature to the field of design history, insofar as they act as bridges between disciplines. One such scholar is the political scientist Anthony D. Smith whose work is relevant in three respects: the particular attention he pays to the role of symbols in the construction of national identities, his implicit use of design, and his reflections on the consequences of the relation between national identity and globalization. Smith's doctoral thesis was entitled *Patriotism and Neo-Classicism: The 'Historical Revival' in French and English Painting and Sculpture, 1746–1800* (defended at the University of London in 1987), and he is particularly interested in the patriotic, symbolic values captured in neo-classical art. Smith was Professor of Ethnicity and Nationalism at the London School of Economics and Political Science until his retirement in 2004.

Smith observes that nationalist symbols and ceremonies are so much part of the world in which we live 'that we take them, for the most part, for granted' (Smith 1991: 77). In his list of symbols that construct national identity, in addition to the obvious attributes of nations (flags, anthems, parades, coinage, capital cities, oaths, folk costumes, museums of folklore, war memorials, ceremonies of remembrance for the nation's dead, passports and borders), he extends the list to encompass more 'hidden' aspects, such as

> national recreations, the countryside, popular heroes and heroines, fairy tales, forms of etiquette, styles of architecture, arts and crafts, modes of town planning, legal procedures, educational practices and military codes – all those distinctive customs, mores, styles and ways of acting and feeling that are shared by the members of a community of historical culture.
>
> SMITH 1991: 77

Although Smith does not explicitly mention the term 'design' in his inventory, his list does mention a number of designed objects. In fact, it is the potential symbolic value of design that makes it suitable for producing symbols of nationhood. Moreover, Smith points out that the study of these symbols and their mechanisms is an insufficiently explored academic field, explicitly stating, 'the field of nationalist symbolism merits more intensive investigation' (Smith 1991: 188). In fact, it remains an under-investigated aspect of nationalism, as Smith reiterates in his book in 2001 (Smith 2001: 7).

Smith's *Nations and Nationalism in a Global Era* (1995) addresses the challenges that globalization poses to the configuration of national identity. Clearly, the continuation of the nationalist logic has become widely contested by globalization. The development of distinctive nations and the parallel growth of a global culture present us with a particular combination of heterogeneity and homogeneity, each revealing the weak points of the other. Accordingly, the tensions and contradictions between the two are reflected in cultural production. The negotiation between the local and the global and their expression in the production and promotion of design is, in fact, one of the major issues addressed by the present study. Therefore, a theory that encompasses an analysis of the formation of nationhood and its confrontation with contemporary, global parameters is extremely suitable.

# What is nationalism?

> Nation, nationality, nationalism – all have proved notoriously difficult to define, let alone to analyse.
>
> ANDERSON 1991[1983]: 3

National identity is considered the product of cultural phenomena, namely nations and nationalism. In that sense, nationalism is linked to the cultural dimension of design, even though at first glance it might appear to be an exclusively political phenomenon. As suggested above, various authors have conceived nationalism as a 'form of culture', and it thus has a much broader meaning than the customary political meaning (Smith 1991: 22). Nationalism does not only inhabit the political sphere, but it also permeates the structure of social relationships and is underpinned through cultural production. As Smith states,

> we cannot understand nations and nationalism simply as an ideology or form of politics but must treat them as cultural phenomena as well. That is to say, national*ism*, the ideology and movement, must be closely related to a *national identity*, a multidimensional concept, and extended to include a specific language, sentiments and symbolism.
>
> SMITH 1991: vii; emphasis in the original

Smith considers nationalism to be an undifferentiated whole in terms of its ideology and core doctrine, its language and symbolism, and its sentiments and aspirations (Smith 1991: 79). Likewise, Billig proposes a similar concept when he argues that nationalism 'covers the ideological means by which nation-states are reproduced' (Billig 1995: 6). Anderson takes a similar position. He argues that nationality, nation-ness and nationalism are 'cultural artefacts of a particular kind' (Anderson 1991[1983]: 4). In fact, nationalism is described as an international ideology, which structures the relationship between citizens and their nation and the relationships between nations themselves. Thus, nationalism does not only play a role at the domestic level, but it also structures 'inter-national' relationships. In this vein, nationalism divides the international context into equal units, regardless of their size and economic potential.

One obstacle to the study of nationalism is its invisibility, precisely because, as an ideology, it has become so widespread. As Billig points out, 'the boundary-consciousness of nationalism has itself known no boundaries in its historical triumph' (Billig 1995: 22). Consequently, nationalism's global presence has made it almost invisible. Like any other cultural construction, nationalism is so embedded in ordinary life that its presence goes unnoticed. Accordingly, Billig admits, 'Nationalism is the ideology by which the world of nations has come to seem the natural world – as if there could not possibly be a world without nations' (Billig 1995: 37). He points out that regardless of their level of success, all other ideologies – Islam, Christendom, Liberalism and Marxism – have borders (Billig 1995: 37). Nationalism is an international ideology, however, and has spread to cover the whole world; nowadays, only Antarctica is not divided into nations.

Whilst its invisibility complicates the study of nationalism as a cultural phenomenon, there are nevertheless several aspects that confirm the 'cultural' nature of nationalism, one of them being its historicity. When the first manifestations of nationalism occurred varies, depending on the historian, from seventeenth-century England and France to the late eighteenth century. Like all modernist scholars, Anderson and Hobsbawm locate the origins of nationalism at the end of the eighteenth century as a product of the Enlightenment, coinciding with the emergence of the first nation-states. As such, the current idea of the nation hinges upon the concepts of popular sovereignty that were forged at that time. Anderson and Hobsbawm argue that the emergence of nationalism somehow compensated for the then decaying concepts of religious community and the dynastic realm, from which the idea of nation took its shape. However, unlike Anderson and Hobsbawm, Smith argues that it is not nationalism in general but the contemporary conception of nationalism that is a product of eighteenth-century Europe, although some of its components were indeed present during the seventeenth and sixteenth centuries. Smith concludes that in any case, such conceptions did not exist prior to the modern era (Smith 1995: 55).

According to Anderson, the arrival of the printed media in the eighteenth century and its subsequent dissemination in accordance with capitalist logic – what Anderson calls 'print-capitalism' – created the feeling of belonging to a community (Anderson 1991[1983]: 44–5). Anderson emphasizes the discursive consequences of this: the daily press created a sense of community by spreading itself throughout the country, whereby all of its readers became conscious of the fact that their compatriots were engaged in the same activity and, maybe most importantly, felt included in the rhetorical 'we' used by journalists to address their readers. Similarly, Billig also situates the study of identity in the creation of a discourse about nation. According to him, we should not approach identity by looking for it in the body or mind of the individual. Instead, the study of identity 'should involve the detailed study of discourse' (Billig 1995: 8), that is, the way a given issue is described using common language.

The cultural origins of nationalism have been analysed through its paradoxical nature, one more piece of evidence of their cultural nature. Anderson points out several of these paradoxes (Anderson 1991[1983]: 5):

The objective modernity of a nation from a historian's perspective, versus its subjective antiquity in the eyes of nationalists.

Anderson later explains, 'If nation-states are widely conceded to be "new" and "historical", the nations to which they give political expression always loom out of an immemorial past, and, still more important, glide into a limitless future' (Anderson 1991[1983]: 11–12). This can be observed in the use of ancient emblems in what are clearly new territorial administrations. For example, as we shall explore in Chapter 5, when European regions in the 1970s and early 1980s drew their symbols from history in an attempt to legitimate their new institutions at the expense of their past.

The formal universality of nationality as a socio-cultural concept (like gender, for example) versus the irremediable particularity of its concrete manifestations.

This means that in the modern world, everyone should 'have' a nationality, just as he or she 'has' a gender. In fact, gender can be described as exhibiting universal features. However, whilst nationality is as universal as gender, each nationality is unique – such that, by definition, 'Greek' nationality is *sui generis*. And even within a shared nationality, it is not unusual to find individuals who understand this nationality differently.

The 'political' power of nationalism versus its philosophical poverty and even incoherence.

Although nationalism has become a meeting-point for political parties from different ideologies, its doctrine has hardly evolved.

Admittedly, the academic understanding of nationalism as a cultural phenomenon differs from its customary use. In the academic understanding, nationalism is not reduced to extremist movements that defend the principle of self-government, but is seen as a common feature of all nations, whatever their political status. Smith describes this conception of nationalism as 'an ideological movement for attaining and maintaining autonomy, unity and identity on behalf of a population deemed by some of its members to constitute an actual or potential "nation"' (Smith 1991: 73). He clearly expresses that this entails 'attaining or maintaining' the autonomy of either an 'actual or potential' nation. Consequently, nationalism does not disappear once a nation has become politically and administratively established, but remains present. It is at this point that nationalism proves to be most pervasive and most invisible at the same time. The fact that it permeates different spheres of everyday life calls for a proper understanding of the phenomenon, in order to discern the role played by design in national identity.

In the customary use of nationalism, nationalism is often defined as involving the actions of given communities – generally circumscribed by larger national orders – to achieve sovereignty over their own territory, with these generally being relegated to the status of exalted attitudes, not established nations. For example, in 1998 a group of Belgian artists and intellectuals published a manifesto in *De Standaard* newspaper that was entitled 'Enough of this nationalistic madness' (*Gedaan met nationalistische dwaasheid*). The signatories included the choreographer Anne Teresa De Keersmaeker, the writer Tom Lanoye, the philosopher Dieter Lesage and the photographer Marie-Françoise Plissart. They made a plea for a multicultural Belgium and, first and foremost, for an end to the ceaseless demands by the regional governments, particularly

Flanders, for self-government, as well as the attempts by the French-speaking community to 'annex' Brussels. They wrote:

> We refuse to behave like Flemish or French-speaking soldiers. We do not belong to any front, any tribe. Dutch-speakers and French-speakers do speak from one mouth. The language is not important. We only know the language of solidarity. . . . It is time that both in Flanders and in the French Community, some voices can be heard that break with the suicidal logics of the ethnic fronts.
>
> ABRAMOVICZ et al. 1998

These sentiments reflect the customary concept of nationalism: the authors invoke Belgian unity as a possible way of escaping nationalism. However, according to both Billig and Smith, 'Belgian nationalism' should be considered as nationalist as Flemish or Walloon nationalism. Federal Belgium is not free of nationalism; in as much as Belgium is considered a nation and uses symbols to create links between institutions and people, it is also nationalist. One is more likely to find the words 'patriotism' or 'chauvinism' associated with Belgium and 'nationalism' with Flanders or Wallonia, as the latter do not constitute nation-states. There might be differences in the means they use and in the degree of exaltation, but not in the fact in itself; they are only different versions of the same phenomenon. As Özkirimli states:

> It is true that the Serbian militia in Kosovo or the ETA militants have different motives than ordinary French or American citizens, yet all these motives, despite their varying forms and intensity, belong to the same family. What unites them is the nationalist discourse: both the ETA militants who commit acts of terrorism and the French citizens who sing *La Marseillese* in football stadiums use the nationalist discourse to explain, justify, and hence legitimate their actions. The motives and the actions might take different forms, but they are all of the same kind.
>
> ÖZKIRIMLI 2000: 5

Indeed, the major achievement of accounts of nationalism from the 1990s onwards is that they replaced the concept of nationalism as a 'minorities issue' with that of a larger phenomenon in which every citizen is involved. One example of this is Billig's approach, which focuses on the differences between the diverse meanings of nationalism (see Billig 1995: 6, 15, 17, 19, 24, 37 for various definitions of nationalism). He notes that the customary use of nationalism is usually reserved for peripheral nationalism: that is, extremist positions whereby people want to change actual state boundaries, or political manifestations of nations-as-people demanding a nation-as-state. This meaning of nationalism might inspire either sympathy (e.g. national liberation from colonialism) or feelings of rejection (e.g. fascist movements; Billig 1995: 7). However, when nations are established, this 'nationalism' seems to fade suddenly. Billig argues that nationalism as an ideology remains; though invisible, 'it becomes something surplus to everyday life' (Billig 1995: 44). This familiarity subsequently conceals 'the object to which the "loyalty" or "identification" is being shown: the nation-state' (Billig 1995: 16).

# What is national identity?

According to Smith, national identity is created by an ideological movement – namely, nationalism (Smith 1991: 4) – and is thereby 'an abstract and multidimensional construct that touches on a wide range of spheres of life and manifests many permutations and combinations' (Smith 1991: 144). National identity is thus a collective cultural identity, such as gender, social class or religious identity, which links individuals to a particular space or territory. As the geographer Jan Penrose states, 'the concept of nation is the product of three elements: a distinctive group of people, the territory which they occupy, and the bonding over time (of historical experience) which melds people and land' (Penrose 1995: 406).

Cultural identities have a different relevance at the individual and the collective levels. At the level of the individual, identities are multiple and often situational, for human beings have multiple identities – of family, gender, class, region, religion, ethnic group and nation – with one or another taking precedence over the others at different times, depending on the circumstances. As Smith points out, 'at home we may feel we belong, and in fact belong, to a particular class or region; abroad we may see ourselves, and be seen, as members of a particular ethnic or national group. For some purposes, religious community will define our identity, for others it will be gender or family' (Smith 1995: 123–4).

At the collective level, however, identities are more 'pervasive' than 'situational'. That is, it is not the opinions and feelings of individuals that matter, but the nature of the collective bond: 'Through socialization, communications and sometimes coercion, we find ourselves bound by particular identities from birth . . . This is frequently the case with ethnic and national bonds' (Smith 1995: 124). In other words, individual identity can be seen as a 'mosaic' formed by singular pieces of collective identity, each with a given social 'shape'. Each individual may have a different collection of pieces, depending on their own characteristics. While the form of the pieces can only change very slowly, the individual can prioritize one piece over the others at certain moments, either follow or subvert it, and put it at the centre of his or her mosaic. In this sense, Smith concludes that 'theoretically, then, it would be perfectly possible for the peoples of Europe to feel that they had more than one collective cultural identity: to feel themselves Sicilian, Italian and European, or Flemish, Belgian and European (as well as being female, middle class, Muslim or whatever)' (Smith 1995: 124).

The tension between the collective and the individual will be explored at length in Part Three. One of the authors to have discussed this dichotomy is Tim Edensor. He argues that national identity must be conceived as a process 'constituted out of a huge cultural matrix which provides innumerable points of connection, nodal points where authorities try to fix meaning, and constellations around which cultural elements cohere' (Edensor 2002: vii). According to Edensor, national identity develops in a continual progression. It is not dependent on individual identities, though neither is it fixed, and it can be contested. He argues that '[n]ational identity does not equate with homogeneity; nor is it inherently defensive, conservative or tradition-bound' (Edensor 2002: 29). National identity can therefore acquire different nuances and can be underpinned by different signs.

In this vein, the design historian Jeremy Aynsley cites two opposing examples of the production of 'German-ness', based on their ideological connotations (Aynsley 1993: 7). First, he mentions the Nazi regime's recourse to Gothic typeface in a propaganda initiative that delved deeply into folk motifs, so as to counteract the modernist design that prevailed under the Weimar Republic (Aynsley 1993: 45–7). In totalitarian political systems, the control of national production is patently evident, and, after Hitler's rise to power in January 1933, art, design, film and architecture were pushed to the forefront of the Nazis' ideological campaign. As obvious as this mobilization of vernacular symbols might be, however, there are other ways of reproducing German-ness that appear in more mundane contexts and that do not exploit traditional connotations. Take the electrical goods manufacturer Braun, for example, Aynsley's second example (Aynsley 1993: 59–60). Braun was founded in 1921 by Max Braun in Frankfurt (Germany) and was purchased in 1967 by the Gillette Company (Boston, Massachusetts). In 2005, the new parent company became Procter & Gamble (Cincinnati, Ohio), which acquired Gillette. Since its foundation in 1921, Braun has mobilized German values other than tradition; indeed, its current logo conveys notions of post-war modernist design, technological excellence and efficiency (Julier 1993: 41–2). Even though Braun is no longer German, the trademark and values attached to it continue to convey a sense of German-ness, but certainly one that is not embodied by the Gothic typeface.

What role does national identity play, however, and how does it relate to other forms of collective identity? Regarding this point, there are essentially two positions. The first grants national identity a prominent role, while the second dilutes its importance and situates it among other forms of collective identity. For most authors, national identity is the most relevant of all forms of cultural collective identity. As Stuart Hall states, '[i]n the modern world, the national cultures into which we are born are one of the principal sources of cultural identity' (Hall 1992: 291). According to Smith, the features of national identity are ubiquity, pervasiveness and complexity (Smith 1991: 143). First, it is a global phenomenon, as mentioned above. Second, it is present in the cultural, social and political spheres of life. Third, it is combined with, and often subsumes, other issues and ideologies. As a result, Smith affirms that, 'Today, national identity is the main form of collective identification. Whatever the feelings of individuals, it provides the dominant criterion of culture and identity, the sole principle of government and the chief focus of social and economic activity' (Smith 1991: 170). Anderson also takes this line, stressing the complexity and ubiquity of national identity. He states that 'nation-ness is the most universally legitimate value of the political life of our time' (Anderson 1991[1983]: 3), and that nationalism has undergone a process of 'modulation and adaptation, according to different eras, political regimes, economies and social structure. The 'imagined community' has, as a result, spread out to every conceivable contemporary society' (Anderson 1991[1983]: 157).

Scholars from the cosmopolitan school, by contrast, minimize the importance of national identity. They argue for a strong identification with humanity at large and not with a single nation. Jeremy Waldron is especially critical of Herder, questioning why humans would need to belong to one or another national community. He argues that we should instead create allegiances with non-national communities, such as ideological or professional groups (Waldron 1995: 102). He suggests that humans 'need culture, but not cultural integrity,' and that the frameworks in which we develop our lives do not need to be homogeneous in order to be valid (Waldron 1995: 108).

How is national identity disseminated? Many authors explain the creation and reproduction of national identity as a form of collective identity. Indeed, the most widespread definition of national identity as cultural collective identity is Anderson's notion of an 'imagined community'. He grounds the cultural conception of nationhood in the 'imagined' nature of the nation. As Anderson states, '[i]t is imagined because the members of even the smallest nation will never know most of their fellow-members, meet them, or ever hear of them, yet in the minds of each lives the image of their communion' (Anderson 1991[1983]: 6). Even when individuals do not know all of the other citizens, they feel that they belong to a community because 'regardless of the actual inequality and exploitation that may prevail in each, the nation is always conceived as a deep, horizontal comradeship' (Anderson 1991[1983]: 7). In this sense, the term 'imagined' is not being used as a synonym of 'false', but as a synonym of 'constructed'.

In a critique of Anderson, Billig argues that the action implied by the verb 'imagine' renders it inadequate. National identity is so ubiquitous that individuals do not need to make any effort; instead, they are constantly reminded:

> Once nations are established, and nationalism becomes banal, the poets are typically replaced by prosaic politicians, and the epic ballads by government reports. The imagined community ceases to be reproduced by acts of the imagination. In established nations, the imagination becomes enhabited, and, thereby, inhibited. In this sense, the term 'imagined communities' may be misleading. The community and its place are not so much imagined, but their absence becomes unimaginable.
>
> BILLIG 1995: 77

Billig relates this routine perception of nationalist elements to Bourdieu's concept of 'habitus', which refers to the dispositions, practices and routines of the familiar, social world (Billig 1995: 42). A certain degree of automatism is implicit in 'habitus'. It should be stressed that Bourdieu's concept refers to social class and the associated, unconscious practices that both define and emanate from it. Yet, as Billig suggests, it can easily be translated from the field of class identity to the field of another social identity, namely national identity. According to Bourdieu, the 'habitus' functions both as an active 'structuring structure' and as a passive 'structured structure' (Bourdieu 2002[1979]: 170). This means that it acts as an interpretative framework of a cultural fact, and at the same time is produced by this very same cultural fact. The most relevant feature of 'habitus' is that it appears as a common-sense structure and is therefore unconscious. To explain 'habitus', Edensor uses the example of an actor who is so used to playing a role that certain actions become second nature. Thus even when derived from cultural assumptions and schemas, the 'habitus' is experienced as natural behaviour (Edensor 2002: 89). Lash and Urry equate 'habitus' with pre-judgements or 'shared, unreflexive orientations and predispositions', which they place at the very heart of culture (Lash & Urry 1994: 317). Hence, national identity – as 'habitus' – is both the producer and the product of nationalism, and tends to be experienced unconsciously. Performed manifestations of nationalism (e.g. the salutation of the flag or a preference for consuming national products) are therefore framed in a 'habitus' and appear natural.

The communities in which national identity operates are more numerous than the nation-states. As mentioned above, nationalism is not exclusive to present-day nations, but can be related to regions or other territorial divisions as long as a collective identity is cultivated and emanates from them. Therefore, according to Smith:

> The modern nation is a 'political community' in its exercise of self-government and autonomy in relation to other nations, either within a federation of nations or as a sovereign national state among other sovereigns. It is a national political community insofar as it requires government to be national self-government of the whole community.
>
> SMITH 1995: 55

Consequently, we can state that subnationalisms are one more product of national identity, as are other communities based on geographical and historical ties. In that sense, there are similarities between regions with a sense of collective identity and subnationalisms. They might not aim for self-government or greater autonomy, but constitute regional identities that are compatible with wider national and supranational identities.

# Why is national identity constructed?

Due to its ubiquity and complexity, national identity is present in several areas of everyday life. Smith distinguishes both the external and the internal functions of national identity (Smith 1991: 16). The external functions of national identity are:

- Territorial. Nations define a definite social space within which members must live and work.

- Economic. Nations underwrite the quest for control over territorial resources, including manpower.

- Political. National identity underpins the state and its organs, or their pre-political equivalents in nations that lack their own states.

The internal functions of national identity are:

- The socialization of the members of the nation as 'nationals' and 'citizens'. Collective dignity is restored by means of an appeal to a golden age. Citizens are offered personal renewal and dignity in and through national regeneration; to belong to the nation is to become part of a political 'super-family'.

- Nations create social ties between individuals and classes by providing repertoires of shared values, symbols and traditions; in other words, the realization of fraternity through symbols, rites and ceremonies, which bind the living to the dead and fallen of the community. 'By the use of symbols – flags, coinage, anthems, uniforms, monuments and ceremonies – members are reminded of their common heritage and cultural kinship and feel strengthened and exalted by their sense of common identity and belonging. The nation becomes a "faith-achievement" group, able to surmount obstacles and hardships' (Smith 1991: 17).

- Nationality provides a powerful means for defining and locating individual selves in the world. Oblivion is transcended through posterity.

Smith's analysis tends towards the objective; he does not consider whether national identity is beneficial or not. Other authors express more biased opinions. The political theorist David Miller (1995) defends the role of national identity as a generator of a shared sense of justice, mutual obligation and trust among the members of modern societies. According to him, national identity allows us to avoid situations in which people operate on the basis of strict reciprocity in impersonal, large modern societies (Miller 1995: 98). Conversely, Billig and Anderson attach quite negative meanings to the concept of national identity. According to Billig, national identity keeps citizens in a 'stand-by' state that is activated when a crisis breaks out (e.g. attack) and the population has to be mobilized (e.g. support the use of armed force) (Billig 1995: 7). In a similar fashion, Anderson points out that 'the great wars of this century are extraordinary not so much in the unprecedented scale on which they permitted people to kill, as in the colossal numbers persuaded to lay down their lives' (Anderson 1991[1983]: 144). For him, it is remarkable that at certain times, something might be considered more precious than one's own life. Even more remarkable than this is the public recognition that such acts can generate:

> Dying for one's country, which usually one does not choose, assumes a moral grandeur which dying for the Labour Party, the American Medical Association, or perhaps even Amnesty International can not rival, for these are all bodies one can join or leave at easy will.
>
> ANDERSON 1991[1983]: 144

Anderson states that 'nations inspire love, and often profoundly self-sacrificing love. The cultural products of nationalism – poetry, prose fiction, music, plastic arts – show this love very clearly in thousands of different forms and styles' (Anderson 1991[1983]: 141).

# How is national identity constructed?

The contribution of design historians to the debate on national identity is most salient when they elucidate the symbolic mechanisms that lie behind a particular national identity. There is agreement in the literature that a sense of community is achieved by the mobilization of 'ordinary' elements that refer to a shared time and place; that is, both the imagined history and territory of the national community. These immaterial concepts are embodied in elements that are laden with meaning, the symbols of the nation:

> By means of the ceremonies, customs and symbols every member of a community participates in the life, emotions and virtues of that community

and through them, re-dedicates him- or herself to its destiny. By articulating and making tangible the ideology of nationalism and the concepts of the nation ceremonial and symbolism help to assure the continuity of an abstract community of history and destiny.

SMITH 1991: 78

The historians Eric Hobsbawm and Terence Ranger's concept of 'invented tradition' has been broadly used to depict the construction of symbolic conventions in processes of nation-building and to describe the role played by the intelligentsia. It specifically focuses on how apparently eternal habits such as traditions are in fact consciously and newly created, serving to legitimate interests. The term 'invented traditions' includes

> a set of practices, normally governed by overtly or tacitly accepted rules and of ritual or symbolic nature, which seek to inculcate certain values and norms of behaviour by repetition, which automatically implies continuity with the past. In fact, where possible, they normally attempt to establish continuity *with a suitable historic past*.

HOBSBAWM & RANGER 1983: 1; emphasis in the original

They state: 'In short, they are responses to novel situations which take the form of reference to old situations' (Hobsbawm & Ranger 1983: 2). Hobsbawm and Ranger distinguish between 'customs' and 'traditions' by means of an example: custom, they write, 'is what judges do; "tradition" (in this instance invented tradition) is the wig, robe and other formal paraphernalia and ritualised practices surrounding their substantial action' (Hobsbawm & Ranger 1983: 3).

Seen from an historical perspective, a paradigmatic example of the use of a given style as a suitable political symbol is the expansion of Empire style during the reign of Napoleon I (1769–1821), initially as First Consul from 1799, and primarily as Emperor (1804–1815) (Fleming & Honour 1977: 404–6). Already present in the Directoire period and even at the end of Louis XVI's reign, Napoleon's reign saw the highpoint of classical style. Empire style adorned official interiors, clothes, furniture and objects, all of which were inspired by classical forms (see Figure 1.2). The classical revival in dress defined a period characterized by imperial expansion and thereby became an 'invented tradition'. In this vein, sartorial references to Greek clothing spread from France, particularly in feminine dress. This was characterized by a simple type of long dress with short sleeves and a high waistline, which fell practically under the bust, creating an almost columnar silhouette. The high waistline and the fabric – which was often thin, almost sheer, cotton – produced a richly draped effect. The colour was generally white for grand occasions. White denoted prosperity, as the colour is easily spoiled and only rich ladies could afford to wear pristine white dresses (Ribeiro 1995: 133–81). In a mixture of Greek and

Roman forms, Napoleon's emblem featured the eagle and the laurel crown. His plans for conquest covered the whole of Europe and beyond. The assimilation of the emblems of the glorious Roman Empire symbolically legitimated Napoleon's own imperial plans. They acted as 'suitable' references in which to cloak the Napoleonic expansion, and thereby its wars.

As mentioned above, shared time and space provide this sense of community. National institutions are fragile when newly created, and therefore construct an aura of longevity through the use of what are presumed to be ancient symbols, as if the worst thing that could happen would be for such an institution to be novel. Therefore, as Hobsbawm and Ranger state, 'plenty of political institutions, ideological movements and groups – not least in nationalism – were so unprecedented that even historic continuity had to be invented, for example by creating an ancient past beyond effective historical continuity' (Hobsbawm & Ranger 1983: 7). Such situations are likely to occur when political regimes break up and new ones assume control. Examples include the new institutions that emerge after processes of federalization or political devolution. As we shall see in Chapter 5, symbols were sought to provide a sense of 'continuity' when branding the institutions.

Hobsbawm and Ranger's account stresses the application of constructivist methodology to the discipline of history. They state that by using this methodology, historians can contribute to the study of these 'invented traditions,' particularly because

> [t]hey are highly relevant to that comparatively recent historical innovation, the 'nation', with its associated phenomena: nationalism, the nation-state, national symbols, histories and the rest. All these rest on exercises in social engineering which are often deliberate and always innovative, if only because historical novelty implies innovation.
>
> HOBSBAWM & RANGER 1983: 13

In answer to the question, 'What benefit can historians derive from the study of the invention of tradition?', they state that:

> [F]irst and foremost, it may be suggested that they are important and therefore indicators of problems which might not otherwise be recognized, and developments which are otherwise difficult to identify and to date [and] second, it throws a considerable light on the human relation to the past, and therefore on the historian's own subject and craft.
>
> HOBSBAWM & RANGER 1983: 12

As mentioned above, Smith criticized the modernist approach taken by Hobsbawm and Anderson by specifying that some elements of the modern concept of the nation could be found prior to the eighteenth century. His second critique of these theories relates to the authors' marked 'top-down' approach. By this, he means their overly-schematic approach, one that starts from the intervention of ruling classes and continues on down to the masses, and its subsequent negation of certain pre-existing elements derived from ethnicity. As a result, top-down approaches can only deliver a partial account of the creation of national identity. In Anderson's and Hobsbawm's accounts, nations are formed by groups from the intelligentsia and are largely based on an economic rationale. Smith contests this conception; he points out that even when the nation and its symbols are very new, they rely on previous ethnic symbols to which the national community feels attached (Smith 1995: 29–51). In fact, Hobsbawm's and Anderson's approaches explain how the symbols are created, but they do not explain their reception. Smith's account includes a parameter that can explain why some symbols are preferred over others and why they are either accepted or rejected. This does not mean that Smith's account ignores the role played by governments. On the contrary, nation-building processes are decisive for the creation of national identities, though other elements also have to be taken into account.

Authors who defend the notion of nationalism from below have questioned the overemphasis on the state as the creator of national identity. These authors generally acknowledge the value that Billig attaches to the everyday, but they expand the role played by citizens by making them both the active creators and creative recipients of symbols of national identity. It is both in the creation and dissemination of these symbols and in their interpretation that the citizenry shapes discourses of national identity. Particularly because national identity is seen as a 'habitus,' if we take the state as the only source of national identity, we fail to capture the multifarious and complex ways in which national identity originates.

# Global culture

Nationalism as a doctrine met stark opposition in communism and proletarian internationalism, at least in theory. In practice, nationalist traits were present in communist regimes, which had implications for theories of nationalism. Indeed, the introduction to Anderson's book acknowledges that Marxist regimes have been involved in wars against each other. He cites the Vietnamese invasion and occupation of Cambodia in December 1978 and January 1979, and China's assault on Vietnam in February that year. He concludes that the end of the era of nationalism, 'so long prophesied, is not remotely in mind' (Anderson 1991[1983]: 3). Indeed, nationalism has been able to defeat its enemies and even draw strength from them. Although it might threaten nationalism in other ways, globalization has so far proven to be an ally, rather than an enemy, in the propagation of nationalism.

Smith explores the role of culture in relation to the global geopolitical landscape. He notes the emergence of transnational forces since the end of the Second World War, which have by definition shaped nationalism and national identity (Smith 1991: 154). The global parameters that should be taken into account are:

- Regional power blocs (e.g. the European Union, Latin American associations).

- Transnational economic corporations; multinationals that link the economic interests and political destinies of different countries. According to Smith, their influence is equivalent to that of nation-states.

- Global telecommunications systems, which help to create a global culture.

- Massive population movements, which seem to be making the nation-state an obsolete institution.

- The growing importance of environmental pollution and disease on a regional and global scale. These factors add a new dimension of the sense of community, in that they are problems that affect the whole world. While nations were a practical solution in an industrial world, with its technological and market needs, the nation needs to be superseded as part of the move to a 'post-industrial' society.

Nevertheless, these forces are not impeding the growth of nationalism. Indeed, as Smith states, 'Paradoxically, therefore, these trans-national economic forces may end up reinforcing the nations and nationalisms they were expected to supersede' (Smith 1991: 157). One force that is more pervasive today than when Smith wrote his book is that of the Internet. In his article 'Nationalism and the Internet', the social anthropologist Thomas Hylland Eriksen (2007) argues that for nations, the assumption of territorial integrity is no longer an important factor. New technologies support communication between members of nations that are not tied to a particular territory. He cites the example of nations that have lost their territory (such as Afrikaner-led South Africa) or nations that have dispersed for political reasons (Tamil Sri Lanka or Kurdistan) (Eriksen 2007: 1). The Internet might function as a portal to disseminate and sustain nations without states. However, these virtual nations reproduce themselves following the symbolic conventions of established nations. If the Internet contributes to the creation of hybrid national platforms, it does not present an alternative to nationalism.

Smith defines global culture as the cultural product of globalization; not as a rootless culture, but as anchored in the intertwining of local and global features:

Broadly speaking, recent cultural developments in the West combine a veneer of streamlined modernism with a pastiche of post-modern motifs, themes and styles. This is essentially an eclectic culture. On the one hand we are deluged with a torrent of standardized mass commodities uniformly packaged for mass consumption; on the other hand these commodities – from furniture and building to TV films and advertising – draw their contents from revivals of earlier folk or national motifs and styles, torn from their original contexts and anaesthetized or treated in whimsical or satirical vein. From Stravinsky to Poulenc in the 1920s to Hockney and Kitaj today, this pastiche of parodied styles and themes has come to stand for the possibility of a post-modern, even a pseudo-classical, mass culture.

SMITH 1991: 157

Remarkably, Smith does not define global culture as the vanishing of national motifs or styles, but as their 'delocalisation'. The study of new national/regional identities must therefore deal with the struggle between the delocalization of culture, derived from globalization, and the localization of national references, derived from nationalism, which gradually affects smaller communities. As Smith argues, 'a memory-less culture is a contradiction; any attempt to create such a global culture would simply accentuate the plurality of folk memories and identities that have been plundered in order to constitute this giant *bricolage*' (Smith 1991: 159). The outcome of this paradoxical construction of identity must somehow combine cosmopolitan references with the wider trend of branding creative products as one's 'own'.

In this vein, the combination of global culture and national-building processes is compatible in the sense that, as Hall explains, it 'constructs identities which are ambiguously placed between past and future' (Hall 1992: 295). Hall cites the example of Thatcher's narrative of the nation, which combined some symbols that referred to a heroic past with others that seemed to challenge the future:

During the 1980s, the rhetoric of Thatcherism sometimes inhabited both these aspects of what Tom Nairn calls the 'Janus-face' of nationalism: looking back to past imperial glories and 'Victorian values' while simultaneously undertaking a kind of modernization in preparation for a new stage of global capitalist competition.

HALL 1992: 295

The characterization of the nation can point in different directions, stressing the nation's past or its future. Whatever the nature of the products, national labels, imposed by national-building processes, transform them in representations of nationhood. The chameleon-like character of nationalism, as described by Smith, then comes to the fore.

# Regions and sub-nations

The concept of the region needs to be reconsidered. Traditionally, the regional has been linked to the rural, in contrast to the shifting dynamics of the urban metropolis. Regions have thereby been depicted as the guardians of traditions and folk culture. In many cases, the regional has provided the symbols that are used to represent the national. As Edensor points out, elements of national identity – whether they are landscapes, rituals or material production – necessarily hail from a particular region, as a country is little more than a relatively cohesive sum of its regions. The problem is that while some elements are elevated to the national level and thus recognized globally, others are neglected. Edensor points to the pampas landscape of Argentina, which supersedes the country's deserts, swamps and mountains in the popular imagination (Edensor 2002: 39). Hence, the construction of nations in traditions involves a process of regional selection. Edensor argues:

> European nations, whose emergence is in many cases coterminous with the development of modern romanticism, are clothed in this rhetoric of the rural, a rural which most frequently encapsulates the *genius loci* of the nation, the place from which we have sprung, where our essential national spirit resides.
>
> EDENSOR 2002: 40

Obviously, it is difficult to fit this description to all regions, as they have the dynamics of small countries – with their own urban metropolises – rather than rural sites. For his part, Smith traces an historical sociology of nationalisms and national identity. In so doing, he presents the evolution of nationalist theories, illustrated with case studies. These include first, ethnic separatism in the old empires in the nineteenth century, and second, ethnic nationalism emerging in the overseas territories of European colonial empires in the early to mid-twentieth century. A third wave of demotic ethnic nationalism swept industrial societies from the late 1960s (Smith 1991: 125). The earliest manifestations of this included the Quebecois in Canada, and the wave also incorporated the Catalan, Basque, Breton, Scots, Welsh and Flemish movements. The major features of these are:

- They are autonomist rather than separatist.
- They recognize the possibility of dual identities.
- They take place in well-established states that generally enjoy a higher standard of living than most developing states.
- They are directed against modern nation-states.

- They are movements of 'subject peoples' against dominant 'ethnies'.

- They involve processes of vernacular mobilization and cultural politicization.

- Intellectuals and intelligentsias play an important role.

Nevertheless, by generalizing, Smith fails to pinpoint the nuances of each particular case. I will argue that the third wave has not only been a movement of 'subject peoples' against dominant 'ethnies', but also of replacing old definitions of place with new ones. It has been a process of purification from both external 'national' intrusion and internal regional concepts. In this struggle, regions have not only eliminated foreign elements, but also a part of themselves. For example, Petr Pithart (b. 1941), the former Prime Minister of Czechoslovakia, reflecting on the country's dissolution, stated that:

> In the last 55 years, the Czechs have lost – as co-tenants in their common house Germans, Jews, Ruthenians, Hungarians and Slovaks. They are now, in effect, an ethnically cleansed country, even if it was not by their own will. It is a great intellectual, cultural, and spiritual loss. This is particularly true if we consider central Europe, which is a kind of mosaic. We are still living touristically from the glory of Prague, which was a Czech-German-Jewish city and a light that reached to the stars. But you cannot win elections with that kind of argument.
>
> Pithart quoted in KYMLICKA 2001: 117

Of all of the characteristics identified by Smith, as listed above, the second (dual identities) is especially interesting for this study. The possibility of combining regional identity with national and supranational identity creates a 'vertical' sum of identities that do not exclude each other, meaning that aspects of the three levels can coexist. In this case, defining a pure subnational identity becomes a complex undertaking. Subnational identities tend to present themselves as monolithic and defined in opposition to the national identity in which it is embedded. In such cases, a dominant subnational identity emerges, based on distinctive aspects, such as language and ethnic origin. The 'vertical' sum of identities is therefore not always acknowledged when defining subnational identities. On the contrary, the diverse understandings of the sub-nation are then replaced by a militant definition of the nation, which assumes that pro-autonomist or pro-independence positions are more legitimate than unionist ones. Through the engineering of symbols, definitions of sub-nations are validated or contested. Negotiations about which symbols to use reflect the tensions surrounding the definition of subnational identities. Regions thus range from being peripheral national units to potential nations in themselves. The whole spectrum can be condensed into a single region, with citizens defending one or the other extreme. Choosing one definition as the dominant definition implies denying the other. If the region secedes, then a redefinition of place occurs. The definition of 'subject people' as dominant 'ethnies' then proves to be too simplistic. Regional identities must be seen as processes, as holders of diverse, even contradictory, identities.

Smith distinguishes three overlapping cultural phases in the formation of ethnic nations and the replacement of previous signs of belonging to a collective identity for a new one. These phases are especially suitable to ethnic nationalist movements of the late twentieth century, where 'there has been concern for a dying language, fear for ethnic and cultural admixture and decline, anxiety over the loss of traditional life-styles, and a sometimes violent desire to mobilize the populace against the dominant ethnic power, the French, the English and Castilians' (Smith 1995: 71).

The first stage is the re-appropriation of one's culture, which involves the rediscovering of the communities' ethnic past by indigenous intellectuals. Through these activities, first the intellectuals, then the wider stratum of professionals or intelligentsia, and finally other classes, 'are brought back to their real or presumed indigenous traditions and customs, languages and symbols, myths and memories' (Smith 1995: 65). Second, the symbols mentioned above are later endowed with new national meanings. He adds that not only the past but also the folk culture of the present can take on a political aspect. Smith provides the example of movements of political romanticism in the early nineteenth century, in which arts, literature, architecture, crafts, song and dance, dress and food, 'were all imbued with the creative, yearning spirit of the people, and demonstrated their native genius' (Smith 1995: 68). Third, the purification of the community involves, first of all, 'jettisoning all "alien" cultural traits – words, customs, dress, food, artistic styles – and reappropriating vernacular traits for a renewed indigenous culture' (Smith 1995: 69).

Smith's account introduces the dialectical relationship between previous dominant cultures and new ones in order to explain the new construction of national identity. However, at this stage some critiques can be raised with regard to his schema. The stages, albeit analytically distinguishable, must be studied under the less 'intentional' framework of the 'habitus' and amplify the possibilities from the vernacular to the modern features to construct national identity. First, the stages must be inserted into the logics of nationalism. Consequently, the different actors must be considered not as fully responsible of the construction of the national identity, but rather embedded in the cultural field of nationalism. It is only from this interaction between the actors that the shaping of a national identity can be forged. Second, historicist and vernacular features are only one possibility for constructing national identity, though it is, as discussed later, not the only one.

# Conclusion

According to the literature that has been reviewed in this introductory chapter, nationalism appears to be a common phenomenon; one that is not relegated to exalted minorities, but that underpins a world divided into nations. This ideology structures social life by producing nations, which are not only political units, but also cultural phenomena. The effect of nationalism – or national culture, according to Stuart Hall – is the creation of a national identity, which some authors believe to be the most pervasive of all cultural, collective identities. As such, it should be addressed not only as a product of social interaction, but also of cultural representation. The various discursive strategies that represent the nation together constitute the national identity. The social construction of national identity is partly a task for politicians, and insofar as the nation has a state, then primarily for the state. Recent accounts have prioritized the role of the citizenry in producing and reproducing the nation. While it is true that national identity is not exclusively shaped by the state, it is also true that the discursive production emanating from state-building processes plays an authoritative role in reproducing the nation. Presenting national identity as collective identity sheds light on the way in which individuals can be linked to this construct. At the same time, these theories contribute a second relevant point; that is, that the mediation of different actors explains how the discourse on the nation is constructed.

# PART ONE

# Primordialism: Nations as Perennial Entities

This section explores the primordialist conception of the nation, considering its formulation, its critique, the controversies it sparked and the extent to which the concept persists today. Focusing on the theories of Johann Gottfried von Herder (1744–1803), four main tenets of primordialism are identified:

- belonging to a nation is a process of socialization;
- there is a national canon: it is not the case that any cultural product of a nation can be considered national art;
- every nation is unique, and this uniqueness is reflected in its national character;
- cultural expression in general and design in particular reflect this national character. Analysing the cultural production of a nation reveals its specific national character.

Over the centuries, design has provided one means by which nations can create a past for themselves. Since at least the late eighteenth century, history and folk art have been a source of inspiration and a recurrent theme of national symbolism. Nevertheless, designers have interpreted this theme in diverse ways.

Finally, this section analyses the essentialist nature of primordialism. Regardless of the critique of essentialist methodology, this position remains valid since it provides a convincing account of how nations have been communicated and conceptualized. Essentialist interpretations of national design are the result of a world dominated by nationalism as a universal ideology.

# Chapter 1
# A National Character

*The first rule which we have to follow is that of national character: every people has, or must have, a character; if it lacks one, we must start by endowing it with one.*

Rousseau quoted in SMITH 1991: 75

There has often been a pronounced identification between designed material culture and national collective identity. The history of European costume offers myriad examples of this, especially in the sixteenth and seventeenth centuries, when national styles were utterly diverse. This diversity is exemplified by Baldassare Castiglione's (1478–1529) *The Book of the Courtier* (1528), written in the form of a discussion between a group of friends at the Ducal Court of Urbino. In an illustrative dialogue, one of the characters, Magnifico Giuliano, asks Federico how a courtier ought to dress, given the wide range of options; for, he notes, some 'dress after the French fashion, some after the Spanish, some who wish to appear German; nor is their lack of those who even dress after the style of Turks: some who wear their beards, some not' (Book II: 26). The account also makes it clear that not every European nation had a distinctive style; Federico wonders why there is no dress that is recognizable as Italian, and why Italians wear foreign fashions. A similar story, this time referring to English styles, can be found in Andrew Borde's (1490–1549) account of his European travels in the 1540s. In his poem, 'The Natural Disposition of an Englishman', which accompanies a depiction of a naked man with a pair of tailoring shears, he denounces the lack of a national English costume and the acceptance of foreign attire in England (Ribeiro 1986: 65). These examples reveal that specific outfits denoting national identities were either worn in the country of origin or disseminated abroad, preserving their original features. Accordingly, some countries were depicted as creators of national fashions and others as recipients. In any case, the country of origin was recognized in the outfit.

Strictly speaking, nationalism as such emerged in the aftermath of the eighteenth century as a product of the French Revolution. As a doctrine, it defends the existence of a nation whose sovereignty resides in the people. The historian Joep Leerssen, however, argues that 'national thought' preceded the French Revolution; a body of thought that included all of the source traditions and ramifications of nationalist ideology. He thereby defends the notion that nationalism, rather than appearing out of nowhere, was the result of a long tradition in which the term 'nation' was used prior to 'nationalism'. Leerssen defines 'national thought' as 'a way of seeing human society primarily as consisting of discrete, different nations, each with an obvious right to exist and to command loyalty, each characterised and set apart unambiguously by its own separate identity and culture' (Leerssen 2006: 15).

In the systematizing thought of Renaissance Europe, nations were also characterized by their inner national characters. Julius Caesar Scaliger's *Poetices libri VII* (1561) reduces nations to their national characteristics:

> The Swedes, Norse, Greenlanders and Goths are bestial, and so are the Scots and Irish. The English are perfidious, puffed-up, cross-tempered, arrogant, of a mocking and quarrelsome disposition, divided amongst themselves, warlike when united, stubborn, independent and pitiless. The French are attentive, mobile, nimble, humane, hospitable, spendthrift, respectable, martial; they scorn their enemies and are heedless of themselves; they are self-controlled, brave, not very tenacious, and by far the best horsemen of all. The Spanish have a dour life-style, they live it up when they sit at another man's table, they are fiery drinkers, talkative, busy, their arrogance is hellish, their disrespect infernal, their stinginess amazing; they are strong in poverty, their religious steadfastness is priceless, they are envious of all nations and all nations are envious of them.
>
> Quoted in LEERSSEN 2006: 56

Being as it would seem a product of observation, these definitions of national character permeated literature, shaping the perceptions of readers and defining how Europeans looked at the world (Leerssen 2006: 57). Such stereotypes continue to resonate even today, suggesting how powerful essentialist conceptions of the nations can be. Similarly, sartorial characteristics proved to be powerful conveyors of national ideas, just as they are today. Clear ideas circulate about what was meant by French, Italian or Belgian fashion. In the present day, when the production of clothing is outsourced and there is a global traffic of goods, it is proving increasingly difficult to maintain these stereotypes. Nevertheless, both tradition and the construction of discourse fuel stereotypes in the field of design in general, and in fashion in particular. The question that then emerges is what should we consider to be 'national fashion': that which is designed in a country, or which is consumed in a country? In the sixteenth and seventeenth centuries, there was a greater correspondence between national sartorial habits and the definition of a nation. Nowadays, this is obviously not the case.

The identification between a garment or outfit and the country of origin made that the idea of a country was evoked by sartorial means. During the French expansion in the mid-seventeenth century, Spanish defeats were represented metaphorically in engravings by means of sartorial references. It was common to depict characters being stripped of their Spanish clothes and dressed again in the French style. This is shown in an engraving of 1642–1643 entitled 'Facetious piece regarding the taking of Perpignan: The Spaniard undressed' (*Pièce facétieuse relative à la prise de Perpignan: l'Espagnol despouillé*), which shows a man being stripped of his typical Spanish attire consisting of a cloak, a hat called a *copotain*, doublet and breeches (Figure 1.1). These garments were usually dyed black and were characteristic of Spanish fashion during this period. In the middle of the engraving a man, dressed only in his underwear and ruff, kneels as his cloak is removed by a Frenchman, his hat by a Portuguese, his

**Figure 1.1** Anonymous, engraving 'Pièce facétieuse relative à la prise de Perpignan: L'Espagnol despouillé', publisher A. Boudan. exc., 1642–1643. Bibliothèque nationale de France, département Estampes et photographie, RESERVE QB-201 (36)-FOL.

doublet by a Dutchman and his breeches by a Catalan. These actions made reference to the loss of the Portuguese Crown, the former Spanish territories in France and the Netherlands, and the revolt in the Principality of Catalonia that started in 1640. Looking at the Frenchman on the left-hand side of the image, the comparison between French and Spanish dress becomes salient. At that time, French styles were looser and more colourful than those in Spain, and profusely decorated with ribbons and lace, in great contrast to the sober, black Spanish garments. In this case, Spain is represented in sartorial terms, with the loss of hegemony being symbolized by the act of undressing a man. This defeat was transmitted to a larger audience by making reference to national sartorial habits, symbols that were widely recognizable at that time.

In other engravings, not only is defeat represented by the act of undressing, but conquest is also represented by the act of imposing new clothes on the defeated. A very similar example is to be found in a 1659 almanac entitled 'Flanders despoiled of Spanish garments and redressed in the French fashion' (*Flandre despouillée des habits d'Espagne et revestue a la Françoise*), evoking the loss of a significant amount of Flemish territory to the French after successive invasions (Figure 1.2). A woman kneeling before the allegory of Victory conveys a similar message. The woman is being violently stripped of her Spanish garments before being dressed in French ones. The corsage at the top of the image is in the French fashion and will be imposed on the female figure representing Flanders.

Language, food and customs became as decisive as design in specifying the differences between European nations. Costume represented the nation and was connected to all of the other aspects that together created a distinctive national character. In 1696, the Dominican priest Johann Zahn (1641–1707) produced a matrix of national characteristics comparing five European nations on points such as physical build, clothing, manners, style of beauty, eating habits, language, discretion, education, religion and so forth. Leerssen remarks that these myriad characteristics were captured morally in types of character and disposition, whereby external characteristics were motivated by a nation's internal essence. He concludes that it was in this period that a new national essentialism emerged. Nations were forced to be essentially different in every single respect. In a development of Zahn's matrixes, a 'Tableau of Nationalities' (*Völkertafel*) was printed between 1690 and 1720. In this table, the various nationalities differed from one another on a number of parameters. All of them had to be represented and each had to be unique. European nations were considered to be distinctive and different from each other; their identity resided in difference. Common traits were ignored, as if they did not contribute to defining the identity of a nation. Something that was characteristic of one nation could not be shared with another (Leerssen 2006: 64).

**Figure 1.2** Lepautre, Jan, engraving 'LA/FLANDRE/Despouillée des/habits d'Espagne/
et revestue a la/Françoise,' Publisher I. Le Potre In. et Exc. – N. Poilli Exc. – P. Mariette
Excudit Cum Priv. Regis, 1660. Bibliothèque nationale de France, département Estampes
et photographie, RESERVE FOL-QB-201 (43).

# Culture-based nationalism

On the whole, modernist theorists have tended to be fierce critics of primordialism. Unlike modernists, primordialists defend the existence of nations prior to modernity, and modernist criticism has focused on this essentialist position. Although the critique is sound and even though primordialist theories might seem obsolete, the primordialist depiction of the nation as a 'given' offers a key to understanding both past and present interpretations of national identity. The tension between the apparent naturalness of the canon and its constructed nature has been highlighted by the design historian John A. Walker, and corresponds as a cultural phenomenon to the remark made by Pierre Bourdieu in his *Outline for a Theory of Practice* that 'every established order tends to produce . . . the naturalization of its arbitrariness' (1977: 164). It is precisely this tension between the constructed nature of nations and their natural appearance that has defined theories of nationalism.

Tony Bennett (2001) acknowledges the strong tendency of nations to construct themselves as homogenizing cultural formations governed by the logic of 'one people, one culture, one history'. In this sense, national canons in general and national design canons in particular contribute to what is often a monolithic construction of national identity. Various sources contribute to the establishment of a national design canon, such as historiography, design exhibitions, museum collections and journalism. In this sense, the art historian Michael Camille (1996: 198) states that canons are composed of representations of objects, not of objects themselves. When the canon is consolidated, there is a close identification between these objects and the nation.

The main proponent of primordialism was Johann Gottfried Herder (1744–1803), a pioneer of a form of political nationalism that was rooted in culture, whose theories must be set against the backdrop of the Enlightenment. His work provides the most relevant characteristics of primordialism for the study of culture in general and of design in particular. These characteristics will be explained in detail in this chapter and discussed in the rest of the book. The expansion of French as a *lingua franca* provoked Herder to respond in defence of minority languages. Herder's initial intention was to preserve diversity in the face of the homogenizing forces of the universalist Enlightenment, which, in his *Another Philosophy of History for the Education of Mankind*, he mocks as follows: 'And then – state of bliss! – the golden age shall be upon us again "when all the world will have one tongue and language and there shall be one flock and one shepherd." National characters, where have you gone?' (Herder 2004b[1774]: 65). His defence of cultural diversity and the uniqueness of every culture lay in stark contrast to the homogenizing trends of the period. It was precisely in the eighteenth century when the sartorial diversity of the previous two centuries was diminished by the homogenizing power of French fashion. In this sense, dress was symptomatic of the situation that was being denounced by Herder, one that was in stark contrast to the representations of different national costumes in the examples given above.

In the context of the present book, one of the most significant concepts from Herder's thought is that of 'national character'. As the political scientist Alan Patten notes, Herder never gave a proper definition of 'national character', nor of the closely-related term 'people' (*Volk* in German) (Patten 2010: 666–7). As for 'character', it is mentioned along with language as an important property of nations and peoples. He believed that thought is dependent on language, and that a particular language is conditioned by the sensibility and the ways of thinking of its speakers (Patten 2010: 667). This resulted in the origination of unique, nation-specific characteristics. These were transmitted from generation to generation and arose 'from family traits, from the climate, from the way of life and education, from the early transactions and the deeds peculiar to them. The customs of the fathers took deep root and became the internal prototypes of the race' (Herder quoted in Wilson 1973: 822). Since all of these circumstances were unique and thus impossible to repeat, every nation was distinctive. This offers an alternative explanation to that of the late-seventeenth-century taxonomies. Herder focuses on the combination of characteristics and thus not on the characteristics themselves, and thereby departs from the above-mentioned 'Tableau of Nationalities'. For Herder, the combination that resulted had to be unique, but not the characteristics themselves. By contrast, in the 'Tableau of Nationalities', nations were expected to be different in every single respect.

Since Herder's cultural ideas are deeply grounded in political considerations, it is essential that we first address his political thought. Even though he expounded a culturally based form of nationalism, this model had clear political implications. Herder objected to the conquest of one community by another, and argued for the separation of nations (*Völker*) (Leerssen 2006: 101). This is where his political thought is most evident. In the second volume of *Outlines of a Philosophy of the History of Man* (1784), Herder argued that the most natural state is that which contains one people, with one national character (Herder 1800[1784]: 249). He did not defend the idea that each nation should have its own state; a nation could be spread across different states – such as eighteenth-century Germany – or might flourish in the absence of any state. Nevertheless, he objected to the notion of one state spreading beyond a single nation and thereby dominating other nations. As the political scientist Frederick M. Barnard states, Herder's political goal was the same as that of Jean-Jacques Rousseau (1712–1778): the replacement of force by culture. The expression of this goal was as radical in Herder's writings as it was in Rousseau's (Barnard 1983: 245). Accordingly, his ideal is a nationally bounded state in which every nation is free to develop its own unique culture (Patten 2010: 658–9).

In the same way that politics and culture were closely interrelated in Herder's thought, so, too, were the community and the individual. Humans were embedded in national groups in a process of socialization. Herder believed that humans were defined by their capacity for language, which could only be learnt in a community. In his 'Treatise on the Origin of Language' (1772), he states that language is the defining agent of humanity. He points out that animal language is instinctive and innate, that 'the bee hums just as it sucks, the bird sings just as it makes a nest' (Herder 2004b[1772]: 80). By contrast, human language is the product of reason (Herder 2004b[1772]: 82). Humans were made for humanity, and it must be 'the goal of our strivings, the sum of our exercises, our guiding value' (Herder quoted in Wilson 1973: 823). In the absence of categorical definitions, Herder's concepts are explained in terms of their functionality and mutual relations. The folklorist William A. Wilson has observed that like Giambattista Vico (1668–1744), Herder explained the nature of a thing by studying its origin, and also like Vico, he equated the nature of a thing with its end, its final cause. Vico argued that humans were made for civilization, while Herder held that they were made for humanity (*Humanität*) (Wilson 1973: 823). Even then, humanity was not innate, but had an *a posteriori* character. Herder admitted that 'although admittedly it is the deepest self in us', cognition is 'not as autonomous, voluntarily choosing, and unbound as is believed' (Herder 2004a: 212).

Herder's account of cognition has two distinctive features. The first is that it is strongly contingent. A person's framework of thought is the accumulated, empirical product of a process of socialization that occurs in a specific natural and social environment. The second is the fundamental importance of language as the medium by which the process of thought compares, measures and combines sensory material. Speech provides the 'heavenly spark' that unites all the senses to make thought possible and to awaken 'slumbering reason' into a vital power (Patten 2010: 664). Likewise, language is an instrument for the intergenerational transfer of ideas. A person's inner language is based on the external language of his or her community, which is acquired through imitation and learning. In itself, a language is based on environmental factors, including history, the way of life of its speakers, the climate, the terrain, innovations used by poets and writers and contact with other peoples and languages, political and administrative institutions and 'culture' (Patten 2010: 664–5). Under this last category, Herder mentions a region's products, food and drink, mode of life, the forms of labour in which individuals are employed, clothing and ordinary attitudes, and arts and pleasures (Herder 1800[1784]: 174). Other authors, such as Benedict Anderson, have moved the focus from socialization to cultural representation in describing how the nation is disseminated and national identity appropriated.

# Design as an index of the nation

Herder believed that the national character was embodied in culture. One consequence of this essentialism was that by analysing this cultural production, one could describe the national soul. For this reason, and because thought is derived from language, every community has its own mode of thought. The same applies to customs, traditions and the like, all of which shape a 'community' (Özkirimli 2000: 18). Nevertheless, a nation's distinctive identity could never be known directly, but only approached through its forms of expression. Art expressed this identity, and was only authentic when it was a spontaneous expression of this inner identity (Oring 1994: 226). Herder expressed his admiration for peasants as the custodians of the national character. It was here that ancestral German traditions could be found, and not in the emulative art of this period (Wilson 1973: 832). Medieval art was the real reference for the development of a true form of national art. The peasantry had for the most part remained unspoiled by foreign influence and therefore connected Germany with its past (Wilson 1973: 826). Moreover, only art that was spontaneous, natural and unconscious could reflect the true identity of a people (Oring 1994: 222).

It should come as no surprise that for Herder, the most cherished art forms were those based on language. His interest in popular culture was reflected in his collection of popular songs (1778–1779), in contrast to the high culture favoured by Enlightenment elites (Leerssen 2006: 99). For Herder, folk poetry bridged the gap between the present and the authentic German soul that would guide the future of the nation (Wilson 1973: 825). He called folk poems 'the archives of a nationality', 'the imprints of the soul' of a nation, 'the living voice of the nationalities' (Herder quoted in Wilson 1973: 826). Wilson notes that Vico likewise claimed that poetry reflected the socio-cultural patterns of the society in which it originated. In his eyes, Homer was nothing less than a projection of Greece (Wilson 1973: 825).

The development of a nation's own art, literature, religion and customs as expressions of the national soul had two purposes, one nationally and the other internationally oriented. It strengthened the unity of the nation on the one hand, while on the other, through the cultivation of its own national characteristics, each nation contributed to the development of humanity. 'All nations,' wrote Herder, 'each in its place, should weave [their part of] the great veil of Minerva' (Herder quoted in Wilson 1973: 823–4). Nonetheless, he did not advocate a national normativism, but on the contrary, a cultural relativism. If individuals were to foster and be faithful to their own national art, in the same way, they should be able to appreciate other national cultures that were valuable in themselves. Correspondingly, in order to appreciate art properly, one should take distance from one's own national framework of reference and be open to other aesthetic ideals:

Admittedly, there are peoples who introduce their national character into their representation of the ideal and stamp its image with their own individual features; but it is also possible to wean oneself from this idiosyncrasy that is both inherited and acquired, to extricate oneself from the irregularities of excessive singularity and ultimately, unguided by the taste of a particular nation or age or individual, to savor the beautiful wherever it manifests itself, in all ages and in all peoples and in all arts and in all varieties of taste, to taste and experience it in its purity, freed everywhere from all foreign elements. Happy he who savors it thus!

HERDER 2004a[1846 posthumous]: 202

According to Leerssen, this cultural relativism lay at the basis of the 'national awakenings' that took place in Central and Eastern Europe in the nineteenth century, from Germany to Bulgaria and from Slovenia to Finland (Leerssen 2006: 97). In Herder's thought, a defence of the national does not preclude an interest in the international. His national thought is thus different from that of traditional nationalists, who promote their own nation as the ideal of virtue. On the contrary, Herder advocates diversity and the right of each nation to be appreciated on the basis of internal parameters, not standard values. This position thus represented a shift away from Enlightenment thinkers who focused on common traits of humanity. Herder reflected on humanity, but he believed that it had limited power to define who we are; rather, it is culture that shapes humans. Arguing that it is impossible to judge foreign cultures is an argument against ethnocentrism. In the Herderian vision, some cultures might be more sophisticated and advanced technologically than others, but they are not therefore more valuable (Crowder 2013: 24–5).

Despite its proto-multiculturalism, Herder's conception of the nation and its embodiment in cultural manifestations is essentialist in two ways. First, it is essentialist to think that a nation is a natural given and that as such, every human belongs to one. For Herder, it is only in the context of a community that individuals can achieve humanity and fulfil their mission. Since socialization leads to the formation of nations, every person should belong to one. Accordingly, the relation between the individual and the nation is deterministic, as there is no other way in which humans can develop. Second, the cultural manifestations of a nation reflect its national character, and the latter can only be deciphered by studying the former. There is a necessary correspondence between a national character and the objects belonging to that culture. This principle – that outward appearance is motivated by inner essence – can be called essentialist. Cultural products are connected to the national character in a symbolic relation. Considering cultural products as signifiers and the nation as the signified, their symbolic relation, using Charles S. Pierce's nomenclature, would be one of indexicality according to this vision. In this category, the relation between the two is based on a real connection, and not in virtue of an interpretive habit. So just as smoke is an index of fire, so, too, are cultural products a reflection of the national character.

It is striking, however, that in Herder's indexical relation between cultural products and the nation, some products reflect this relation better than others. Herder defines folk poetry as all poetry that embodies the national inner identity, and that folk poetry is the ideal and highest type of all poetry (Schütze 1921: 119). For Herder, this is because folk poetry emerges from the people and has not been mediated by authorship. This absence of individualism is key when attributing national authorship to products. Indeed, when we examine the relation between design and the nation, his belief that a particular kind of art better represents the identity of a nation is recurrent. As we shall see in Part Two, various reasons have been given for connecting one kind of design to the nation, while other forms of design have been denied this status. Such reasoning has tended to champion the vernacular. In this sense, the practice of granting objects a place in the category of national design has been underlined by a primitivist logic. Needless to say, this correlation is debatable in a number of respects, since the vernacular is a fluid category. It is debatable first, how foreign elements can be distinguished from the national, and second, whether these foreign products do not also define the identity of a nation. For Herder, French-inspired art made by Germans could not be called German art. Paradoxically, the classification of national art is unconnected to the nationality of the artist, and on the contrary seems to reside in what is claimed are the permanent characteristics of the nation.

# Dreaming the primitive nation

As long as essential national traits are open to discussion, there will be myriad possibilities for defining and redefining the nation by prioritizing some cultural products above others. Wilson observes that the past cherished by Herder's followers was, for the most part, a mythic past, and that the great and noble nation they wished to re-create was largely the product of their own imaginations. They believed that there had once been such a Germany (Wilson 1973: 829–30). This is a typical characteristic of primitivist thought, a trend in which Herder could be included (Lovejoy and Boas 1997[1935]: 8). Primitivists look back on a Golden Age in which life was superior to that of their own time. For Herder, medieval Germany was the example to follow. An approximation to that lost age could be achieved if one was able to learn from contemporary peasants, who safeguarded the knowledge and attitudes stemming from that cherished past. Herder's thinking combines the two categories of primitivism that Arthur Lovejoy and George Boas describe as 'chronological' and 'cultural primitivism' (1997[1935]: 1–11). While thinkers in the former category look for the ideal in past times, those in the latter shift their attention away from the past to focus on the present, and generally consider the figure of the savage or the peasant as closely linked to the ideal.

Chronological primitivism, in turn, is divided into a number of categories, depending on the recurrence of the Golden Age in history and its relation to the present. Herder's account could be consistent with what Lovejoy and Boas describe as the 'Theory of Decline and Future Restoration'. This form of primitivism maintains that the best age of mankind to date occurred at the beginning of time, that there was a decline in the past, but that at some time in the future there will, or may, be a restoration of man's goodness. The only difference is that Herder does not locate the ideal age at the beginning of history, but in the period before the decadence, that is, before the Enlightenment. Thinkers in this vein argue that the move from decline to restoration can be achieved either by a sudden intervention on the part of some external power, such as in Christian chiliasm, or, as in Herder's case, by the recognition of the superiority of the primeval mode of life and a return to it, or some form of close approximation (Lovejoy & Boas 1997[1935]: 3). Herder's view that the parenthesis of the Enlightenment could be overcome by returning to pre-existing values, which had been preserved by contemporary peasants, is clearly consistent with the second category.

As Eugene Reed has noted, the categories of chronological and cultural primitivism overlap in Herder's thought, and the distinction is blurred (Reed 1965: 553). The diachronic and synchronic aspects of primitivism merge, since the ideal is a period from the past that is nevertheless incarnate in the contemporary peasantry. Lovejoy and Boas argue that this hybrid model merges the characteristic moods of youth and age, since chronological primitivism tends to idealize the past, which they characterize as typical of the elderly. On the other hand, cultural primitivism cherishes a love of strangeness, which according to them is an impulse that is strongest in adolescence and youth (1997[1935]: 8). With his belief that national identity can be found in artefacts from the past or in folk art, Herder's primitivism resonates in different episodes of the history of design, as will be discussed below.

The interest in the primitive evolved in the nineteenth century, but it did not meet with equal appreciation in art and design. The art historian Ernst Gombrich observed that the word 'primitive' became a term of praise towards the end of the eighteenth century. He cites as an example the atelier of the French neo-classical painter, Jacques-Louis David (1748–1825). His pupils regretted that their master had not explored more grandeur and simplicity in his paintings; in other words, a more 'primitive' style (Gombrich 1996[1979]: 297). The influence of Rousseau's writings questioning the progress of civilization, and Johann Joachim Winckelmann's (1717–1768) exaltation of the beauty of Greek art, are paramount when attempting to understand the origins of this trend. For Winckelmann, Greek art reflected the Greek soul in all its nobility and restraint.

These ideas actually conflicted with Herder's cultural relativism, whose appreciation of the self-expression of each nation departed from Winckelmann's one-dimensional canon. If each nation had to search for its own character, then the international imposition of Greek values prevented each nation from finding its own national art (Gombrich 1996[1979]: 305–6). Herder argued that the soul of the German nation was to be found in gothic art, and this call for variety contributed to the re-evaluation of the gothic and the medieval in Europe. Gombrich wonders why the acceptance of the primitive in art was then delayed until the early twentieth century, with the avant-garde movement, even though the taste for the primitive had arisen some hundred years earlier. He points out, however, that this delay applied to representational art, but not to design. Fidelity to nature remained embedded within art, but less so in the decorative arts (Gombrich 1996[1979]: 307).

In his chapter entitled 'The Priority of Pattern', Gombrich describes an evolution that is well known in seminal design-historical accounts. He refers to August Pugin's (1812–1852) taste for flat ornamentation, derived from his study of gothic ornament. Ideas on decoration lay at the heart of public debates in the first half of the nineteenth century. The reasons for this were partly aesthetic and partly economic, since poor design would result in poor sales. Later, Gombrich refers to the design reforms put into effect by Henry Cole (1808–1882) and Richard Redgrave (1804–1888), who started looking to non-European styles of decoration and their flat motifs. The 1856 edition of Owen Jones' *The Grammar of the Ornament* forms the next episode in Gombrich's genealogy, followed by Gottfried Semper's claim that decorative patterns should be flat in order to fit easily into ordered arrangements. Gombrich's account finishes with John Ruskin (1819–1900) and the latter's discussion of the flatness of stained-glass windows. The chapter concludes with Ruskin's influence on William Morris (1834–1896) and the Arts and Crafts movement, along with that of Japanese art on art nouveau (Gombrich 1996[1979]: 311–21). Gombrich interprets the predilection for flat decoration as an early adoption of primitivism in the field of design, a trend that arrived only later in the visual arts. In this sense, it is worth studying how these ideas were defended and developed by design theorists. At times, their primitivism followed Herder's ideas, but they also presented points of dissent. Studying these theorists helps us to understand the early adoption of the primitive in the field of design and its resonance in design thought; understanding Herder thus allows us to trace the preservation of Herder's ideas in design theory.

# Primitivism in design theory

One exponent of chronological primitivism was the designer and theorist William Morris. Morris' thinking was informed by Pugin's and Ruskin's emulation of gothic style, and emerged as an alternative to what was seen as the poor-quality design presented at the 1851 Great Exhibition in London. Imbued with Victorian medievalism, Morris' socialist model of society gave prominent place to the manufacture of goods. The object of his critique was the capitalist system of production that prevented workers from experiencing the production process as something that was pleasurable. In his primitivist account, he argued that an ideal relation had existed between the worker and the product in the Middle Ages, and that this no longer existed in industrial society. In 'The Revival of Handicraft' (1888), Morris argued that 'the produce of all modern industrialism is ugly, and that whenever anything which is old disappears, its place is taken by something inferior to it in beauty' (Morris 1888: 151). He admired the Middle Ages for its individualistic methods of production and for having little or no division of labour, since the workman worked for himself and was not dependent on any employer (Morris 1888: 150). Similarly, Morris' ideal of work relations was that of the medieval guild, in which he saw forms of association that guaranteed the equality of freemen (Waithe 2006: 137). He did not argue for a literal return to the Middle Ages, however; Morris did not believe that feudal society would lead to a better future *per se*. On the contrary, he believed that an egalitarian and socialist society would bring happiness.

The combination of cultural and chronological primitivism is manifest in Morris' vision, but he also added a future-oriented element derived from his socialist ideas. While Morris admired the life of the fourteenth-century peasant and guild members, he nevertheless believed their time to be inferior to that of the coming socialist era. They provided inspiration for the socialist cause, but if progress were to be made, it would be necessary to break with their way of life (Waithe 2006: 142). This strong belief in the progression of history towards a socialist society tempered Morris' primitivism and created distance between his ideas and those of Herder. Morris argued for the resurrection of certain medieval values, but at the same time, he located his ideal society in the future and not in the past. He described his ideal society in *News from Nowhere* (1890), locating it in the mid-twentieth century. There was no class division in this society, but neither were there courts nor any authority whatsoever, and there was no monetary system.

Morris' ideas stemmed partly from his admiration of Ruskin, whose medievalism was based on two key suppositions: first, that the artistic standards of an age are an index of its religious and ethical values; and second, that these standards are shaped by the conditions under which artistic labour is carried out (Arscott 2006: 10). For Ruskin, as for Herder, cultural production was an indexical reflection of the character of a society. If in Herder's case, this was a national character, for Ruskin, the character of a society lay in its religious and ethical values. The connection that Morris made between a society, labour and artistic production links him to both Ruskin and Herder, and the conception of culture as an index of society reverberates in his work.

Another component of Herder's theories, the reference to the spontaneity of truly national design, was explored by the Japanese craft theorist Yanagi Sōetsu (1889–1961). Yanagi led the *Mingei* (folk crafts) movement, which aimed to revitalize folk art in Japan in the 1920s. Yanagi studied not only Ruskin and Morris, but also other thinkers, and knew about the expansion of primitivism in art. One of his most characteristic contributions to the theory of craft – one that was very much connected to Herder's condemnation of individual authorship – was his 'criterion of beauty', and more specifically, the state of 'no-mindedness' that guaranteed true beauty. He differentiated between folk arts and artistic crafts. The former (*getemono*) were the most authentic expression of the people. He wrote that these 'reflect a purely Japanese world. *Getemono* clearly reveal the identity of our race with their beauty rising from nature and the blood of our homeland, not following a foreign technique or imitating foreign countries. Probably these works show the most remarkable originality of Japan' (Yanagi quoted in Kikuchi 2004: 50). In these words, one can discern Herder's view that spontaneous art is the most authentic national art. The major merit of such art was to reflect the beauty of the country better than other forms of art; in Yanagi's words, the 'nature and blood of our homeland'. As for Herder, originality and lack of contamination from foreign influence were assets that should be nourished, since these gave a nation character. Hybridity and individuality were to be avoided and thought to be less suitable for reflecting a nation's character. Accordingly, Yanagi praised everyday items that lacked individuality. For example, he praised a specific tea/soup pot (*sansui dobin*) that had been created by the illiterate artisan Minagawa Masu from Mashiko (Figure 1.3). This artisan decorated between 500 and 1,000 of these works per day with rapidly executed, repetitive traditional patterns. Yanagi considered this object to have 'extraordinary beauty' (Kikuchi 2004: 53–4). Through its automatism and connection with tradition, the pot was imbued with a genuinely national character that could not have been achieved had the designer wished to stamp it with his own personality and individuality.

Yuko Kikuchi has analysed the nationalist components of Yanagi's theory. A rise in Japanese cultural nationalism occurred in response to the Westernization of the first half of the Meiji period (1868–1912). From 1868, the Japanese government had promoted industrialization, had hired Western specialists and had sent students to Western universities. Intellectuals were both open to Westernization and simultaneously attempted to protect Japanese identity. This ambivalence was clear around 1919, as shown by the new turn in periodicals such as Yanagi's *Shirakaba*, which started displaying Eastern art again after a period in which Western art had prevailed (Kikuchi 2004: 76–7). In this sense, Yanagi sought in craft an argument to defend Japanese singularity, and his position could therefore be interpreted as that of a follower of Herder's cultural relativism. Yanagi's praise of Korean and Taiwanese crafts has been seen

**Figure 1.3** Minagawa, Masu (ca. 1872–1953), teapot (*dobin*) decorated with a land-scape, 1915–1935, ceramic and porcelain enamel, height 15 cm.

nevertheless as paternalistic. Yanagi was indeed interested in the folk art of Korea, which was then a Japanese colony, and made a number of attempts to preserve and disseminate Korean heritage. He characterized the beauty of Korean craft as the 'beauty of sadness'. Accordingly, he characterized Korean cultural products as being produced by the 'lonely Korean', whereas Japanese colourful ceramics were created by 'cheerful Japanese', and the 'practical and strong Chinese' likewise created ceramics with strong shapes (Kikuchi 2004: 132).

On the other hand, in the singularity of Japanese craft he equally saw an argument for maintaining Japanese colonial dominion. In this case, Yanagi's argument is the polar opposite of Herder's cultural relativism. He developed a vision of Asia as the 'Other', as opposed to the Japanese 'Self'. In doing so, he became part of what Kikuchi has coined 'Oriental Orientalism'. In this vein, he used the same argument to safeguard Japan from Western influence and to elevate Japan to the centre of Asia, thereby justifying colonial dominion (Kikuchi 2004: 123–5). His political stance against colonialism was ambiguous, at the very least. Yanagi argued fervently against Japanese military domination of Korea, but not against liberal rule to 'civilise' the Koreans. At the same time as he denounced the Japanese oppression of Korea in the 1920s, he called upon

Koreans to reflect on their lack of 'self-awareness' and on the fact that they had not protected their own country (Kikuchi 2004: 139). Similarly, he praised Taiwanese bamboo crafts for their naturalness and intrinsic Oriental character, while at the same time he considered the Taiwanese to be unaware of the beauty that only the Japanese could see, and whose responsibility it was to preserve it (Kikuchi 2004: 182).

# Chapter 2
# Rethinking National Romanticism

*What is perhaps more remarkable is that the formation of national identities was less the result of national introspection than a large-scale international exchange of ideas, theories and savoir-faire. The various national identities that exist today, while individually specific, are in reality similar in their conception.*

THIESSE 2007: 16

Primitivism in design, either through the construction of a Golden Age or through the elevation of peasant culture, has functioned as a tool for reaffirming national identity. Since the emergence of nationalism in the nineteenth century, theorists, designers and the state have been heralding a revival of either historical circumstances or of traditions and folklore. Historical revivals were key to defining the identity of nations. Folk art played an important role, as seen by the establishment of folklore studies, the representation of countries at world fairs and the establishment of artists' colonies. The relation between primitivism and the nation developed in the cultural climate of romanticism and the political climate of nationalism. In many respects, these two phenomena were interconnected and served each other. Leerssen thus refers to Romantic Nationalism or Nationalist Romanticism, the epicentre of which he locates in North-western Europe around 1800. He points out that developments in the late eighteenth century contributed to the formulation of the two (Leerssen 2013: 11). Herder's thought is a clear example of how the two interconnect; his interest in the gothic as an alternative to classicism resonated in romanticism. On the other hand, his interest in the origin and autonomy of nations abounded in nationalist thinking. This way of thinking continued in the nineteenth century; romantics explored the subject of the nation in their works and nationalists used art to persuade the citizenry.

Leerssen defines these two categories as: 'The celebration of the nation (defined in its language, history and cultural character) as an inspiring ideal for artistic expression; and the instrumentalisation of that expression in political consciousness-raising' (Leerssen 2013: 28). He sees the two as interdependent, and as two sides of the same coin. The use of one or the other depends on whether there is greater emphasis on the poetical ('art inspired by nationality') or the political ('art instrumentalized for the national cause'). He would accordingly use the term 'National Romanticism' for the former and 'Romantic Nationalism' for the latter, although he insists that as the two are so closely interrelated, differentiating between them can be an arduous task (Leerssen, 2014: 5). The nomenclature of design history is equally ambiguous. Whereas in Kirkham and Weber's book *History of Design. Decorative Arts and Material Culture, 1400–2000*, the authors use the term 'National Romanticism' (2013: 431), in David Raizman's *History of Modern Design,* 'Romantic Nationalism' is preferred (2010: 140). I will use the term 'National Romanticism'. Bearing in mind that this book is about the intersection of the poetical and the political, if one of the two should be prioritized, then it is the poetical.

National Romanticism has been related to the revival of craft traditions in the late nineteenth century (see Bowe 1993; Lane 2000; Kirkham & Weber 2013: 431–3). A clear distinction is therefore made between the development of historicism in the first part of the century and the vernacular revival in its latter part. As such, these accounts equate National Romanticism with cultural primitivism, overlooking the role played by chronological nationalism (historicism) in recreating the nation. Accepting cultural primitivism alone as an expression of nationalism ignores strategies to create national symbolism that were based in historicism. At the end of the eighteenth century and beginning of the nineteenth century, interest in the past was linked to a search for national identity, the romantic attempt to find one's place among other nations and cultures. A nation's uniqueness could only be understood in a historical context. For those disappointed by Enlightenment ideas, the past played an instrumental role, as these thinkers hoped that having a historical understanding of their nation would help them to build a better future (Kirkham & Weber 2013: 422–6).

I propose to examine both cultural and chronological primitivism as two facets of National Romanticism, thereby bringing its definition in design history closer to cultural history (Leerssen 2013, 2014). This conception acknowledges the continuity between developments in nineteenth-century design and the emergence and evolution of nationalism. When analysing this evolution, in general terms, an early interest in chronological primitivism is followed by cultural primitivism. If the former prioritized a nation's past, the latter did the same for folk art. The evolution of anthropology as a discipline and the mechanization of daily life imbued the figure of the peasant and folk art with the essence of the nation. This evolution has been characterized by Leerssen as the shift 'from past to peasant' in nineteenth-century Romantic Nationalism (Leerssen 2014: 13).

As explained in the introductory chapter, one of the contributions made by the theoretical debates of the 1990s was to reformulate the concept of nationalism. The concept now reaches beyond peripheral positions to cover the reaffirmation of the nation in general, be it old or new, whether it has its own state or belongs to a larger one (see Billig 1995: 7). If our understanding of nationalism reaches beyond extremist positions to embrace the everyday presence of established nations, then the nineteenth-century historicism of the decorative arts, oriented to the reaffirmation of established nations, should be considered representative of National Romanticism, just like the late nineteenth-century Arts and Crafts movements in Central Europe, Scandinavia and Russia. Neo-gothic, neo-Renaissance, neo-baroque, neo-rococo and neo-Moorish; in different ways, all gave substance and a sense of continuity to nations.

A second implication of extending our understanding of National Romanticism is that it goes beyond countries such as Germany and Scandinavia, and becomes a pan-European phenomenon (Lane 2000). The French historian Anne-Marie Thiesse has elaborated further on this in *La création des identités nationales* (1999). Her book gives an overview of the way in which idealized notions of folk culture have played a role in the construction of the national. Referring to a wide range of European countries, it shows that the veneration of folk art was an international phenomenon. Thiesse concludes that the creation of national identity was quite a transnational phenomenon. Every national identity was underpinned by similar aspects and followed similar paths. In all of the countries studied, objects of folk art such as folk costumes, furniture and objects related to festivities – Easter or Christmas, for example – were collected in museums as tokens of the national. Thiesse therefore refers to 'the cosmopolitan of the national' and states that 'there is nothing more international than the formation of national identities' (Thiesse 1999: II and 64).

# Historicism, the vernacular and the nation

In the first half of the century, design focused on historicism, drawing on references to official culture from the past. The interest in the Middle Ages was most salient in what has been called 'troubadour style'. At that time, contemporaries viewed the Middle Ages as a period that ran from the twelfth to the sixteenth centuries. Albeit very much connected to romanticism, however, the medieval revival was already present in late-eighteenth-century France. In 1774 the comte d'Angivillier (1730–1789), the Director of State Buildings, commissioned a series of paintings and sculptures for the royal palace depicting the medieval past, in order to 'inspire virtue and patriotic sentiment' (McClellan: 1994: 82). In the same year, the coronation of the new king Louis XVI (r. 1774–1791) coincided with a campaign to enhance the figure of the Renaissance king Henry IV. The latter founded the Bourbon dynasty and was an exemplary ruler, in stark contrast to the then unpopular Louis XV (r. 1722–1774), who was blamed for the financial crisis that had resulted from the Seven Years' War (Mackrell 1998: 33). Medieval details were incorporated in court costume. Queen Marie-Antoinette (r. 1774–1792) appropriated the Medici collar – a raised lace collar – associated with the French queen Catharina de Medici (r. 1547–1559). In masquerades, the slashed fabrics that had been popular in the Renaissance were also used in feminine and masculine dress (Mackrell 1998: 34–5). This fashion was continued in the First Empire (1804–1814/1815) by the Empress Josephine (1763–1814), who incorporated medieval details within the dominant style of the period, clearly inspired by classical dress (Mackrell 1998: 37–41).

The romantic period, which stretched from the end of the Napoleonic Wars to the revolutions of 1848, saw a revival of old styles. Nationalism imbued the arts and design with a historicist fever. There was an interest in reviving the history of the different nations, with a preference for the period before the Napoleonic years and the Enlightenment. Women's dress revealed conscious attempts to revive certain elements of historical costume, such as neck ruffs and the practice of slashing clothing, typical of the sixteenth century (Tortora & Eubank 2005: 280). In a portrait by Jean-Auguste-Dominique Ingres (1780–1867) of Marie Marcoz, the Viscountess of Senonnes, the model wears a red velvet dress typical of Empire fashion, with the waistline positioned right under the bust (Figure 2.1). The sleeves of the dress are slashed, allowing the white lining to come through, a technique typical of the sixteenth century. The ruff neck and cuffs are equally inspired by sixteenth-century dress (Ribeiro 1999: 132). Likewise, Elizabethan leg-of-mutton sleeves were in vogue from 1824, and gained in volume until 1829. In the late 1830s, dresses from the 1660s were the model to follow (Ribeiro 1999: 148). Bodices with an open neckline, a narrow waist and voluminous sleeves starting below the shoulders were combined with increasingly full skirts. Hairstyles also followed seventeenth-century models. Parted in the middle, hair was pulled smoothly to the temples, where it was arranged in hanging, sausage-shaped curls. At the back, hair was pulled into a bun or chignon (Tortora & Eubank 2005: 287).

In furniture, neo-styles came to replace the Empire style favoured by Napoleon. Along with classical references, there was an increasing fashion for gothic style. It is striking how recently created countries attempted to recreate a Golden Age; Belgium, for example, sought to reaffirm its national identity by drawing on examples from the past. Belgium's founding as a nation-state had been the result of the 1830 Belgian Revolution, whereby the Catholic Southern Provinces seceded from the United Kingdom of the Netherlands. Due to the liberalization of trade and the rapid development of the Industrial Revolution, Belgium became the most industrialized country in Continental Europe. Its central geographical

**Figure 2.1** Ingres, Jean-Auguste-Dominique, 'Portrait of Madame Senonnes', 1916. Nantes, Musée des Beaux-Arts.

position favoured commerce, the country was rich in raw materials and entrepreneurs financed industrial endeavours. The concentration of the coal and steel industries in the southern half of the country complemented the developing textiles, glass and ceramics industries. Industrial products were displayed in four Exhibitions of National Industry that were organized and financed by the Ministry of Internal Affairs in 1830, 1835, 1841 and 1847. At these exhibitions, participants aimed to demonstrate the superiority of industrially manufactured products to crafts. Despite this, the exhibits were largely inspired by styles from the past. Models from the Ancien Régime were preferred to neoclassicism, which was associated with the 'unification' under the Napoleonic Empire. Flemish-Renaissance and gothic revivals were also considered to be references for a new Belgian cultural identity (Leblanc 2005: 10–15, 24–6).

Historicism came to represent one variation of the one-sided revival of neoclassicism. In the Americas, for example, North America had adopted neoclassicism as a vocabulary to express its independence from Britain in 1783. South America however, combined European styles with indigenous traditions. Neoclassicism was seen as a response to the excesses of rococo and therefore as representing democracy (as opposed to monarchy). It continued to be prevalent until the early nineteenth century, when various other revival styles became popular, including the Greek, Roman gothic and Egyptian styles (Kirkham & Weber 2013: 467). Independence movements in the first three decades of the nineteenth century resulted in newly independent states. Haiti was the first to declare itself a free republic in 1804, Brazil seceded from Portugal in 1822, and by 1830 all of the Spanish territories in the Americas had achieved independence, with the exception of Cuba and Puerto Rico. The iconography generated by movements opposed to autocratic or colonial rule – such as the Phrygian cap and the Roman fasces – was adopted by the newly independent countries of Latin America. Along with these elite symbols, others were derived from folk art and intertwined to define a new national iconography of design. Many workshops produced 'Republican-style' furniture in Puebla (Mexico), Lima and Ayacucho (Peru), Quito (Ecuador), Bogotá (Colombia) and Rio de Janeiro (Brazil). For example, Joseph W. Whiting (1800–1849), who was based in Caracas, produced *butaca*-style chairs, a typology derived from the seats of the pre-Columbian era, between 1824 and 1845. These armchairs featured United States Federal decoration, complete with gilt stencilling (Kirkham & Weber 2013: 459).

As with historicism, an early interest in folk art can be located in the late eighteenth century. The first collections of folk culture were chiefly concerned with popular songs and tales. The years of Napoleonic occupation and those following its end in 1815 witnessed a search for national identity in the occupied states. Inspired by Herder and his praise of artless popular culture, Jacob and Wilhem Grimm collected folk tales and fairytales. Based on oral tradition, their collection was published between 1811 and 1814 as a compendium of essential German culture (Leerssen 2006: 122). The new scholarly discipline of folklore studies flourished in the wake of this romantic interest: tales, proverbs and ballads were collected in Russia, Sicily and Norway. Inventories were made of festivals, rituals, superstitions and customs in a sort of ethnography-turned-inward, which focused on traditional dress, farmhouse architecture, dialects and folk dances (Leerssen 2006: 195). The influence of Herder is clear as a source of inspiration for this search for popular culture (Leerssen 2006: 97). From the 1830s onwards, interest in popular culture expanded to cover material objects, especially clothing and jewellery. After the first decade of the century, series and collections of engravings depicting folk costumes multiplied. The influence of historical illustration and theatrical costumes contributed the most spectacular fashions, such as headdresses featuring ever higher and more vivid patterns of colour. Tailors and seamstresses created ceremonial outfits for rich clients. In emerging nations, wearing national costume was a manifestation of political ideology, and patriotic balls in Central and Eastern Europe proved to be particularly good occasions for wearing such outfits (Thiesse 2000: 58).

From the mid-nineteenth century, folklore studies in Europe began to cover popular domestic objects – furniture, crockery and carpets – as well as rural architecture. Indeed, these popular arts and crafts were facing more and more competition from industrial production. New values were attributed to the production of crafts, as the fruit of human skill and individual creation (Thiesse, 2013:13). While the world fairs chiefly disseminated national manufactured goods, they were also increasingly seen as showcases for more traditional national culture. The historian Angela Schwarz (2012) has described the way in which ethnographic displays came to complement industrial products at the exhibitions in Paris in 1867 and 1878 and Vienna in 1873. At the Paris exhibition of 1867, the organizers had invited the 44 participating countries to construct typical edifices outside the exhibition building, in what was known as the 'foreign park' (*Parc étranger*). Some chose an iconic building, others folkloric architecture. Austria-Hungary and Russia even created small villages with representations of different regions. The interiors were furnished with folk crafts and mannequins were shown in folk dress. The erection of model houses and peasant cottages became a standard feature of later exhibitions, such as those of Vienna in 1873 and Paris in 1879. In Vienna, there was a village of nine farmhouses that mainly represented the regions of Austria-Hungary. The houses were inhabited by real peasants, performing everyday activities. While manufacturers presented their industrially made products to the world, alongside them their nations were represented with the vernacular. The two worlds were separated from each other, both physically and symbolically.

These scientific displays of peasant life accentuated the distance between rural peasant interiors and urban life. The objects in use represented a lifestyle that contrasted with that of the visitors. The relationship between the visitors and what seemed to be ordinary objects thus became 'museumized'. In 1878 in Paris, the Dutch contribution got a good press. Visitors could enter a fully furnished room inhabited by mannequins in folk dress, representing a typical interior from a Frisian fishers' village (Schwarz 2012: 107–10). Instead of looking at the objects and dresses from a distance, the visitors were able to enter another dimension. The Dutch entry rivalled that of Sweden, which was put together by Artur Hazelius (1833–1901). Hazelius was the founder of the Nordic Museum (*Nordiska Museet*), the first ethnographic museum, which was established in 1873 in Stockholm – although the museum building was only completed in 1909. In the Swedish display, visitors were not allowed to enter the exhibition space, but could only look at it from afar. It was in such exhibitions that the value of craft as a token of primitivism and a representation of different national identities was at its clearest. Handicrafts acquired a symbolic value that went beyond the utilitarian, one that encapsulated the more stable values of national character in a world where mechanization was producing a wide range of functional goods that would ultimately threaten the survival of handiwork.

Attempts to bridge these two worlds were made by designers who sought to preserve the craftsmanship of folk craft and adapt it for daily use. These initiatives contained a political message, a critique of modern society and a proposition for a better world. The best-known example is that of the British Arts and Crafts movement, influenced by William Morris, as mentioned above. In 1861, along with Charles Faulkner and Peter Paul Marshall, Morris established the firm Morris, Marshall, Faulkner & Co., with Dante Gabriel Rossetti, Edward Burne-Jones, Ford Madox Brown and Philip Webb as partners. The firm produced furniture, jewellery, stained glass, embroideries, wallpaper, carpets and so forth. Morris' ideal of society entailed a redefinition of material culture that could improve the labour conditions of producers and improve the life of consumers. Taking its name from the Arts and Crafts Exhibition Society, founded in London in 1887, the Arts and Crafts movement flourished in Britain and Europe between the 1880s and 1916. Nostalgia for the countryside and vernacular traditions were central to the movement's meaning (Livingstone 2008: 242–4). The British representatives were all established in the 1880s and included the Century Guild (1882–1883), the Art Workers Guild (1884) and the above-mentioned Arts and Crafts Exhibition Society. They worked as cooperatives, gathering a number of designers who operated as a group, sharing their workshops and presenting their work collectively at exhibitions. Particularly influential were the exhibitions of the Arts and Crafts Exhibition Society that were regularly covered in the magazine *The Studio*, and reached beyond Britain. Invitations to exhibit at the world fairs of Turin (1902), St Louis (1904), Ghent (1913) and Paris (1914) contributed to the dissemination of the society's ideals (Livingstone 2008: 247). These were disseminated to other Anglo-Saxon countries, such as the United States and Ireland (Bowe 1991), and reached the European Continent and Japan. The interpretation of the Arts and Crafts movement that emerged in the Continent and Japan took peasant and folk art as its main reference, whereas the British Arts and Crafts movement drew mainly from medieval sources. In Continental Europe, these groups developed alongside a manifest interest in anthropology, reflected in the many museums that opened during that period. Examples of these include the Scandinavian ethnographic collection (*Skandinavisk-etnografiska samlingen*) in Stockholm, 1873, which has been known as the Nordic Museum since 1880; the Museum of Ethnology (*Museum für Völkerkunde*) in Vienna, 1876; the Ethnographic Museum of the Trocadéro (*Musée d'ethnographie du Trocadéro*) in Paris, 1878; the Danish Museum of Ethnography (*Dansk Folkemuseum*) in Copenhagen, 1879; the Museum for German Traditional Costumes and Handicrafts (*Museum für deutsche Volkstrachten und Erzeugnisse des Hausgewerbes*) in Berlin, 1889; and the Norwegian Museum of Cultural History (*Norsk folke museum*) at Bygdøy in Oslo, 1894.

Design inspired by folk art had political overtones, especially in Central Europe, a region characterized by a complex mix of political powers, which led to a search for a specific national identity in Hungary, Poland and the Czech region. The search for the vernacular contributed to the redefinition of national identity beyond traditional constellations of power. Austria-Hungary introduced constitutional reforms in 1867 to grant limited autonomy to its provinces. The empire remained heterogeneous, however, and comprised national movements based on Germanic, Slav, Polish and Magyar cultures. The rapid growth of metropolises such as Vienna and Budapest and the industrialization of provinces such as Bohemia contrasted with the agriculture-based economies in the eastern provinces. Similar situations could be found in Sweden; in Norway, under Danish rule until 1814, when it passed to Sweden before achieving its independence in 1905; Finland, which was passed from Sweden to Russia in 1809 and became independent only in 1918; and Denmark, where newly established independence and the revision of national boundaries had a similar effect. The case of Russia, albeit under different political circumstances, saw similar developments.

# Nation versus modernity in Russia and Central Europe

According to Karen Livingstone and Linda Parry, the Arts and Crafts movements in Continental Europe were less of a response to the effects of industrialization than those in Britain and America. They argue that these economies were rather rural, and saw little industrial development compared to Britain (Livingstone & Parry 2005: 30–1). While this may be true to some extent, in some cases, such as Sweden, industrialization was an issue. At any rate, these vernacular revivals emerged as an alternative to modernization in general. Anxieties about modernization, similar to those that characterized the British Arts and Crafts movement, were present in Central Europe and Russia. The lack of industrialization in the countryside was of less importance, since these movements originated in the cities. The movements were started by urban elites who experienced first-hand the changes brought by industrialization, to a greater or lesser degree, and by modernization.

Even when these cases are similar, they offer a rich variety of attitudes towards the vernacular. Thiesse has argued that a new status was conferred on objects of folk art, as they were disappearing under modernization. This new status was 'that of "relics" in an almost religious sense, appropriate to the new "secular religion" of modernity' (Thiesse 2013: 29). The range of ways in which designers interacted with folk art was nevertheless diverse. At times, these objects were indeed almost relics, at other times much less so. The interest in the vernacular was often mixed with the designer's own style. Far from remaining 'uncontaminated', vernacular inspiration was in some cases combined with modern styles, blurring the distinction between the vernacular and the modern. The veneration and faithfulness of these designers to their sources of inspiration reveals an artistic interest, rather than an archaeological one. Since they differ from case to case, it is worthwhile analysing them in detail and drawing some conclusions.

Interest in the vernacular often developed for political reasons. Peasant culture was considered in opposition to centralized government and elites. Especially where designers' colonies were established in remote places, people were keen to preserve the unique character of the nation against the homogenizing processes of modernization. New forms of collective living outside the cities were mainly motivated by two factors: first, by the need to escape from civilization and practise an alternative lifestyle; and second, to get closer to remote places imbued with some pristine national quality. These places tended to be isolated and therefore to have retained their unspoiled character. In Russia, in the aftermath of rapid industrialization, design reformers looked to the era prior to the modernizing policies of Peter the Great (r. 1682–1725). The Abramtsevo colony near Moscow developed under the auspices of Savva Mamontov (1841–1918), who purchased the village in 1870. An art devotee, he set about bringing together writers, musicians, painters, sculptors and dramatic artists, whom he invited to stay and work at Abramtsevo in order to foster high quality, nationally inspired art. Initiated by his wife Elizaveta, a collection of folk art was established in 1881, intended to inspire the work of artists at Abramtsevo. The director of the workshop, Elena Polenova (1850–1898), created 'handcrafted' objects in this spirit. She designed furniture that borrowed motifs and shapes from objects still being used by the peasants. On a bigger scale, the Abramtsevo Ceramics Factory was founded in 1890 and revived Old Russian majolica ware and decorative architectural tiles (Salmond 2000: 391–2). By 1899, when Savva Mamontov was accused of financial irregularities and his business collapsed, artistic workshops based on the Abramtsevo model had been founded on the

Solomenki estate, owned by Maria Yakunchikova, and in 1898 on the Talashkino estate, owned by Princess Maria Tenisheva (1858–1928). Sergey Malyutin (1859–1937) worked on the latter. He was credited with creating the *matryoshka* doll in 1890, presented at the 1900 world fair in Paris, probably the best known symbol of Russia (Kirkham & Weber 2013: 433).

In Germany, several workshops were created, including the Munich United Workshops for Art in Handicraft (founded in 1897 as the *Verenigte Werkstätten für Handwerk*) and the Dresden Workshops for Arts and Crafts (*Dresdener Werkstätten für Handwerkskunst*). Another colony was promoted by the Grand Duke Ernst Ludwig (1868–1937), ruler of the small Protestant state of Hesse. Ernst Ludwig was inspired by the British Arts and Crafts movement, and in 1899 invited seven artists to Darmstadt, the capital of Hesse, to lead the local production of arts and crafts in a colony founded on a hilltop near the city. Another important influence for Ernst Ludwig was Alexander Koch, a leading crafts reformer and German nationalist who urged artists to find links between modern art and the German people. The Viennese Josef Maria Olbrich (1867–1908) and Peter Behrens (1868–1940) accepted the invitation. The result was a small village, with houses designed in the spirit of the *Gesamtkunstwerk*, or 'total work of art', from the buildings to the furniture and utensils. These realizations have been analysed as examples of art nouveau, but were largely based on a collection of generalized South German peasant traditions. These were stylized and adapted for modern tastes, and therefore not immediately recognizable (Lane 2000: 132–8). Indistinct inspiration from the regions conferred a national character on these creations, one that was not necessarily connected to one region or another, but to the country in general.

The next two examples are centred on the cult of what Anthony D. Smith has called 'poetic places', places that symbolize the historic home of a people and the repository of their memories (Smith 1991: 65). These poetized spaces were not only embodied in the landscape or in monuments, as Smith describes, but also very much in the peasant community that remained at the margins of modernization. This pristine state was reflected in the cultural objects produced by these peasants, who served as inspiration for designers. The interest in their work was not driven by its antiquarian value – as tokens of the past – but for its value as a form of living fossil, as an embodiment of uncontaminated national character. This living heritage formed a source of inspiration for designers' colonies that sought a revival of national design tradition. In Hungary after 1902, an interest in peasant culture lay at the heart of the Gödöllő Workshops run by the artist Aladar Körösfői-Kriesch (1863–1920), who sought to revive the art of weaving. These workshops were based in the region of Kalotaszeg in Transylvania (in modern day Romania), which had a particular meaning for Hungary, as it was inhabited by Székely (ethnic Hungarians) and had retained a degree of independence under the Turkish occupation. It was one of the less developed regions in the country and was therefore untouched by the modernization processes that had transformed much of Hungary. The artists and designers lived in a colony near the village of Gödöllő, producing leatherwork, stained glass and furniture alongside their weaving. Women from the village and the artists' wives were trained and employed as weavers. As David Crowley states, this immersion in peasant culture was driven by a search for a new Hungary and a new Hungarian-ness, an alternative to international academic and historicist traditions (Greenhalgh 2000: 356–9). In this case, the emergence of ethnographic studies in Hungary coincided roughly with this interest in peasant culture. The Hungarian Ethnographical Society was formed in 1889 and the Society's journal, *Ethnographia*, was launched in 1890.

During the same period, the Zakopane style was launched in the Polish Carpathians. Zakopane was the regional centre of Podhale, the northern foothills of the Tatra Mountains. This was a very poor area under Austrian rule, populated by the Górale (highlanders) who subsisted as peasant-farmers and shepherds. Poland had been divided into three in the late eighteenth century, between Russia, Prussia and Austria. Since then, and until the country's reunification in 1918, the idea of Polishness had been preserved. The town of Zakopane was the centre of an impoverished community of peasants, as well as a small imperial bureaucracy and a small business class. From 1873, trips were organized from Warsaw to visit the region. Among other things, the recitation of stories and dialects was one of the major activities. Stanislaw Witkiewicz (1851–1915), an art critic, artist and architect, created a style inspired by local traditions for rich residents in this new tourist region, drawing upon the knowledge of his colleagues, architects and local craftsmen. The villas and their interiors were inspired by local styles, following a *Gesamtkunstwerk* aesthetic. By the end of the 1910s, a significant number of villas, a chapel, two hotels and a sanatorium had been built in the Zakopane style (Crowley 2001: 110). As Crowley points out, redefining Polish-ness as embedded in the peasantry was groundbreaking at that time. In late-eighteenth-century political discourse, peasants were not even considered to be 'Polish' – a category that was reserved for the gentry and the aristocracy (Crowley 2001: 108).

# Museums and the vernacular in Scandinavia

In Scandinavia, the ethnographic and open-air museums that opened in the 1870s and 1880s represented a communal Scandinavian past based on peasant traditions. The open-air museum founded by Nicolay Nicolaysen (1817–1911) brought together farms and churches in Bygdøy (Norway) between 1881 and 1888. Similarly, Artur Hazelius collected examples that expressed the communal traditions of the Scandinavian people in the above-mentioned Nordic Museum, founded in 1873 in Stockholm, and an open-air museum in Skansen. Bernard Olsen, inspired by Hazelius' display at the world fair in Paris in 1878, established the Danish historic-ethnographic museum of peasant life in Copenhagen in 1885 (Lane 2000: 39–40). In addition to these, museums of decorative arts played a central role in promoting folk crafts. In Norway, three such museums were opened in the late nineteenth century: one in Oslo (then Christiania) in 1876, a second in Bergen in 1887, and a third in Trondheim in 1893. Norway had been under Danish rule until the end of the Napoleonic Wars, when it was passed to Sweden, despite having had its own Constitution since 1814. These museums aimed to study the region's craft heritage in order to improve contemporary industry and crafts. At that time there was little industrial production in Norway, but traditional handicrafts were seen as a means of modernization and development. In this case, the vernacular offered a path towards modernization that was perfectly compatible with nationalistic sentiment, unlike in the Hungarian and Russian cases, for example (Livingstone & Parry 2005: 286–8). Along with these museums, the Lysaker colony continued to develop the interest in wooden architecture that had started in Bygdøy. This group was organized around the artist Erik Werenskiold (1855–1938), and situated five miles from the centre of Oslo. Sigrun Sandberg (1869–1957) and Sophie Werenskiold (1829–1926) produced textiles. The painter-turned-designer Gerhard Munthe (1849–1929) produced plain, colourful, interior designs that combined old Norwegian furniture, self-designed furniture and peasant textiles. He collected medieval textiles that served as an inspiration for his own work, on which he collaborated with his wife, Sigrun Sandberg (Lane 2000: 82–6).

The situation in industrialized Sweden was different from that in Norway. Denise Hagströmer notes that while in 1840, 80 per cent of domestic textiles were home-woven, by 1900 the same percentage was machine-made. In the 1890s Sweden saw an increase in urbanization, with a consequent housing shortage and industrialization. The textile arts were the first to borrow from peasant crafts. The Association of Friends of Textile Art (*Föreningen för Handarbetes Vänner*) was founded in 1874 to defend peasant techniques from cheap industrial products and to enhance textile art in an 'artistic and patriotic manner'. After a visit to England in 1890, the artist Carin Wästberg (1859–1942) declared that Swedish textile producers should stop imitating the German Renaissance and develop their own style, based on Swedish nature and the Swedish imagination. This combination of inspiration from nature and personal style was evident in Wästberg's textiles and in the furniture of Gustaf Fjaedstad (1868–1948). His *Stabbestol* chair (1901) was hollowed out of a tree trunk, displaying bark, cones and branches as decorations (Livingstone & Parry 2005: 278–9). Moreover, a similar retreat experience to that of the Lysaker circle developed around Carl and Karin Larsson, this time in the region of Dalarna, where they theorized on the home from a rural enclave (Lane 2000: 112–17). They created the artistic home *Lilla Hyttnäs* (1888–1910, largely completed by 1893), which was transformed from a small family cottage into a combination of an idyllic past and peaceful present. Colourful rooms inspired by peasant interiors coexisted with lighter areas reflecting an eighteenth-century Gustavian revival (Kirkham & Weber 2013: 431).

In Finland, the region of Karelia was the repository of the national Finnish essence. Elias Lönnrot (1802–1884) collected popular songs from the area, which were later published as the *Kalevala*, the first version of which appeared in 1835. Debates around the expression of Finnish national identity emerged in textile crafts, promoted by The Friends of the Finnish Handicrafts (*Suomen Käsityön Ystävät*), a society founded in 1879 to preserve national handicrafts. Its initiators, Fanny Churberg (1845–1892) and Jac Ahrenberg (1847–1914), sought to preserve traditional Finnish craft, which they believed to have been corrupted by outside influences, and, echoing its Swedish counterpart, 'to refine it in a patriotic and artistic direction' (Churberg quoted in Livingstone & Parry 2005: 268). Hagströmer notes that the folk craft revival served different interests in Sweden from those in Norway and Finland. While in Sweden it served to create a national ethos, in the two other countries it developed around an independentist need (Livingstone & Parry 2005: 279 and 284). At any rate, craft emerged as a symbol of the nation in both an established nation and in cases of subnationalism. Although their goals might have been different, their invocation of nationalism was very similar.

In the 1890s, when Finland experienced large-scale Russification under Tsars Alexander III (r. 1881–1894) and Nicholas II (r. 1894–1917), artists made frequent pilgrimages to Karelia, which was divided between Russia and what was then the Grand Duchy of Finland (itself a Russian province). Akseli Gallén-Kallela (1865–1931) believed that the farmhouses and crafts of Karelia represented ancient Finnish culture. He moved there with his wife and produced, among other things, *ryijy* rugs, the traditional deep-pile wool rug-making technique commonly used for bedcovers and sleigh rugs (Lane 2000: 94). Another visitor to Karelia and a friend of Gallén-Kallela, the half-Italian, half-Swedish Count Louis Sparre (1863–1964), founded the Iris Workshops in 1897 in the small city of Porvoo. This workshop was inspired by British Arts and Crafts examples and produced everyday objects in a 'Finnish style' (Livingstone & Parry 2005: 272–3). The work of the above-mentioned designers contributed to the success of the Finnish pavilion at the 1900 world fair in Paris, designed by Eliel Saarinen (1973–1950), Herman Gesellius (1874–1916) and Armas Lindgren (1874–1929). The well-known 'flame' bench-cover by Gallén-Kallela was on display at the Iris room. Made using the *ryijy* technique, it was draped over the back of the bench and the seat and over the floor, thus performing the function of a cover and a rug.

# Folk art and political propaganda in Japan

A contrasting case is presented by Japan, where initiatives to create national crafts ended up serving as nationalist propaganda. The influence of the British Arts and Crafts movement arrived in Japan and developed as the *Mingei* movement, initiated by Yanagi Sōetsu. Yanagi, along with the other members of the Shirakaba group and the potter Bernard Leach (1887–1979), moved to Abiko on the outskirts of Tokyo to establish their own artists' colony in 1914. It was in 1923, however, that Yanagi started to be interested in Japanese folk art. He travelled through Japan collecting examples of folk crafts that were later housed in the Japan Folk Crafts Museum (*Nihon Mingeikan*), which he established in Komaba, Tokyo, in 1936. In setting up the museum, he was influenced by Hazelius' Nordic Museum, which he had visited in 1929. In 1934, the Japan Folk Crafts Association (*Nihon Mingei Kyōkai*) was founded, and became responsible for developing the New Mingei (*Shin Mingei*) movement. The association organized workshops in depressed rural areas to help craftsmen improve their design and manufacturing systems, so that they could make affordable objects for modern lifestyles. These creations were later exhibited along with historical *mingei* (Livingstone & Parry 2005: 296–304). As Kikuchi observes, *Mingei* was constructed as an authentic tradition, while at the same it had the capacity to expand and adapt to the modern context. Between the late 1930s and 1945, *Mingei* was appropriated by the Japanese government as a means of nationalist propaganda. One of Yanagi's books was recommended by the Ministry of Education, and his 'criterion of beauty' became a dominant concept for defining what it meant to be Japanese (Livingstone & Parry 2005: 305).

As mentioned above, Yanagi's theory flawlessly exemplifies Herder's notion of a national canon – gothic for Germans – and his defence of spontaneous art as opposed to authorship. Indeed, this issue caused the break between Tomimoto Kenkichi (1886–1963) and Yanagi. Tomimoto questioned Yanagi's praise of the 'art of the people'. He believed that beauty could be found not only in the serial work of anonymous artisans, but also in the original work of individual artists, and he founded his own group in 1927 (Kikuchi 2004: 212–13). Concurrently, the vernacular was supposed to be a living art, and as such able to incorporate new trends, unlike historicism. The cult of spontaneity was not shared by all vernacular revivals. Folk art was interpreted freely and often subject to the development of a personal style. For example, in Abramtsevo, motifs that were meant to be read in the round were redeployed in flat forms, or patterns stemming from embroidery and lace were applied on carved decorations. In fact, Polenova soon developed her own style, inspired by the vegetation of the countryside, which departed from the original models of peasant art (Livingstone & Parry 2005: 260–1).

The immutability of folk art is questionable. Many designers were attracted to these isolated, poetic places for their authenticity and stability. Motivated by their belief that national identity was one and immutable, designers sought authenticity in practices that they also believed to be pristine. For example, Polenova encouraged artists to look for inspiration in folk art, as they did not need to rely on published material, drawings or museum objects. Instead, her goal was 'to capture the still-living art of the people, and give it the opportunity to develop. What turns in publications is dead and forgotten . . . The thread is broken and it is terribly difficult to retie it artificially' (Polenova quoted in Hilton 1995: 233). She followed this by saying that for a peasant, copying from the past would be similar to copying from a different country, such as Mauritania or Greece. In this way, she presented folk art as something that was disconnected from history and geography, granting it both permanence and contemporaneity.

Perhaps due to its living character, folk art has also been subject to historical mutations. Charlotte Ashby explores this aspect in her study of The Friends of the Finnish Handicrafts. Ashby notes that in the 1880s, this society was promoting Finnish design as distinct from Western imported traditions, especially French ones. Its designs consequently emulated geometric patterns and strong colour contrasts, and the wall-hangings, curtains and ceiling cloths created an Eastern, tent-like space, referencing the peasant practice of hanging cloth and festive clothes from the beams and walls. The 1900s saw a period of collaboration with contemporary artists and the development of new designs, reflecting a spirit of openness and a will to distance themselves from the intensive Russification of the country. The 1910s saw a return to the more traditional geometric arrangements of the eighteenth- and early-nineteenth-century Finnish *ryijy* preserved by collectors. These were different from the sources from the 1880s. These antique *ryijy* reflected the slow filtration of late-baroque and classical patterns from other textile mediums into Swedish *ryijy*, and from there on to Finland. The revival of such patterns in the 1910s coincided with the return of classical forms to design more generally (Ashby 2010: 356–62).

Thus the isolation of folk craft from history is only relative; when connecting with the vernacular, designers had to select what vernacular would best represent their nationalist aspirations. This was most salient in the Norwegian case, where museums of decorative arts tried to make rural art schools and artisans operate in accordance with their standards. As the art historian Ingeborg Glambek observes, not all artisans were appreciated equally, but some were used as examples. One was Lars Kinsarvik (1846–1925) from Handanger, who produced wooden furniture in the Viking-inspired 'dragon style' (Figure 2.2). Another was Ole Moene (1839–1908), who made vases, mugs and tobacco boxes in a style that was paradoxically influenced by baroque acanthus ornaments (Livingstone & Parry 2005: 289) (Figure 2.3). Moreover, other designers, such as Gerhard Munthe in Norway or Carl and Karin Larsson in Sweden, were happy to

**Figure 2.2** Kinsarvik, Lars, chair, ca. 1905. Oslo, Norwegian Museum of Cultural History (Norsk Folkemuseum).

**Figure 2.3** Moene, Ole Olsen, spoon, undated, acquired in 1915. Oslo, Norwegian Museum of Cultural History (Norsk Folkemuseum).

combine peasant art with historic furniture in their interiors, without creating any sense of opposition between chronological and cultural primitivism.

If folk art could merge with historicism, it could also merge with modernity and international trends. For example, in Darmstadt, a very abstract interpretation of folk art was promoted that drew as much on the stylistic language of art nouveau as it did from the preservation of folk craft. Similarly, the Finnish pavilion by Saarinen made use of vernacular Finnish elements combined with the semicircular doors introduced by the American architect Louis Sullivan (1856–1924) (Greenhalgh 2000: 378). This combination of international and local elements was most present in the Finnish Iris Workshops. According to the design historian Marianne Aav, the workshop founder Louis Sarre believed that 'Finnish Style' did not need to borrow from Finnish folk art. His furniture also displayed influences from medieval English furniture (Livingstone & Parry 2005: 272). Likewise, Ede Toroczkai Wigand (1878–1945), one of the Gödöllő designers, found that the Hungarian vernacular patterns paradoxically emulated the British Arts and Crafts movement, a movement that he greatly admired. The British magazine *The Studio* commented in 1901 that his furniture 'might have been planned by an English designer' (Livingstone & Parry 2005: 246). These last examples show how the national vernacular could leave some space for hybridization, calling Herder's ideas on an immutable national canon into question.

Inspiration in folk art was a common denominator for a number of very different initiatives. Although they were searching for distinctiveness, these groups actually looked to similar sources. Moreover, the resulting experiences were all initiated by an educated urban elite that generally, but not always, drew on folk art as an alternative to international trends such as art nouveau and historicism. Their confidence in their task was such that in some cases, they even started teaching folk art to peasants, as happened in Russia and Japan. Nevertheless, the instrumentalization of folk art differed in each case. In many cases, the veneration of folk art was only relative, as designers incorporated folk art into their own stylistic development. Anthropological approaches proved to be no obstacle to the search for a new style. As a result, the relationship between modernity, historicism and folk culture was not one of opposition, but of intersection. In theory, the modernity and internationalism of art nouveau was counteracted by folk art. Both, in their turn, were in stark opposition to little original historicism. In practice, however, these three trends coexisted and intermingled, resulting in hybrid styles.

# The afterlife of National Romanticism

If National Romanticism was a product of the nineteenth century, its propagation did not stop there, but was prolonged in the twentieth century. Leerssen states that after 1919, state-endorsed artistic expression and popular culture were the two fields in which the phenomenon survived (Leerssen 2014: 22). As mentioned above, in the case of Japan, non-official initiatives were later endorsed by the state. The state found primitivism to be a suitable representation of the nation when consolidating its presence among the citizenry. Notwithstanding this, National Romanticism had to compete with internationalist trends. It had done so in the past with art nouveau and now did so with modernism, too.

As Jeremy Aynsley has demonstrated, the internationalist trend continued throughout the twentieth century in the formulation of modernism and its subsequent reinterpretations, especially after the First World War (Aynsley 1993: 7 and 9–29). We can trace the merger between National Romanticism and modernity even in the most unlikely of examples. As Jonathan Woodham points out, the Paris world fairs in 1925 and 1937 presented rich displays of peasant and folk traditions (Woodham 1997: 87–9). Similarly, in Nazi Germany a *völkisch* aesthetic was displayed, made up of a combination of chronological and cultural primitivism. The period following the election of Adolf Hitler (1889–1945) as Chancellor in 1933 saw neo-classical architecture and interiors feature in official designs, combined with a vernacular style for less official decorative schemes (Aynsley 1993: 45). Under the Third Reich (1933–1945), the home was a terrain in which to implement this aesthetic. Furniture made from German softwood was preferred to tubular steel, which was then seen as 'bolshevik'. However, the Beauty in Work (*Schönheit der Arbeit*) movement developed models for furniture, tableware and lighting that mixed modernist and vernacular aesthetics. Moreover, modernism featured in other iconic designs of the time, such as the streamlined *Flying-Hamburger* diesel-electric train, the network of sweeping autobahns and airships such as the LZ *129 Hindenburg* (Woodham 1997: 100). Equally, the small Volkswagen car KDF-*Wagen* was a National Socialist project, though it was brought into production only after the Second World War (Kirkham & Weber 2013: 623).

The embracing of a dual aesthetic of modernity and traditionalism seen in Germany under the Third Reich (Woodham 1997: 96–102) was also a feature of Mussolini's Italy (1922–1945) (Woodham 1997: 102–7; Paulicelli 2004: 17–27), Portugal under the Second Republic (1926–1974) (Bártolo 2014: 141–54), and Spain under Franco (1936–1975) (Pelta 2010: 434–7). In all of these cases, a predilection for folkloric forms did not prevent modern design from developing and becoming a symbol of these regimes. In any case, this duality was not exclusive to dictatorial regimes, but was also a feature of state-endorsed activities in other countries. Woodham acknowledges that this mixture of modernity and tradition was a constant, for example, when marketing Britain abroad as late as the 1950s. For example, in the 1958 world fair in Brussels, a commemorative wall-plaque in the official British display proclaimed that 'in Britain roses grow on tea cups and wallpapers' (Woodham 1997: 89–96).

Rather more mundanely, it was not only state-related fields that succumbed to the pull of historicism and folk art. One example is the early twentieth-century trend known as 'Neo-Indigenism' in Mexico and Peru and 'Nativism' in other Latin American countries. Mexico presents a special case, tinted by the Mexican Revolution (1910–1920), in which anything from the pre-Columbian period was imbued with 'Mexican-ness'. The designer Dr Atl, a pseudonym for Gerardo Murillo (1875–1964), organized a workshop to create modern adaptations of ancient Aztec and Toltec wares. In graphic design, post-revolutionary illustrators such as the muralist Diego Rivera (1886–1957) likewise appropriated a pre-Columbian aesthetic. The cover of the 1926 book *México en Pensamiento y en Acción* (Mexico in Thought and Action) shows an Aztec deity in the shape of a feathered snake (Kirkham & Weber 2013: 585–6) (Figure 2.4).

Another example is that of the Biba boutiques and department stores in London in the 1960s and 1970s. Art deco-inspired clothing was displayed along with art nouveau-inspired furniture. Woodham states that this re-creation of past times 'was closely bound up with notions of tradition and national identity' (Woodham 1997: 205). Biba in particular is one of the examples discussed in Elizabeth E. Guffey's book, *Retro. The Culture of Revival*, which situates the emergence of this trend in the period shortly after the Second World War. In her view, the difference between retro and nineteenth-century revivalism lies precisely in this way of viewing the past with a certain detachment, but no sense of veneration. She states that 'retro does not look backwards in order to dignify or elevate contemporary society' (Guffey 2006: 21). On the contrary, the retro past is associated with a loss of faith in the future (Guffey 2006: 22). Although retro might not involve a celebratory, primitivist attitude, as it does in the nineteenth-century examples, this trend underpinned a sense of national identity, but in a less exalted way, in step with the times. Since the concept of the nation has become established and is ubiquitous, so has its representation. Leerssen identifies this phase, after Billig, as 'banal nationalism' that is nonetheless a continuation of its romantic nineteenth-century precedent. It has escaped detection because, according to him, it has become a *doxa*, a 'habitus' in Bourdieu's terms (Leerssen 2014: 32).

In the twentieth century, established nation-states were confronted by globalizing forces and by subnationalisms, both of which put the primacy of the nation at stake. Globalization did not challenge the idea of a world divided into nations, but it did connect them more intimately. As in the eighteenth and nineteenth centuries, the presence of homogenizing forces prompted a response from the local. As mentioned in the introduction, Smith does not see globalization as rootless, but as composed of national styles that are 'delocalized' (Smith 1995: 157). In fashion, for example, many of the collections of the French designer Christian Lacroix (b. 1951) are inspired by Spanish folklore. This shows how Spanish folklore is an element that has been easy for one designer to

**Figure 2.4** Rivera, Diego, book cover for Rosendo Salazar's book *México en Pensamiento y en Acción*, 1926.

appropriate and make recognizable for a wider public. These associations are not only showcased in world fairs or competitions, but also broadcast daily via television and available on the Internet. Indeed, while products are becoming more and more homogeneous, national stereotypes are still in use, and can arise when tradition proves a convenient connotation. The souvenir industry is proof of this, as is advertising that draws on national conventions. Likewise, the emergence of subnationalism has threatened the configuration of established nations, but not the concept of the nation itself. Subnationalisms aim to become nation-states and therefore to have the right to belong to the same club as long-established nations. Viviana Narotzky, for example, has studied the case of Catalonia in the 1980s and 1990s. Along with the preparations for the 1992 Olympics in Barcelona, a distinct identity, different from that of Spain, was carefully engineered. Modern design was paramount, but referents to tradition were not obliterated. In the case of Catalonia, it was Catalan art nouveau (*Modernisme*) that came to serve as a referent; a style that Catalonia championed within Spain, and which therefore conferred singularity and an appropriate past (Narotzky 2007: 102). In sum, subnationalisms follow a similar path towards the configuration of a national identity to that followed by established nations.

The coexistence of tradition and its multiple re-creations has not prevented folk craft and folk dress from continuing to lie at the basis of multiple formulations of a national canon and a national style. A recent example of this is the recent K-design programme, launched in 2012 by the Korean Institute of Design Promotion (KIDP), in which Korean design is defined through a selection of design elements from the past (Choi 2014: 593–7). This programme aims to boost Korean design through several activities. One of them was a design contest broadcast on television. Young designers undertook weekly challenges in a reality-show format. Whether they passed or failed the challenge determined whether they would continue on the programme. One of the criteria was that their design should reflect 'Korean-ness'. The search for a particular design identity was underpinned by a different part of the programme called 'K-Design DNA', in which experts selected objects that reflected Korean identity. The selection was dominated by artisanal products from the fields of architecture, dress, furniture, pottery and calligraphy, along with a small number of industrially produced objects such as automobiles, TV sets and telephones. The campaign aims to revive Korean tradition and, at the same time, to make Korean design competitive in the global market. The KIDP has expressed its intention to link Korean traditions with a universality that appeals to overseas consumers (Choi 2014: 594).

Another example is the Hungarian fashion contest 'Re-buttoned: Hungarian is in Fashion!' (*Gombold Újra! Divat a Magyar*) (Figure 2.5). After being held nationally in 2011 and 2012, the contest was widened to become the Central European Fashion Days, which since 2013 have included the four countries of the Visegrád Group (the Czech Republic, Poland, Slovakia and Hungary). For this contest, young graduates design a small collection based on the national folk dress of their own country (Zanin 2014: 2–3). Like the K-Design contest, the aim of the organizers is to reward products that are recognizable abroad and at

**Figure 2.5** Models present creations by Hungarian designer Renata Gyogyosi during the fashion contest 'Gombold újra! Divat a Magyar' at the Museum of Fine Arts in Budapest on 8 May 2011.

the same time based on the region's heritage. In both cases, globalization has generated opportunities for countries to extend their global reach, based on differentiation. Crafts and folk dress offer univocal signifiers of the nation, which maintain their character even after being streamlined to appeal to an international audience.

# Chapter 3
# The Logic of National Design

Primordialism expresses a number of essentialist assumptions. The first is that human beings inevitably belong to nations, and the second is that the national character of a nation can be deduced by analysing its cultural production and by extension design, too. One might therefore ask, to what extent does essentialism still represent a valid approach to the humanities and social sciences in general, and to design history in particular? Opinion on this matter is divided. Constructivist theorists have been major critics of essentialism. In this sense, Rogers Brubaker has written that nations are historically-formed constructs, although he acknowledges the relative weight of pre-modern traditions (Brubaker 1996: 15). The sociologists Jack D. Eller and Reed M. Coughlan describe essentialism as a bankrupt concept and argue for its elimination, pointing to its lack of empirical support, inherent social passivity and anti-intellectualism (Eller & Coughlan 1993: 200). Conversely, the political scientist Umut Özkirimli acknowledges the flaws of primordialism as a methodology but recognizes its continued relevance today. He argues that primordialism explains how national identity manifests itself as a 'given' and is assumed as such by the citizenry. It stresses the character of national identity as a perceived belief rather than as a construction, and therefore its power to shape human action (Özkirimli 2000: 72). Consequently, primordialist accounts of design history have not disappeared altogether, but are still to be found in contemporary design discourse.

Thus, far from being obsolete, primordialist positions can be found in the history of design. The idea of 'national character' has frequently been referred to in design history when clarifying national differences. Below, we will discuss three examples from Britain in the 1950s, 1980s and 2010s. The reason for selecting three examples separated in time was to view the validity and survival of primordialist conceptions of the relation between design and nation not as the product of a particular period, but as an historical continuum. In addition, their separation in time allows us to discern certain variations.

# Recurrent essentialism

The first example is that of a paper by Paul Reilly entitled 'The Influence of National Character on Design', given in October 1956 at the Royal Society of Arts. Reilly was deputy director of the Council of Industrial Design and presented the paper a few months after the opening of the London Design Centre in April of the same year. His paper is at least ambivalent and often contradictory when exposing how national character could influence design. It starts on a sceptical note, denying that the national stereotypes of the volatile French, the amorous Italians, the disciplined Germans and the phlegmatic English have an impact on design. Reilly then opens up the possibility that climate, geography, religion and society might influence national design (Reilly 1956: 920). Although he considers folklore and handicrafts to be clear products of national character, he sees design as a hybrid product of both international trends and national character. The English character is visible in the inherited traditions of craft-based industries in High Wycombe, Stoke, Kidderminster and Lancashire. In Germany, heavy Renaissance-inspired furniture is another example. In the United States, due to its shorter history and dynamic industry, national characteristics can be found in popular art such as 'the brazen juke-box, the glamorous automobile, the glittering cooker and the glossy magazine' (Reilly, 1956: 922). Reilly hereby echoes Herder in presenting folklore as the incarnation of the national character.

It is in his take on contemporary design, however, that an essentialist vision becomes clear. It is more difficult to discern national characteristics in contemporary design, according to Reilly, since there are two competing forces guiding designers at present. Climate, customs and social systems shape national variations, while functional technology and the speed of communications tend to obliterate them (Reilly 1956: 923). Reilly did not believe that globalizing trends or universal design parameters would transcend national origins. On the contrary, they would coexist and anchor design in the national and the international. He proceeds to demonstrate this with examples, showing that even 'within the international circle of the modern movement and the functional approach to design, there is in these fields plenty of room for reasonable expression of temperament' (Reilly 1956: 923). He compares various designs of different provenances, such as teapots, cutlery, glassware, chairs, textiles and stamps. For every set of objects, he manages to attribute a national characteristic to the forms on display: the English teapot, for example, is based on historical examples; the German manufacturer is more likely to fit form to function without emulating previous models; the Italians experiment with sculptural forms for the pleasure of it, and the Americans experiment because the market is constantly demanding novelty (Figure 3.1).

In these characterizations, more of the national character – something that Reilly seemed so reluctant to accept – is present than just the climate, customs

**Figure 3.1** Teapots illustrating Paul Reilly's article are: (1) Wedgwood, Shape 146 in 'Queen's ware', produced since 1768, Josiah Wedgwood and Sons Ltd, Stoke-on-Trent, Britain; (2) Gariboldi, Giovanni, 'Ulpia', Richard Ginori Spa, Italy; (3) Loewy, Raymond, 'Form E', Rosenthal Porzellan GmbH, Germany; (4) Zeisel, Eva, 'Hallcraft', Hall China Company, East Liverpool, Ohio.

and social systems. Thus, the English teapot is based on an 'already proven shape' that owes more to a character trait than to the context, and the same is true of the German 'intellectual exercise' and Italian forms 'for pleasure and fun'. The only example that relies on contextual aspects is that of the American market (Reilly 1956: 924). Here, Reilly echoes Herder in viewing material culture as an expression of a specific community. Accordingly, a unique national character is reflected in every single cultural product of a given community. In other words, since a teapot is produced within a nation, it is impregnated with the national character. Analysing the formal characteristics of the teapot allows us to elucidate the characteristics of the nation.

The second example is the exhibition on 'National Characteristics in Design' that was organized by the Boilerhouse Project in 1985. The catalogue was written by the architecture and design critic Jonathan Glancey, who later became the architecture and design editor of *The Independent* (1989–1997) and architecture and design correspondent for *The Guardian* (1997–2012). This exhibition brought together products from Britain, France, Germany, Italy, Japan, the Soviet Union, Sweden and the USA, and promoted the notion that national characteristics could be detected in the products. Like Reilly, Glancey maintained that contemporary products had some standard characteristics. This was clearer from the way they worked than from the way they looked; for example, although they looked different, a Swedish Saab and an Italian Lancia shared the same engine (Glancey 1985: 1). Glancey characterizes the USA as 'big and brash' (Glancey 1985: 3); he calls Italian design 'erratic', reflecting its governmental instability and the relative importance of the regional capitals to the detriment of Rome (Glancey 1985: 19); and emphasizes Germany's functional aesthetics, due to the fact that the country 'has purged itself of its aristocracy' (Glancey 1985: 1). The backbone of British design sense, he avows, is the racehorse. Exactly like a racehorse, English design is 'well groomed and, muscular but in a lean and smoothly curvaceous way: tame and well mannered' (Glancey 1985: 23). These curves can also be seen in telephone boxes and red pillar boxes, and harmonize with Routemaster buses and black taxis. He concludes that all these products 'mask their workings with a garb of well tailored, well mannered clothing' (Glancey 1985: 25). Again, Glancey is making clear distinctions and drawing near-caricatures of national characters. This need to find singularities must be interpreted as a reaction to the homogenizing impact of globalization. Essentialism proves to be a strategy for convincing visitors of the truth of these statements.

The third example is that of the 2012 exhibition at London's Victoria and Albert Museum entitled 'British Design from 1948: Innovation in the Modern Age', which coincided with the London 2012 Olympics and presented the work of designers 'born, trained or working in the UK' (Breward & Wood 2012: 8 and 16). The exhibition displayed more than 300 examples, ranging from architecture to fashion and illustration. The catalogue was an edited volume featuring contributions from a dozen authors, including designers and historians of architecture and design. The editors of the catalogue, Christopher Breward and Ghislaine Wood, acknowledged that:

> It has become almost a truism to suggest that Britain's creative role in the world can be described through often opposing qualities that range from the eccentric and transgressive, through the romantic and sentimental, to the pragmatic and ingenious, but few have attempted to document the ways in which these characteristics have been consciously developed or inscribed in the nation's material landscape over time.
>
> BREWARD & WOOD 2012: 23

This latter was precisely the goal of this exhibition. Initially, the exhibition attempted to follow the attributed qualities of British design and their origins by assessing a number of past exhibitions that had presented 'the best of British' (Breward & Wood 2012: 24). At least, this was what was announced in the introduction to the catalogue, because what followed were rather conventional historical essays on the history of design in Britain.

The catalogue was divided into three sections whose headings referred to these qualities, namely: 'Tradition and Modernity 1945–79', 'Subversion 1955–97' and 'Innovation and Creativity 1963–2012'. Only a few essays addressed the formation of these qualities, however, and these were mostly written by the editors themselves. For example, the essay on the period 1949–1979 stated that '[t]he war had brought to the fore the importance of preserving British tradition, stability and conservatism governed' (Breward & Wood 2012: 31). In the introductory chapter to part two, one could read that

> the so called baby-boomers tested previous assumptions about racial and sexual identity, social class and gender roles in a manner that changed the cultural landscape for ever. In Britain, as elsewhere, much of this was expressed materially, especially through the media of fashion, magazines, music, interiors and film.
>
> BREWARD & WOOD 2012: 144

In the introduction to the final chapters, the editors stated that

> [s]ince the mid-eighteenth-century the concept of inventiveness has constantly been used to characterise British industrial and design culture, from the introduction of new spinning and weaving machines in the 1780s, through the launching of ships and opening of bridges in the 1840s, to the development of computer codes in the 1950s, '60s and '70s and the invention of the World Wide Web in the 1980s.
>
> BREWARD & WOOD 2012: 257

The editors sought to embed those qualities in historical and social aspects, such as the impact of the Second World War, the reaction of the next generation and technological achievements; something that Reilly had advanced, but not carried out.

The justification of these qualities with contingent reasons seems to distinguish this catalogue from the essentialist attitudes voiced by Reilly and Glancey, who instead stereotyped national characteristics. Nevertheless, these justifications cultivate the myth, rather than deconstruct it. The connections that are made between historical and social facts and the resulting designs are easy to accept, but remain unsubstantiated. The only essay in the catalogue that follows a truly constructivist methodology is Maurice Howard's 'Nation, Land and Heritage', in the sense that it focuses on the theme of the re-creation of tradition in various contexts. This article follows the depiction of the country house in films and interiors, book illustration and photography, inspired by a timeless past and the display of the land itself in ceramics (Breward & Wood 2012: 99–113). Even though this exhibition conceptualized the nation more reflexively than the two previous examples, there is still a tangible traditionalist approach to the national that reaffirms stereotypes, rather than questions them.

Yet, it is the starting point of this exhibition that brings it closer to Herder's thought than the other two. The exhibition defines British design as the product of designers who were born or trained or worked in Britain. Even when the category of 'British' designers is expanded beyond those born in the country, the vision of the national character is still based on the persons and not on the products. This definition thereby excludes designs that circulate within the community and are consumed by nationals, but that do not stem from British minds. Although the categorization of national designers is broadened slightly, by contrast, the categorization of national design products remains strictly limited. This is something that is addressed in the section below and further in Chapter 7. It is worthwhile reflecting, however, on how Herder's ideas, despite being criticized, still dictate the way in which material culture in general and design in particular are 'nationalized'.

# Herder today

It is not the intention of this book to defend Herder's theories, but rather to acknowledge how they can be useful when attempting to understand design. If Herder has been something of a 'straw man' for constructivists, we should acknowledge that he captured the way in which a nation is experienced. Recent accounts have restored the richness of Herder's ideas, in contrast to the flatness imputed by constructivists. In this sense, the cultural geographer Jan Penrose has identified two key reasons for the persistence of primordialism today, even though few scholars support the idea that nations represent natural divisions of humanity. The first is that the primordialist conception of nations as essential has become embedded in a 'common sense' understanding of nations (Penrose 2002: 287). Penrose states that nations have been ideologically essentialized, because nationalist doctrines define the independence of the nation in terms of its natural origins. When nations are depicted as natural phenomena that have existed for centuries, they are indeed portrayed in a primordialist way (Penrose & Mole 2008: 272). When the nation is evoked in these terms, the nation's character becomes inseparable from naturalness and primordialism, thus giving it legitimacy. After this message is spread and the nation is assumed to be natural, observation will provide verification of this belief; it thus becomes acceptable to define the world as composed of different national groups. It is easy to make this assumption, as long as we do not need to draw finite boundaries between these groups. Penrose explains the view that nations are essential as 'the result of eliding the process of group formation with one of its products', that is, the resultant culture and the resultant nation (Penrose 1995: 407). In this way, it is assumed that because group formation is essential, nations are essential, as are national cultures. Likewise, Smith (1995: 34) argues that primordialism enables us to understand the enduring power and hold of ethnic ties. Özkirimli, in turn, argues that 'the concept underlines the importance of perceptions and beliefs in guiding human action' (Özkirimli 2000: 83). Consequently, reconsidering Herder's philosophy contributes to a better understanding of nationalism in these two respects, and also allows us to reconsider stereotypical interpretations of his work.

The second reason for the persistence of primordialism is that it has functioned as a foil, against which alternative perspectives have been developed. This makes a proper understanding of primordialism a prerequisite for understanding subsequent theoretical formulations (Penrose 2002: 287). As explained above, modernist and ethno-symbolist theories were shaped in opposition to primordialism. Below, it will be argued that the difference between Herder and the modernists is sometimes not as great as it might seem, and that there are some connections between them.

# Canons

Although essentialist visions can help us to understand how national identity is perceived to be natural, the question remains as to whether essentialist national canons are appropriate for today's scholarship, and if not, what the alternatives might be. Diana Fuss opens her book *Essentially Speaking* by recalling how one of her students criticized her for circulating a text written from a clearly essentialist perspective. The student argued that the text was therefore undeserving of serious consideration. Fuss answers that

> the question we should be asking is not 'is this text essentialist (and therefore "bad")?' but rather, 'if this text is essentialist, what motivates its deployment?' How does the sign 'essence' circulate in various contemporary critical debates? Where, how, and why is it invoked? What are its political and textual effects?
>
> FUSS 1989: xi

Thus the best use of an essentialist discourse is, paradoxically, to serve as the basis for a constructivist analysis.

For the purposes of this book, we need to discern the implications of first, 'essentialist', and second, 'national' canons of design. It seems clear from the discussion above that essentialism helps us to understand how national identity is experienced, but that it is not valid as a methodological tool. Regarding national canons, Kjetil Fallan distinguishes between an 'analytical category' and an 'actor's category' when defining 'Scandinavian design' (Fallan 2012: 2). National design canons as analytical categories refer to design produced in a given country in all its variants. The term as such corresponds with the customary meaning of 'Scandinavian design' and is a tool that historians might use to describe and categorize historical phenomena. Conversely, national canons as an actor's category refer to an object of research in itself, its formation and evolution. This is frequently a historically shaped vision of national design that conveys an illusion of comprehensiveness, but does not necessarily include all of the design produced in a country. National design labels as both analytical and actors' categories merge in the historiography of design, yet they are clearly distinguishable. Despite their similarity, though, it is better to consider them as two separate categories.

Fallan makes the distinction between 'Scandinavian design' (with a lower-case 'd') as an analytical category and 'Scandinavian Design' (with a capital 'D') as an actor's category. He notes that the latter is far from being synonymous with the former. A customary definition of Scandinavian design would be 'design that originated in the Scandinavian countries'. Fallan argues that this definition does not correspond with 'Scandinavian Design', since Finnish design has been included in its formation, for example, but Icelandic design has not. This is at odds with the strict definition of the Scandinavian countries, that is, Denmark, Sweden and Norway, with the latter two making up the Scandinavian Peninsula. The formation of Scandinavian Design can be traced back to the mid-twentieth century and was shaped by a series of exhibitions for Britain and North America displaying design from the region, especially high-end design for the home (Fallan 2012: 3). Since then, Scandinavian Design has been identified with a particular style, nurtured by the common characteristics of those exhibited objects. The problem arises when this restrictive definition is no longer examined as an actor's category, but is mistaken for an analytical category. The narrow and partial character of Scandinavian Design then becomes hegemonic and pushes the varied spectrum of design into the background. The same can happen with other national or regional design canons. For example, one can think of a similar blurring of boundaries between analytical and actors' categories in 'Italian Design', 'British Design' or 'Dutch Design'. Paradoxically, the broader the propagation of the term, the narrower its definition. It then works like a brand that achieves increasing credibility and coherence by virtue of its dissemination.

What Fuss proposes in her book is basically the study of essentialist texts as an actor's category. Despite their incompleteness and tendency to stereotype, ignoring the existence of essentialist texts will impoverish our understanding of design. This does not mean that we should take essentialist definitions at face value and grant them a comprehensiveness that they do not deserve.

Conversely, their analysis as an actor's category will contribute to the consideration of design not only as the circulation of objects, but also as the circulation of ideas, more specifically ideas about the production of design as related to a given nation. One example of a constructivist analysis of national design labels is Per Hansen's study of 'Danish Modern', which was the label applied to Danish furniture between 1930 and 1960. He argues that the success of this label should not be essentialized and related to the inherent beauty of Danish furniture. On the contrary, the social network that gave meaning to this concept should be mapped, so that we can understand the emergence and dissemination of the concept. He argues for an implementation of constructivist methods to disclose the narratives attached to objects and to consider concepts such as 'Danish Modern' as brands beyond their customary use. There are two reasons for the development of these labels, according to Hansen. The first is that these narratives allow consumers to make sense of this furniture. The second is that, like brands, these narratives were launched and orchestrated by social networks to create a specific effect. Only then can the narratives and the social networks implicated be situated properly (Hansen 2006).

# The Dutchness of Dutch Design

The problem with terms such as 'Dutch Design' or 'Scandinavian Design' is that they present themselves as implicitly absolute, not overtly partial, and they achieve legitimacy by drawing links with a nation's character and a community's past. We have seen examples above from the 1950s and the 1980s, but the construction of these essentialist design canons also continued later into the twentieth century. One good example is the configuration of 'Dutch Design' that emerged in the 1990s and was disseminated worldwide, inspired by the Droog Design exhibitions. 'Dutch Design' has come to characterize design from the Netherlands that is critical, ironic and conceptual, while excluding more commercial, industrial and perhaps less intellectual examples. The essentialist approach would be to attribute these characteristics to the Dutch national character, whereas the constructivist approach would be to map the steps that led to this identification.

The exact origin of the term 'Dutch Design' is debatable, but it can be traced back to the emergence of the designer-entrepreneur in the 1980s and, as part of this trend, to the activities of the designer Gijs Bakker. Bakker taught his students not to wait for a commission, but to generate their own ideas that could later be manufactured industrially. This approach was supported by a generous public funding policy, which made it possible for experimental designers to subsist. The engagement of public bodies with the less commercial side of design dates back to the early 1980s, with their support for the exhibition 'Design from the Netherlands', also curated by Bakker. Celebrating the designer-entrepreneur, he put together this travelling exhibition. Bakker selected twenty designers on the basis of an 'obviously visually perceptible concept', which was the common denominator in a diverse selection (Bakker & Rodrigo 1980: 3). The show included serially produced works, prototypes in experimentation and one-off designs. Furniture, electric appliances, jewellery, textiles and fashion of an artistic, craft-based or industrial character were showcased. Examples included Frans de la Haye's bicycle, whose frame involved fewer iron segments than an ordinary frame and was stabilized with the use of stretched metallic cables, and Reinder van Tijen's DIY cement mixer made out of an oil drum. Bakker's ideas were later echoed in the 1993 Droog Design exhibition. Bakker himself participated as a veteran among the recently graduated designers, both showcasing his own work and acting as art director alongside Renny Ramakers. The Droog works shared a strong underlying concept that was patently visualized, recalling Bakker's 'obviously visually perceptible concept' of his 1980 exhibition. Throughout the 1990s, conceptual design and Dutch Design became synonymous with one another.

Droog Design had been founded in 1992 and mainly showcased the work of recent design graduates of that time, such as Tejo Remy, Piet Hein Eek and Jurgen Bey. The company achieved global recognition after being shown at the Interieur Biennale in Kortrijk (Belgium) in 1992 and the International Furniture Fair in Milan in 1993 (De Rijk 2010). Its minimalist, conceptual work with a humorous twist became a dominant design theme and gave meaning to the term 'Dutch design' abroad. Forging an established notion from Dutch Design granted the Netherlands a place of its own in exhibitions and publications celebrating national design. For example, despite the international fame of Dutch graphic designers, the Netherlands had not been included in the *National Characteristics in Design* exhibition (Glancey 1985). Design from the Netherlands had likewise been excluded from the exhibition on *Neues europäisches Design* (New European Design) as late as 1991, an exhibition that had conversely showcased design from Austria, Britain, France, Germany, Hungary, Italy and Spain (Branzi 1991). When the Italian architecture and design magazine *Abitare* finally decided to produce a special issue on the Netherlands in 1985, the country's architecture and city culture were widely covered, but the compilers could only find enough material to fill a mere four pages on Dutch design (Abitare 1985). In sum, the Netherlands was absent from the framework of national design exhibitions and publications, and the notion that there was such a thing as design that was typical of the Netherlands consolidated in the early 1990s. The situation changed fast, though, and Dutch Design gained unprecedented momentum. By the mid-1990s, Dutch Design had gone from being a non-existent to an internationally renowned term, and design from the Netherlands gained a firm position in the international design world. When the editors of *Abitare* returned to the Netherlands in 2002, a quarter of the magazine was occupied by designs illustrating the breadth of current Dutch Design (Abitare 2002). Indeed, according to the design historian Damon Taylor, the term 'Dutch Design' is characteristic of a certain approach to design that combines 'quirky conceptualism and expressive functionalism' (Taylor 2010: 438). This means that at the same time as Dutch Design was stabilized as a 'notion', it became associated with a specific type of practice: that of conceptual design.

Droog Design shared a number of characteristics with the Italian Alchymia and Memphis groups. Like them, Droog displayed a cohesive selection of statement-like works and, like Memphis' collaboration with Barbara Radice, Ramakers drafted the group's self-authored texts, describing its aims and trajectory. One example of this, the book *Droog Design: Spirit of the Nineties* (1998), presented Droog as quintessentially Dutch, linking its austere character to an abstract geometry, the artificial nature of the Dutch landscape and a mercantile spirit embedded in Calvinist ideology. This book traced a lineage back to restrained seventeenth-century Dutch portraits, followed by sober, early-twentieth-century Dutch Modernism (Ramakers & Bakker 1998: 40–63). As well as exaggerating the Dutch Calvinist mentality, these essentialist statements also neglected the multi-religious nature of the country, with its Catholic and orthodox Protestant nuclei, not to mention a considerable number of Muslims. Despite its stereotyping vision, this characterization of Dutch Design has become widespread as synonymous with Droog and conceptual design, that is, experimental work in which the conceptual core clearly dominates, enriched by a humorous twist.

Droog Design epitomises the creation of a genealogy to legitimate contemporary production, mostly furniture and product design. It is nevertheless remarkable that this trend was followed by works on Dutch fashion and Dutch typography. For example, Jan Middendorp's book *Dutch Type* (2004) elaborated on the innovative character of Dutch type design and emphasized its historical openness, as the country had been occupied by Spanish, Austrian, French and German forces, had been able to take advantage of sea routes, and was a multi-religious and politically varied country. According to the author, all of these factors fostered 'a practical attitude' (Middendorp 2004: 9). It would be inaccurate to seek the origins of this stereotypical vision in authors such as Middendorp; they were probably not intending to minimize the diversity of Dutch design production, but were indebted to previous accounts. For example, Ramakers quotes Benno Premsela's 1995 exhibition 'Made in Holland', characterizing Dutch Design as rectilinear. Needless to say, numerous counter-examples can be found in Dutch design before and after 1998, such as Wim Gilles' rounded kettle of 1954. Ramakers did not question this essentialist statement, however, but justified it with reference to the linear Dutch landscape, with its absence of mountains (Ramakers & Bakker 1998: 40–1). In turn,

Middendorp quoted Alston W. Purvis' book on Dutch graphic design of 1992, in which Purvis states that the climate and the water have forged the recalcitrant and self-confident character of the Dutch, and that they are 'averse to improvisation, to the non-essential and the arbitrary, and they have a distinct proclivity for simple logic and basic common sense' (Middendorp 2004: 10).

The creation of a discourse hinges not only on purely textual elements, but also on contextual aspects that might prove difficult to identify. The main pillars underpinning the construction of 'Dutch Design' were Droog Design, the Dutch subsidy policy and Design Academy Eindhoven. The Dutch Art and Design Fund financially supported a whole range of schemes for designers and artists: with the aid of a starter's grant, an office or studio could be set up, the equipment required could be financed by the Facilities Fund (*Voorzieningenfonds*), and the rent for a studio reimbursed from another source. Other grants were also available for participating in international shows and exhibitions, and government-financed studios and workshops in various large capitals were available for limited periods of time. Mienke Simon-Thomas describes a paradoxical situation in which the more defiant, critical and non-conformist a designer or artist was inclined to be, the greater their cultural standing seemed to become, and the more financial aid they were able to attract (Simon-Thomas 2008: 233). Design Academy Eindhoven has focused on conceptual design since the early 1990s, abandoning its traditional programmes on technological aspects. The academy has trained its graduates in this philosophy, to represent and export 'Dutch design' abroad (Simon-Thomas 2008: 231–2).

As discussed above, the canonical discourse on Dutch Design is markedly essentialist and rather restrictive in its definition of the Dutch nation, since it describes the Dutch as a coherent ethno-national group sharing a communal history and territory. The result is thus a discourse inserted into an essentialist tradition that links current production to a primordial past. In this sense, it corresponds to Bourdieu's 'habitus', as it tends 'to reproduce the regularities immanent in the objective conditions of the production of their generative principle' (Bourdieu 1977: 78), the 'generative principle' in this case being the ideology of nationalism. This does not mean that the authors are keen to shape an essentialist vision of design, but that they are writing within the logic of nationalism as a dominant ideology. If nations have been propagated as essentialist units, it is unsurprising that this ideology permeates all discourse involving the nation, including national design canons. As Bourdieu explains, the 'habitus' as a product of history itself 'produces individual and collective practices and hence history, in accordance with the schemes engendered by history' (Bourdieu 1977: 82). Habitus is thus the way in which history becomes a structuring structure, since it lies at the basis of its own generation and reproduction.

# National design canons

The evolution of theories of nationalism stretches from the scholars who condemned or defended the nationalist cause in the nineteenth century to more recent attempts to discern the causes that led to the configuration of a given national identity (Özkirimli 2000: 12–62). Even when Özkirimli defends the value of the primordialist vision, he bases his approach on the theories of the anthropologist Clifford Geertz, who stated that, 'Believing with Max Weber, that man is an animal suspended in webs of significance he himself has spun, I take culture to be those webs, and the analysis of it to be therefore not an experimental science in search of law but an interpretative one in search of meaning' (Geertz quoted in Özkirimli 2000: 73). Therefore, although he defends primordialism as a way of understanding the weight of national identity in society, Özkirimli sees its analysis as a process of disentangling webs of significance in order to grasp meaning. As Rogers Brubaker (2002) has observed, the arguments of nationalists should not form the basis for the analysis of nationhood. I would add that they should not be taken for granted either, but their pervasiveness should be acknowledged.

That nationalism is a widespread doctrine today is clearly apparent. The nation-state would seem an obvious basic unit of study, and brings with it a well-defined analytical framework. Nevertheless, we have to bear in mind that nations are in themselves cultural constructions, and that they should be considered artificial entities and studied accordingly. In view of this, we will consider two current debates in the humanities and the social sciences, regarding first, national canons, and second, methodological nationalism. The historians Maria Grever, Kees Ribbens and Siep Stuurman have argued that national canons reproduce the hegemony of the nation-state. They see national canons as a product of the nation-state that has served the purposes of nation-building when used in education. The current situation, characterized by trans-national movements, migration and supra-national entities, calls these national canons into question (Grever & Ribbens 2004: 4). Accordingly, these authors argue for an understanding of competing historical perspectives, rather than for the replacement of old historical canons by new ones (Stuurman & Grever 2007: 12). Their claim is that contesting historical perspectives reveal the lack of comprehensiveness of historical national canons.

In sociology, methodological nationalism, defined as 'the equation between nation-state and society', is likewise up for discussion (Stuurman & Grever 2007: 9). The sociologist Daniel Chernilo explains the acceptance of this equation both in historical terms – since the expansion of the nation-state from the Enlightenment onwards has proved unstoppable – and conceptually – since national categories have been used extensively to shape the most abstract conceptions of society (Chernilo 2007: 1–2). Following Smith, he argues that there are good reasons for the primacy of methodological nationalism, but warns that when we accept methodological nationalism at face value, the nationalist order of things is reproduced and reinforced and therefore exerts an imperceptible influence (Chernilo 2007: 11–12).

These and other authors agree that both national canons and methodological nationalism have a limited ability to reflect current historical developments. This section will concentrate on three of them and link their positions to design history. First, Grever and Stuurman argue that national canons do not reflect multiple allegiances. Nationality can be strongly rooted in the citizenry, but Dutch citizens, for example, can also see themselves as Amsterdammers, Surinamese, Turks or Muslims (Ribbens 2007: 67). Second, methodological nationalism establishes a hierarchy between the national and the international, whereby the former precedes the latter and the latter is consequently seen as a product of the former. The sociologist Szusza Gille argues that even when the interrelations between the two are acknowledged, these assume the pre-existence of the national and its power to condition the international (Gille 2012: 91). Third, Chernilo holds that methodological nationalism does not capture the complexity of the nation-state, which is presented as a single form of socio-political arrangement. He considers this conceptualization to be historically elusive, sociologically equivocal and normatively ambiguous (Chernilo 2007: 3).

National canons tend to be based on a cohesive community that justifies the choice of the nation as a framework. Acknowledging the heterogeneous nature of the national community would then open up other possibilities. National canons become problematic when expressing multi-layered and dynamic identities, and very much so, as Ribbens states, when the canon marginalizes or even excludes 'the perceived primary identity of a given group' (Ribbens 2007: 67). As expressed above, the discourse around Dutch Design has been reductionist when expressing the essence of the nation, its religious character and ethnic formation. Histories of design in the Netherlands have nonetheless accommodated foreign designers. Mienke Simon-Thomas' book covers the Frenchman Pierre Paulin, who joined the Artifort team in 1959, and the Amsterdam-based Czech Borek Sipek, who was awarded the Kho Liang Ie prize in 1989 (Simon-Thomas 2008: 157 and 217). National canons contain designers that have studied, worked or lived in the country, but they are nevertheless presented as exceptions to the rule. One could say that this integration has happened in spite of, rather than thanks to, the methodology that is employed.

Yet, if foreign designers have proved difficult to 'nationalize', canons have been stricter when it comes to the design objects themselves. Their inclusion is more problematic if their authorship is not national, even if they are consumed in the country in question. In these cases, the vertical allegiances of being of foreign design and foreign manufacture but national use, for example, exclude products from the national canon, as seen in the case of the above-mentioned exhibition on 'British Design from 1948: Innovation in the Modern Age'. Kjetil Fallan and Grace Lees-Maffei have recently proposed that we look at nations as sites for design, for manufacturing and for the mediation and consumption of design (Fallan & Lees-Maffei 2013: 5). If products are as configured by their mediation and consumption as they are by their design and manufacture, then their nationality should also be found wherever they have been used. Although this concept is clear in theory, methodological nationalism does not yet lend itself to include, for example, Tupperware products in a survey of design in the Netherlands, even though Tupperware products are consumed in this country.

Subsuming the international in the national has been the other flaw of methodological nationalism. As Gille argues, this framework 'becomes a built-in obstacle to the discovery that the international may in fact precede and even affect the social space of the nation' (Gille 2012: 91). Methodological nationalism looks for common characteristics among national designers, grouping them into stylistic schools, or explaining the emergence of local manufacturers in terms of local material resources. However, in a world where influence spreads through the Internet and where it is increasingly difficult to locate corporations nationally, methodological nationalism falls short. The global exchange of influence need not necessarily take place between nationals, but between individuals, who, in turn, do not necessarily need a national framework to communicate. Physical proximity does not guarantee a homogeneous style, since designers may be more influenced by what happens in a remote studio than by their fellow nationals. The national indeed has an impact, but it is insufficient to explain the international traffic of influences and goods. In this sense, Smith's idea that the global is a delocalization of national characteristics seems insufficient. There are more possibilities for the origins of design than the nation.

The sociologist Daniel Chernilo has exposed the inability of methodological nationalism to capture the complexity of the nation-state, as it presents the nation-state as historically invariable, transparent in its mechanisms of legitimation and its normativism for the future of nations. He claims that the nation-state has evolved historically, becoming totalitarian, democratic or imperialist, and that methodological nationalism does not reflect this evolution over time. His second critique is that the nation-state enshrines continuity and, at the same time, the capacity to re-invent itself. Finally, Chernilo questions the normativism of the state as the only construction to legitimize nations (Chernilo 2007: 23–4). In this light, a national history of design that wants to escape methodological nationalism should acknowledge the capacity of the nation-state to evolve, change and reinvent itself, and not present it as a permanent reality. In this sense, the embedding of design in mechanisms to legitimize the nation-state would need to be addressed; national exhibitions, national symbols and the establishment of museum collections being some examples. An analysis of national symbols and the circumstances of their creation and dissemination could contribute to attempts to reveal the state as a changing entity. Likewise, the analysis of national design canons would reveal the authoritative role of design in creating supremacy.

The question remains as to whether the nation is a proper analytical framework, and if so, how to study it. These authors acknowledge the relevance of methodological nationalism, on the grounds that nation-states have been decisive forces in shaping history. Chernilo acknowledges that for conceptualizing the nation-state, methodological nationalism is necessary, and that 'in small portions, and under strict doctor's supervision, some form of methodological nationalism may be a necessary evil' (Chernilo 2007: 162). If the nation-state is conceptualized with the necessary sophistication and self-reflexivity, it can be a useful analytical framework. To achieve this aim, the generation of conflicting narratives can work as an antidote to the flaws of traditional methodological nationalism. As long as design history is concerned and in consonance with the above-mentioned critiques, when recurring to methodological nationalism this needs to be done in a reflexive manner and reconsider what is at stake when labelling a designer or a product as 'national'. Second, the nation-state should be embedded in a global logic. Lastly, we need to explore design as an element for the reproduction of the nation.

# Conclusion

The existence of the nation is superimposed on processes of globalization, and the survival of essentialism is inherent to the survival of nationalism. Design forms part of this dichotomy. In this vein, we can affirm that both systems are superimposed: that of global interaction and that of national divisions. Far from threatening one another, they seem to act as reciprocal stimuli. This contradiction is found in the concept of national design, whose 'national' products have conversely been created in a global creative broth of multidirectional inspiration. Hence, the tension between the real, global traffic of inspiration and the superimposed national schemas produces multiple creative contradictions and hybrid artefacts. One example of this is the search for specificity in Dutch Design. Second, the creative output of a given country shows a great heterogeneity, as individual creators reveal that they have more in common with foreign trends (such as Lacroix's inspiration from Spanish folklore) than with their national colleagues. Indeed, the interaction of the two systems bears fruit; the paradox arises when one of the two attempts to prevail. In her account of globalization, the geographer Doreen Massey proposes a view from a satellite, by which the communicational and social relations of people can be mapped (Massey 1993: 63). This view renders a continuous flux of interchanges that do not follow the logic of boundaries. Hence, she argues that the duality of Space as (Being) and

Time as (Becoming) is challenged in what she calls a time–space compression, which forces us to address places under the concept of a 'progressive sense of place'. Remarkably, she wonders whether this state of affairs should generate any sense of insecurity, as other scholars suggest, and questions people's need for attachments of some sort. However, as argued in this study, as soon as we leave the satellite and come closer to Planet Earth, we observe that the disorganized relationships between people are boxed into concentric collective identities, like Russian dolls, and related to places that range from continental to local identities. The place-bound collective identity *par excellence* is the national identity, whose boundaries do not necessarily match those of an established state, however, as will be argued in Part Two. On the basis of the above analysis, it is evident that national identity is constructed, launched and promoted, creating cultural frameworks based on nations. Design participates in the production and reproduction of these national frameworks.

# Modernism: Top-down Approaches to National Identity

Unlike the primordialist, modernist scholars maintain that the emergence of nations dates back to the late eighteenth century. According to them, predating national communities can not be labelled as nations strictly speaking. Their methodology is rather constructivist than essentialist, since they trace the means through which a sense of nation is recreated. They prioritize the state and the elites as the artifices behind this construction. The nation as a concept is created top-down, stemming from the state and percolating into civic society.

Regarding national symbols, Part One has explored the symbolic strategies to re-create an ancient nation. This is not the only option to symbolize the nation, but modernity must be considered, too. Depending on what is considered a suitable projection, one of the two options might be used. The establishment of a national symbol occurs through discursive association and both are possible. Nevertheless, there is a manifest preference from traditional-looking symbols above modern-looking ones.

The conceptualization of the state passes through its singularization as a privileged entity and its embeddedness in civic society. This fluid position defines the influence of the state on design, not only as long as design for the public sphere is concerned but also with design for the private sphere. The divide between the public and the private is both blurred and accentuated through the ways in which the state influences design.

# Chapter 4
# National Symbols and the State

Modernists seek to reconstruct the creation and dissemination of nations. Their rhetoric is more specific than the rather abstract rhetoric of primordialism. For modernists, it is individual or collective actors who are capable of having agency. In the world of primordialism, nations, myths and memories also have agency. Smith points to the states not as the only actors but rather as the main ones who build up national identity. He distinguishes between the cultural origin of nations and the political nature of states, which, however, acquire a complete identification in many contemporary societies. He points out that:

> In our day, too, the symbiosis of state and nation has been intensified through growing ministerial control over all aspects of cultural and social policy. This is patently clear in the field of education, and especially higher education, but it has become increasingly manifest in other areas like regulation of the press, radio and television, medicine and health services, the liberal professions, labour law, family status and benefits, genetic engineering, criminal justice, policing and prison services.
>
> SMITH 1995: 94

Likewise, Billig acknowledges this idea by admitting, '. . . political discourse, which is grounded in the national context, set in the metaphorical eye of the nation, and employed in the practice of representation, will typically flag nationhood. Such flagging is part of the "normal", habitual condition of cotemporary state politics' (Billig 1995: 98). Accordingly, both the state (the political institutions) and the nation (cultural construct) have achieved a total identification. Consequently, the discourse emanating from the state can be seen as a permanent reproduction of the national order. Nevertheless, the relation between nation and state is not always univocal what originates different kinds of nation-states. For Smith not all the states are nation-states. On the contrary, insofar as most modern states are plural, they are clearly not nation-states. Smith (1995: 86) prefers to call them 'national states'.

> Strictly speaking, we may term a state a 'nation-state' only if and when a single ethnic and cultural population inhabits the boundaries of a state, and the boundaries of that state are coextensive with the boundaries of that ethnic and cultural population [. . .] In this sense, there are very few nation-states. Portugal, Iceland, Japan (except for the Ainu and Koreans), Denmark (except for the Faroese), are examples [. . .] Most states are polyethnic in character and many are severely divided along ethnic lines, some of them with numerically significant ethnic minorities and others divided into two or more large *ethnies* – such as Burma, Indonesia, Malaysia, Kenya, Nigeria, Belgium, Canada and Britain.
>
> Emphasis in the original; SMITH 1995: 86

The distinction between nation-states and national states is relevant with regard to terminology but not as much with regard to methodology. National states combine a central/federal configuration of national identity with peripheral/regional equivalents. However, its methodological study will remain exactly the same, similar to Billig's account discussed above on the equivalence between patriotism and nationalism. If both regions and countries may be studied as nations, then their processes of nation building may also be comparable. The difference with 'pure' nation-states is that in the same territory, diverse nation-building processes cohabit, and hence their respective processes establish a foreseeable dialectical relationship.

The state can then be seen as agencies of nation building and hence their activities as producers of national identity. Anderson's account introduces the term 'official nationalism', which is described as 'something emanating from the state, and serving the interests of the state first and foremost' (Anderson 1991[1983]: 159). This process shows 'a genuine, popular nationalist enthusiasm, and a systematic, even Machiavellian, instilling of nationalist ideology through the mass media, the educational system, administrative regulations, and so forth' (Anderson 1991[1983]: 163).

Smith distinguishes between nation making and nation building, the former limited to administrative task and the latter more specifically oriented to creating a national consciousness. First, the measures of state-making may include: creation of a single code of law and system of courts throughout the territory, creation of a single taxation system and fiscal policy, formation of professional cadres of skilled personnel for the key administrative institutions, or the creation of effective military institutions and technology under central control (Smith 1995: 89). Even when these processes of state-making develop a strong national consciousness, it is mainly through the overlapping, if analytically separable, processes of 'nation-building' where this national consciousness is forged. Both terms are often used interchangeably, but their emphases are rather different. According to Smith, nation building includes:

1   The growth, cultivation and transmission of common memories, myths and symbols of the community;

2   The growth, selection and transmission of historical traditions and rituals of community;

3   The designation, cultivation and transmission of 'authentic' elements of shared culture (language, customs, religion, etc.) of the 'people';

4   The inculcation of 'authentic' values, knowledge and attitudes in the designated population through standardized methods and institutions;

5   The demarcation, cultivation and transmission of symbols and myths of a historic territory, or homeland;

6   The selection and husbanding of skills and resources within the demarcated territory;

7   And the definition of common rights and duties for all the members of the designated community.

Numbering absent in the original; SMITH
1995: 89–90

When design is involved in processes of nation building, it relates normally to the fifth and sixth nation-building activities. Impinged on either cultural or economic politics, design equally participates in creating a national consciousness at the service of nation-building processes.

Critical voices on the overemphasis of the state have come from scholars such as Edensor. He argues for a greater recognition of the civic society in creating national identity but nonetheless acknowledges the role of the state in creating a legal, bureaucratic framework for individuals. It ranges from the paying of taxes to broadcasting regulations, environmental measures or employment rights. Thus, the state is 'responsible for enforcing and prioritizing specific forms of conduct, of inducing particular kinds of learning experiences, and regulating certain "good habits amongst its citizens"' (Edensor 2002: 20). Yet, he criticizes the visions of Hobsbawm and Ranger, who insist too much on the ruling class as the only ones responsible for the national ideology and who are seen almost as ideological manipulators. On the contrary, he affirms that

once the nation is established as a common-sense entity, under conditions of modernity, the mass media and the means to develop and transmit popular culture expands dramatically, and largely escapes the grip of the state, being transmitted through commercial and more informal networks. The rise of popular forms of entertainment, leisure pursuits, political organisations and a host of vernacular commonalities is not generated by national elites but is facilitated through the mobilities engendered by advances in transport and communication technologies.

EDENSOR 2002: 4

Thus, Edensor points to the state as the agent that develops a national 'habitus', but not as the one ultimately responsible for maintaining and reproducing it. Once created, the 'habitus' as a common-sense framework generates those experiences and visualizations that transform the abstract concept of nationality into a concrete reality. This point of view might seem to coincide with the abstract rhetoric of the primordialist and contrast with the more person-bound language of modernists. The main difference is that Edensor extends agency from the state to civic society and then defines a framework in which the nationalist logic works. Primordialists such as Herder, on the contrary consider the nation in itself as an abstract entity, capable of agency. Modernists attribute agency to inanimate actors, too, under the condition that they are physical and not abstract. In this sense, national symbols and cultural representation contribute to the dissemination of the nation. The grandiloquent and romanticized language of primordialists is however absent in modernist accounts.

# Modernity and the national

Of the elements that indicate banal nationalism, many things are designed, such as: flags, coins, bank notes and anything bearing national emblems (Billig 1995: 41). These could be called the deliberate symbols of nations. According to Smith, these symbols awaken reactions through symbolic value, insofar as they embody 'the tenets of an abstract ideology in palpable, concrete terms that evoke instant emotional responses from all strata of the community [. . .]. The emotions it unleashes are those of the community directed to itself, self-consciously extolling itself' (Smith 1991: 77–8). Along these lines, Anderson adds the tombs of Unknown Soldiers (1991[1983]: 9), emblems, national anthem and poetry (1991[1983]: 145) to this inventory. Hobsbawm also enhances their importance as community makers: 'Indeed most of the occasions when people become conscious of citizenship as such remain associated with symbols and semi-ritual practices (for instance, elections), most of which are historically novel and largely invented: flags, images, ceremonies and music' (Hobsbawm and Ranger 1983: 2).

To which extent are some elements more suitable than others for becoming national symbols? In this vein, Hobsbawm and Ranger explain that 'objects or practices are liberated for full symbolic and ritual use when no longer fettered by practical use' (Hobsbawm & Ranger 1983: 2–4). As mentioned above in the

Introduction, Hobsbawm provides the example of the robes and wigs of judges as the 'traditional' features which he distinguishes from the activity of judging itself – what he calls the 'custom'. Relatedly, in Part One, we have seen the preference for the historicist and the vernacular to represent the nation. Historicism conveys intrinsic references to the past. In the case of the vernacular, its use as a national source of legitimacy was largely acquired when those artefacts and modes of production were made obsolete by modernization, thereby acquiring similar historicist connotations. Likewise, in Hobsbawm and Ranger's account, wigs acquired their modern, symbolic significance as soon as other people stopped wearing wigs. In this vein, a coat of arms will be more easily perceived as a symbol of a nation than the government's logo, ancient art more than contemporary art, and folk costumes more than fashion. Yet logos, art and fashion are included in the agendas of the nation-building practices. Even unnoticeably, they are conveying national values, not because of bearing the national emblems but because of being discursively related to the nation. Sociologist and one of the founders of Cultural Studies Stuart Hall, points out:

> National cultures are composed not only of cultural institutions, but of symbols and representations. A national culture is a *discourse* – a way of constructing meanings which influences and organizes both our actions and our conception of ourselves [. . .]. National cultures construct identities by producing meanings about 'the nation' with which we can *identify*; these are contained in the stories which are told about it, memories which connect its present with its past, and images which are constructed of it.
>
> Emphasis in the original; HALL 1992: 293

Smith's account is mainly focused on the mobilization of the historical and vernacular. Billig's account concerning the ubiquitous presence of national reminders should open up the limits of symbols to more ordinary goods still demarcated within the category of state symbols such as coinage, flags or emblems. The examples of the Gothic typeface or Braun products mentioned above in relation to Germany show that not only do vernacular symbols convey national identity but also modern artefacts can act as such symbols. In fact, Smith acknowledges this a bit further. He affirms, 'These processes of nation-building also tie in with our working definition of the nation as "a named human population which shares myths and memories, a mass public culture, a designated homeland, economic unity and equal rights and duties for all members"' (Smith 1995: 90).

Following Billig's 'banal nationalism', Edensor develops the less discussed, but paradoxically more ubiquitous, holder of national symbols, namely popular culture. He comments on modernists like Anderson, Smith, Hobsbawm and Ranger for their exaggerated focus on high culture and tradition (Edensor 2002:

10–11). Yet he acknowledges some virtues in Anderson's approach to print-capitalism and Smith's references to 'common mass public culture', in as much as they turn the focus from the official to the quotidian (Edensor 2002: 9). Nevertheless, Edensor insists on their lack of attention to the vast realm of everyday life and argues that Billig only skims the surface on this subject, though his work constantly suggests its importance. Edensor argues that even though high culture has formed the most visible elements of national pride and international prestige (e.g. national galleries, opera houses or national theatres), as marks of status on which 'governments are often happy to lavish funds' (Edensor 2002: 15), there are many other unattended elements of popular culture which underpin the daily experience of the nation. Edensor acknowledges that these elements are generally unnoticeable for they are seen through the common-sense screen of national 'habitus'. Yet in our workplaces, public spaces and homes, individuals are constantly performing their nationness and being reminded of the nation that they inhabit.

According to Edensor, the best way to discover the national colour of one's everyday existence is by moving from one's home country. Then we realize that it is not only a question of a different language, but that in a different country we are

> dumbfounded by the range of everyday competences which we do not possess, where we come across a culture full of people who do not do things the way we do them, who draw on different practical resources to accomplish everyday tasks.
>
> EDENSOR 2002: 93

He acknowledges how unmarked his way of dressing was until he arrived in India. His dress code suddenly became marked as 'British' when confronted with different outfits. According to Edensor, everyday activities, albeit unconsciously, are 'nationalized' and remind us of the 'peculiar' status of our nation and, by performing these activities, we perform our national identity. Thus, national feeling is underpinned by small specific everyday experiences and visualizations (i.e. architecture, weather, food or post-boxes) that form a national landscape. The whole set of peculiarities that delimit a national landscape can be extremely different if we are in India or in Britain but can also be divergent in countries so close as Belgium and Spain. For example, let us examine such an ordinary act as taking out the garbage. In Belgium, garbage must be separated into categories, each of which needs a different bag. Those bags are quite expensive, as municipality taxes are paid through the purchase of the bags. Moreover, there are only glass containers in the public space and the garbage truck passes once a week – this day depends on the district. The civil employees will only pick up the 'municipal' garbage bags and the rest will remain on the street. On the contrary, in Spain four kinds of garbage containers invade the public space, namely general garbage, paper, plastics and glass. Citizens may use any plastic bag as garbage bag, as taxes are paid separately. Moreover, the garbage truck empties the container during night time, and consequently citizens can take out the garbage bag every day. According to Edensor, such activities, albeit unconsciously, are 'nationalized' and remind us of the 'peculiar' status of our nation and, by performing these activities, we perform for our nation. Obviously, extracting a simple action out of the whole context that surrounds it can be unconvincing. Nevertheless, putting this irrelevant practice in the whole context of elements that form a familiar, national landscape (e.g. architecture, weather, food or post-boxes) reveals how familiarity and national feeling is underpinned by small punctual everyday experiences and visualizations.

The question is, do those particular experiences still survive in a context of globalization, where similar clothes, restaurants or lifestyles can be found all around? Edensor points out that not every single 'national' symbol must be absolutely peculiar to a concrete nation. That a given element can embody notions of nationness 'is not to imply that they are unfamiliar in other contexts' (Edensor 2002: 108). As symbols, these elements are not univocal and therefore can be domesticated in different contexts to embody different conceptions of nation, since it is in the combination of landscapes, practices and objects where the recreation of national familiarity resides. Unlike other scholars, Edensor does not separate conscious and unconscious activities, since purposeful and reflexive actions have 'blurred boundaries' (Edensor 2002: 71).[1] However revealing Edensor's gaze might be, it is insufficient to study the processes through which some symbols become an element of a nation building or nationhood becomes commoditized and linked to certain objects. Taking out the garbage bag can be part of the performance of a nation in the everyday but obviously, the visualization of a national flag is unequivocally a different experience of the nation. Considering every experience equally does not deliver much information on how the nation is being actively shaped nor does it do so on how these symbols are mediated.

Accordingly, symbols (including symbols of popular culture) are divided into categories depending on their final use and their role in the construction of national identity. Thus, two categories of symbols of nationhood are distinguished: 'deliberated' symbols and 'accidental' ones. In each case, the category of symbol is attained by the more or less arbitrary identification of a 'signifier' with a 'signified'. For example, how a three-banded rectangle black-yellow-red (signifier) (i.e. the Belgian flag) makes a direct difference to Belgium (signified). The 'designer' of the flag was consciously designing an element for the sole purpose of representing Belgium, and therefore it will be called a 'deliberated' symbol. On the contrary, a huge building composed by eight spheres united with tubes can also represent Belgium (i.e. the Atomium building in Brussels). Not all buildings achieve such an intimate relationship with Belgium, but this symbol did so through successive mediation of meanings, and therefore will be treated differently as an 'accidental' symbol. According to Edensor, 'the meaning of symbolic cultural elements cannot be determined or fixed' (Edensor 2002: 5). Indeed, symbols are flexible and can be utilized by different parties for different purposes, but still symbols have a minimal nucleus of meaning which is univocal. This does not mean that the object in itself contains this connotation, but because there might be a dominant interpretation that resists any adjustment. For example, liberals, socialists or conservatives can appropriate the Belgian flag to defend confronted visions of Belgium, but still, the flag will make reference to Belgium and very improbably will ever come to be identified with any other country. In this sense, symbols are flexible although within certain limits.

# Creating modern national symbols

The question is now, how design beyond the historicist and the vernacular can be incorporated in a national discourse. For that, first the characteristics of national art, according to Smith, will be distilled to later discuss specific design examples that have been construed as similarly national. He points out that painting, sculpture, architecture, music, opera, ballet and film are susceptible to being used to reconstruct the history of the nation due to its inherent properties. In his article 'Art and Nationalism in Europe', Smith analyses some late eighteenth- and nineteenth-century works such as Jacques-Louis David's 'The Oath of the Horatii' (1784) or Jean-Auguste-Dominique Ingres' 'Joan of Arc at the Coronation of Charles VII' (1854), in order to explore two historical revivals in painting devoted to national depiction, namely ancient and medieval references.

After this analysis, he concludes that history painting as a category of national art can reconstruct national images on the basis of its qualities. According to Smith, national art is characterized by four main features (Smith 1993: 65–6):

- First, national art is didactic and emulative, because it seeks to depict the public virtues of the commonwealth. It looks in the history of ethnic groups for the public virtues that are valuable for the present.

- Second, national art is often celebratory. It magnifies the nation and its heroes (e.g. the Albert Memorial).

- Third, national art crystallizes the nation by presenting it in a concrete form, thereby endowing it with an enduring, monumental quality (e.g. Nelson's Column in London).

- Fourth, national art evokes the idea of national community through images. Under this category, Smith includes three genres, namely landscape, history painting, and genre painting (e.g. Constable's emulation of a typical English landscape).

Smith's conclusions say much about the references of the studied period but present some problems when this schema has to be translated to today and, in addition, to other creative fields. Their characteristics of national art seem devoted to a concrete form of art from the past. However, some examples may prove that Smith's observations on 'national art' present certain parallelisms to the fields of contemporary design and fashion. Below, some examples are supplied which show certain similarities to the four features mentioned earlier. Agreeing with Per Hansen (2006), the analysis below aims at showing that it is through the creation of a discourse that objects or events become symbols, in this case symbols of the nation. Through the decoding of these messages, the object can be objectively separated from its symbolic value and the social networks identified. The examples below illustrate, following Smith, how design can become national. An exhibition can convey notions of public virtue, an award scheme can magnify the heroes of a nation, a fashion collection can crystallize the nation and local fashion talent can evoke the national community.

In 1985, Spanish designer André Ricard wrote an article in *El País* newspaper on the *Diseño-España* exhibition to be held at the Europalia festival in Brussels. After a difficult negotiation with the Spanish organizers, one of the Europalia exhibitions was committed to recent Spanish design. In the article, he wrote about contemporary graphic and industrial design, concluding that they had roots 'beyond the industrial era, in the anonymous works of the craftsmen, who were the authors of magisterial works, beautiful and useful which denote the ability, inventiveness and sensitivity of our people' (Ricard 1985: n.p.). Whether or not this aim was ever in the minds of the designers, the post-modern creations of Spanish designers were perceived as, and through this article also mediated, the vehicle of ancestral craftsmanship. Thereby, this exhibition responds to the first of Smith's characteristics regarding national art, namely the didactic and emulative function. When Ricard admits that contemporary design denotes the 'ability, inventiveness and sensitivity of our people', he elevates the design pieces from the 1985 exhibition to examples of 'public virtue'. As such, they are not only proof of the mastery of some professionals but also receptors of traditional 'genius'.

Design and fashion awards do generally respond to Smith's second characteristic, namely the celebration of the nation and its heroes. Accordingly, Belgian design awards (since 1993) are named after Belgian designer Henry Van De Velde (1863–1957) and the Spanish Fashion Awards (only edition in 1987) were named after Spanish fashion designer Cristóbal Balenciaga (1895–1972) (El País 1987: n.p.; Valcke 2001: 36–7). National heroes somehow serve as references of what good design is and through this, Smith's second characteristic – the celebration of national heroes – finds an echo in design. Indeed, something like the 'Coco Chanel National Awards for Spanish Fashion' seems at best unlikely to be established in countries with a minimal design tradition. National awards not only reward excellence but prove to be good events to celebrate the nation and to create a sense of national and historical continuity. The awards official status attach the prestige of a nation to a given talent. To actualize that tie, continuity had to be sought so who better than Van De Velde or Balenciaga, both of whom embodied international fame as designers with the fact of being a national talent.

In 1993, the Belgian newspaper *De Standaard* published an article entitled 'Ann Demeulemeester Holds Belgian Honour High in Paris' (*Ann Demeulemeester houdt Belgische eer hoog in Parijs*) (Herten 1993: n.p.). The designer had just presented her collection for the following winter and, as the article claimed, she was second in the top-ten designers list made by the prestigious *Journal du Textile*. Not only the achievements of a single fashion professional were at issue, but also the honour of the country that she somehow represented. Demeulemeester scored in the fashion capital Paris and with her so did the whole country. Through this rhetoric, the collection itself evoked the national community and concretized it in a form. Individual Belgians had little to gain from Demeulemeester's success. However, the particular achievements of a fashion designer became somehow collectivized and a collective pride seemed to emanate from that accomplishment. The language of nationalism is unnoticeable because it is pervasive. Yet an apparently innocuous heading can conceal a complex configuration of assumptions and belongings.

As for the fourth characteristic, namely the evocation of the national community by images, another article can be cited. In 1998, the American music magazine *Rolling Stone* published an article on Belgium with a French title, to which an English translation was attached: *'Belgique c'est chic*. Translation: Belgian style rocks' (Daly 1998: 87–91). It began at the Modepaleis, the Antwerp flagship store of the fashion designer Dries Van Noten. There, a short interview with the owner was carried out. It continued with a description of the Antwerp Royal Academy of Fine Arts, from where the most famous Belgian designer graduated. Then, the article gave a short account of Belgian food – mentioning beer as well as mussels and fries – and the Antwerp shop 'Fish and Chips'. After this short break, the article went back to the fashion issue, mentioning the 'Antwerp Six' phenomenon, including an interview with Dirk Van Saene. Then there was a reference to the 1980s Belgian New Beat, which was followed by a short interview with Walter Van Beirendonck, the third of the 'Six' – with Van Noten and Van Saene – that the article treated. The article ended with a reference to the Antwerp Academy graduation show and the promising new graduate Bernard Willhelm. Alongside the main texts, there were two text boxes, one describing the five most famous beers and a second one describing the professional careers of the 'Antwerp Six'. The nineteen pictures mostly depicted street images of Antwerp, except two from the Ghent Festival. Most of the article covered issues related to fashion, but the title generalized the fashion phenomenon as the agent of a new image of Belgium in general. The article did not state 'Belgian fashion is chic', but affirmed that the whole of Belgium was. Therefore, Belgian fashion somehow represented the nation, acting – according to Smith – as a national art form. Once again, this identification took place at a discursive level. It did not emanate from the designers or from the authorities, but can only be noticed if we do not take the pervasive logics of nationalism for granted.

These four examples come to prove that even though a first reading would locate Smith's characteristics of national art in the opposite pole of contemporary production, the logics of nationalism can still be found today in design production. Precisely, one of the main reproaches of Edensor to Smith is that he focuses on aspects of high culture and forgets the relevance of low culture (Edensor 2002: 11). Apparently, similar aspects can be found in both. The question that this fact raises is whether low culture moves in similar parameters to high culture or whether low-culture artefacts enter the dynamics of high culture precisely when they enter a high culture realm. Chapter 5 will explore this question; there I will argue that the institutionalization of design as national symbols involved entering the dynamics of high-culture. Accordingly, Edensor points to popular culture as a conveyor of national identity and, reasonably, critiques Hobsbawm and Ranger's account as only centred on ceremonial traditions (Edensor 2002: 5). However, their account reveals the undeniable dominance of high culture in the realm of national symbols. For that reason, as I will argue, external elements that enter the domain of institutional national symbols will adopt the manners of high-culture products.

Whilst National Romanticism used the references to history and folk culture, contemporary creative production – with very different references and sources of inspiration – finds itself in a similar symbolic relationship with the nation. This raises the question whether the authors of nineteenth-century national art can be considered nationalist artists and, subsequently, if contemporary designers are nationalist as well. That design can become instrumentalized as nationalist, presumably, in spite of their own designers, is not contradictory to Smith's account. He accentuates that this capability of constructing national identities does not imply conscious manipulation on the part of the artists – because normally the intention of propagating national identity is definitely absent – but that it happens through mediation (Smith 1991: 91–2, 1993: 64–7).

I do not mean to imply that artists were always consciously manipulating the sentiments of the public, in order to create the idea of the nation. While there are, of course, many cases of outright manipulation in propagandist art designed to extol particular regimes or leaders, there are many more examples of periods, schools, styles and works of art which contribute to the formulation of a national identity, and which are influenced by the ideals of nationalism, without any desire on the part of the artist to instil the national idea for partisan political ends. In other words, it is more interesting to examine the artist as purveyor of 'moral historicism' and as 'true believer', if not in the tenets of nationalism, the ideological movement, then in the idea of the national community.

SMITH 1993: 64–7

Thus, national art is not necessarily propaganda art, but a possible channel for constructing national identity. Smith's most interesting observations are his acknowledgements of state mediation. He points to the artists as producers of works of art, which are later nationalist mediated by the intelligentsia. To achieve the national connotation, Smith describes a process of mediation with three main actors. First, the intellectuals 'who create artistic works and produce ideas', then the wider intelligentsia 'or professionals who transmit and disseminate those ideas and creations' and, finally, a still wider educated public 'that "consumes" ideas and works of art' (Smith 1991: 93). As Smith states, visual art and music have been of special importance in the crystallization of authentic national imagery and its dissemination to a wider audience:

The popular reception accorded to certain ethnic and 'nationalist' paintings by David and Delacroix, Mihály Muncasy and Akseli Gallen-Kallela, Vasili Surikov and Diego Rivera, to Eisenstein's or Kurosawa's ethno-historical films, to the operas of Verdi, Wagner and Musorgsky, or the symphonies and symphonic poems of Elgar, Dvorák and Tchaikovsky – or in this century, of Bartók, Janácek and Sibelius – reveal the growing mobilization of wider social groups into the vernacular ethnic culture reappropriated and sponsored by native intellectuals.

SMITH 1995: 67

Chapter 7 will argue that this classification is not as strict as Smith recognizes. Sometimes, the authorship of nationalist works of art is a collective authorship between intellectuals and intelligentsia, and some other times the intelligentsia transforms a work of art into a 'nationalist' work of art. At times civic society creates a nationalist discourse intentionally and sometimes a nationally neutral discourse in origin can be interpreted as national.

Moreover, Smith explores the possibilities art has for being turned into a suitable symbol of nations. First, for aesthetic considerations, 'the feelings of beauty, variety, dignity and pathos aroused by the skilful disposition of forms, masses, sounds and rhythms with which the arts can evoke the distinctive "spirit" of the nation' (Smith 1991: 162). Second, art can display both the revival of ethnic ties and ethnic identification, and especially its commemoration of 'the forefathers' and the fallen in each generation of the community. The latter seems to be limited to the construction of identity based on ancient or 'pseudo-ancient' forms, such as National Romanticism.

Smith's focus on the production of visions of the past neglects other issues that characterize contemporary nations, namely a 'future-oriented' national identity. In these cases, the symbols combine some ancient features with other more cosmopolitan ones that point directly to the future. In fact, Smith admits that 'any cultural element can function as a diacritical mark or badge of the nation – though it may make a considerable difference which is chosen in certain circumstances' (Smith 1995: 150). Yet, he mainly insists on the relationship these symbols have with the past. He admits that there are many ways of reproducing the nation and for each case, suitable symbolic paraphernalia would be applied. The convenient evocations of early nineteenth-century France might not be the same as for twentieth-century Belgium. In this sense, Billig states:

It is a mistake to think that an ideology is characterized by a single voice, or a particular attitudinal position. In common with other ideologies, nationalism includes contrary themes, especially the key themes of particularism and internationalism [. . .] The debate, however, is conducted within parameters that take nationhood for granted as the natural context of the universe. In this sense, the argument is conducted within, and not against, nationalism.

BILLIG 1995: 87

Indeed, past elaborations are not the only possible nationalist references and depending on which nation, it might be recalled in a totally different form. It does not mean that one approach is more nationalist than the other, rather that each nation has its own programme, and even each nation can be approached distinctively, prioritizing some referents above others. Along these lines, Alison Goodrum compares the British clothing manufacturers Mulberry and Paul Smith during the 1980s and 1990s. The former reproduces a nostalgic vision of Anglo-Britishness where tradition, countryside sports – what she calls 'huntin', shootin' and fishin' ' – and an imperial past are reproduced (Goodrum 2005: 77). On the other hand, Paul Smith reworks those notions of good tailoring and nostalgia but merges them with eccentricity and irony, which are also related to 'the other side' of Anglo-Britishness, that of the 1960s Swinging London (Goodrum 2005: 62). These contradictory sartorial references export two different versions of British identity but nevertheless coexist and even have some points in common. Whether one or the other is privileged can depend on the convenience of depicting the nation in one or other way, but still, both may reproduce the nation and therefore, can be used as conveyors of a nationalist discourse.

# Verbalizing the nation

Next to these symbols, there is the language, which of course is here approached in a different way from nineteenth-century theories of nationalism. If for Herder, language was the vehicle for socialization, for Anderson and Billig language serves as the cultural representation of the nation. According to Anderson, language should not be approached as a symbol of nationhood by itself, but the ways of speaking about the community should be pointed out as the generator of sentiments of belonging.

> It is always a mistake to treat languages in the way that certain nationalist ideologues treat them – as emblems of nation-ness, like flags, costumes, folk-dances, and the rest. Much [*sic*] the most important thing about language is its capacity for generating imagined communities, building in effect *particular solidarities*.
>
> Emphasis in the original; ANDERSON 1991[1983]: 133

As mentioned earlier, Anderson believes that 'print-language is what invents nationalism, not a particular language per se' (Anderson 1991[1983]: 134). By extension, any communication medium helps spread this sense of community. He states 'advances in communications technology, especially radio and television, give print allies unavailable a century ago. Multilingual broadcasting can conjure up the imagined community to illiterates and populations with different mother-tongues' (Anderson 1991[1983]: 135).

According to Billig, everyday language plays a determinant role; to the extent to which some common words, pronounced in particular contexts, are decidedly, and unnoticeably, symbolical. The reminding of nationhood 'cannot merely be a matter of the flag hanging outside the public building, or the national emblem, whether bald eagle or furry marten, on the coinage of the realm [. . .]. These assumptions have to be flagged discursively. And for that, banal words, jingling in the ears of the citizens, or passing before their eyes are required' (Billig 1995: 93). Billig includes an analysis of the daily press, evidencing different examples in which the nation is reproduced and which include the reader as part of this community. Like Anderson, Billig emphasizes the use by journalists of the term 'we' to address their readership, for example in the article 'Turning Our Industrial Sunset in New Dawn', published in the British newspaper *The Guardian* (Billig 1995: 115). By using the word 'our' in the title, the journalist takes for granted that the reader would be British, offering the reader an opportunity to perform his/her nationhood. The collective property – 'our' – of the industrial sunset strengthens the invisible ties that bind the 'imagined community'. Inside the article, some sentences, such as 'The revival of Britain's supply side is not just about techniques and reforms; it is about who and what we are', stress the use of 'we' as the 'British people'. The rhetoric of 'we' remains natural when the reader is indeed a Brit. In this case, the 'habitus' of nationalism offers an interpretation framework for this article. Only a non-Brit would notice the conventions linked to this use. Another example that Billig cites is the use of 'the nation', which in British newspapers is obviously Britain, without any more explanation. He points out that these uses of words reproduce the nation daily as well as the sense of belonging of the readers to the same community (Billig 1995: 115).

In the predispositions of Bourdieu's concept of 'habitus' – as 'unreflective background practices' – Lash and Urry see similarities with philosopher Hans-Georg Gadamer's pre-judgements (Lash and Urry 1994: 317). In this sense, Gadamer's hermeneutics attributes a similar power to language when he states 'language is the universal medium in which the comprehension itself takes place' (Gadamer 1960: 467). According to him, the comprehension can only be achieved by the interpretation. The receptor is always interpreting the notions conveyed by language because it is in the use of language where our pre-judgements of the world rest. Gadamer's meaning of pre-judgement does not imply faulty judgement but rather a pre-conception. Pre-judgements underpin the concepts of collective identities exposed above – in the sense that collective identities were socially shaped and had a more or less fixed form.

# Note

**1**  See Edensor's (2002) critique on Judy Butler's concepts of 'performance' and 'performativity' on pages 70–1.

# Chapter 5
# Government Branding

Despite the possibilities for modern design to represent the nation, generally speaking there is a prevalence for the ancient as far as the symbols of nations are concerned. Even new administrative units have often defined their symbolic capital out of presumably ancient symbols. This process has been described by the historian Hobsbawm as the 'invention of tradition', which points out that governments have attempted to create new nations as if they had previously existed (Hobsbawm & Ranger 1983). Similarly, Anderson acknowledges this refusal to create nations without history. He points out how paradoxical 'the objective modernity of nations to the historian's eye vs. their subjective antiquity in the eyes of nationalists' is (Anderson 1991[1983]: 5). He describes these processes as manoeuvres to force the identification of the citizens with the nation and more concretely with the nation-state.

Far from being an outdated strategy, these mechanisms can be found even in the newest nation-state to date, i.e. South Sudan in Africa. This country gained its independence from Sudan in 2011 after a referendum on 9 July and became a state member of the United Nations on 14 July that year. Its flag was adopted from the Sudan People's Liberation Movement, the banner under which the supporters of independence gathered in the two civil wars. Its coat of arms conversely was designed from scratch but reproduces a well-known formula of a heraldic coat of arms and cartouche displayed by many other different countries (Figure 5.1). An eagle holds a shield over a spade and a spear, under which the legend 'Justice, Liberty, Prosperity. Republic of South Sudan' can be read. Anne Quito reflects on the homogenizing character of this coat of arms that is adorned with similar recurrent iconography like the USA, Egypt, Yemen or Moldova. On the other hand, and considering that national symbols not only seek for differentiation but also for legitimization, then it works in placing this brand-new country on a par with long-established nations. She describes that the most difficult element to incorporate was not the commonplace eagle and cartouche but actually the most specific. The shield had to be different to those typical of

**Figure 5.1** Ministry of Culture technical committee, coat of arms of the Republic of South Sudan, 2011.

the constituting tribes of South Sudan, yet representative enough (Quito 2014: 58–62). Up until today the link to tradition, a suitable representation of the composing parts of the country and a validating language seem to be the ingredients for the design of national symbols. History and the vernacular seem to defeat modernity as long as national symbols are concerned. When a national graphic language has been established, nations tend to follow it if they want to be recognized as such.

The nation needs to be conceived as collective and at the same time appeal to every indvidual. This tension is salient in the discourse of the nation. History can be a force to collectivize the nation through the invocation of a shared past. Similarly, the individualization of the nation is evident in the use of language. Anderson describes how, in different languages, the words related to the nation make continuous reference to kinship (motherland, *Vaterland* and *patria*) or home

(*Heimat*). 'Both idioms denote something to which one is naturally tied. . . . [I]n every thing "natural" there is always something unchosen. In this way nation-ness is assimilated to skin-colour, gender, parentage and birth-era – all those things one can not help' (Anderson 1991[1983]: 143).

In this tension, modernity does not play a significant role. Nevertheless, it has been on the agenda of governments, too. The extent to which tradition and modernity coalesce is one characterized with compromise and hybrid solutions. There are a few examples in which the public sector has opted to express modernity through design. The most notable might be the post-war Netherlands. A number of public commissions including the logos for the Post Service and the national currency displayed playful colour combinations and sans-serif typography. A trend of creating coherent corporate identities was initiated in 1963 in the Netherlands by Dutch Royal Airlines (1963) and followed by the oil company PAM (1965) and the supermarket Albert Heijn (1966). Design offices Total Design (founded in 1963) and Tel Design (founded in 1962) were responsible for most of these commissions. The corporate identity for the Dutch Railways – from 1937 until 1995 entirely financed and run by the Dutch state – commissioned in 1967 is a key project of Gert Dumbar (b. 1940) in his period as artistic director of Tel Design (Figure 5.2). Dumbar was asked to make the company's graphic information clearer, including logo, pictograms,

**Figure 5.2** Tel Design, logo of the Dutch Railways (*Nederlandse Spoorwegen*) and graphic design of the train carriages, 1967.

route-planners and timetables. Instead of representing this public body with calligraphic style and heraldic motifs, he designed a clean, schematic logo more typical of private corporations. The blue logos were displayed on carriages painted in bright cadmium yellow. This unusual design met initial resistance from the commissioners, but was finally implemented and is still in use today (Bakker 2011: 168).

The Dutch banknotes were designed by Ootje Oxenaar. His first designs in the late 1960s and early 1970s included portraits of key figures of Dutch history such as composer Jan Pieterszoon Sweelinck (1562–1621), painter Frans Hals (1582–1666) or philosopher Baruch Spinoza (1632–1677) (Figure 5.3). The characters referred to the Dutch Golden Age but were depicted in a stylized style, almost as characters from a comic book. Another series followed in the 1980s characterized by the use of more bright colours depicting nature elements from the Netherlands such as a sunflower, and a snipe or a light tower (Simon Thomas 2008: 177). If the first series made reference to historicist motifs, the second was rather based in vernacular architecture and national nature. The way of representing these motifs was innovative indeed. The motifs themselves however can be rather connected to previous examples dating back to the nineteenth century that represent the nation through its nature or vernacular architecture. This innovative approach towards public commissions met both defenders and detractors. On the one hand, this modern-looking iconography contributed to bringing the government closer to the citizenry by turning power symbols into civic symbols. On the other hand, these corporate identities became ubiquitous and were considered to compromise the seriousness of the country. More specifically, after Studio Dumbar's redesign of the police cars in 1993, the

**Figure 5.3** Oxenaar, Ootje, 1000 guilder banknote, issued in March 1972, obverse displaying the portrait of Baruch Spinoza (1632–1677).

stylization of the public sphere in the Netherlands seemed to have reached a peak. American designer Michael Rock pointed out that this preference for modern-looking design could convey the message that the government is progressive and looks out for cultural improvement. According to him, if the same happened in America, it would be perceived as if the government expended the money of taxpayers in frivolities (Rock 2004: 66). Similarly, an often-quoted reflection of Dutch designer Chris Vermaas argued that the Netherlands had became a 'Legoland' country. He made reference to the broad bands that adorned the police cars and made them similar to children's toys (Rock 2004: 70; Bruinsma 1996). Both external and internal perception pointed to the fact that the designed visual and material culture related to the Dutch government was unusual in its display of modernity. Indeed, official bodies tend to be identified with traditional emblems and the incorporation of a contemporary graphic language could align them too much to the realm of corporations.

But if this unleashed modernity was present in government-related bodies, when addressing the visual identity of the government itself, this modernity became much more constrained. The Dutch government faced the renovation of its house style much later, using a stylized representation of its coat of arms and a blue ribbon to unify the communicational strategy of the different ministries under one house style. The new logo and house style was designed by Studio Dumbar in 2007 and has been implemented since 2008. The legend is positioned on the right side of the ribbon, stating the name of the ministry, department or governmental organization responsible for sending the information. This hierarchical structure announces first the responsible ministry in the top most line, which can be followed by a sub-department and, if applicable, a sub-sub-department. Designer Peter Verheul (b. 1965) designed three typefaces for exclusive use, based on his own Versa typeface (Bavelaar et al. 2010: 159–60). Design critic Marc Vlemmings compared this design to the Dutch stamps and (former) guilder coins and banknotes, recognizing that this house style did not reach the standards of modernity of its predecessors. Indeed, designing national symbolism had been in many ways connected to tradition. The logo of the Dutch government could not be different, especially taking into consideration its pronounced symbolical character for the country.

Previous examples in which a unique logo was implemented to identify national governments and its ministries were the house styles of the federal governments of Canada (1970), Germany (1998) and Switzerland (2007). The Canadian example has been one of the pioneers in implementing the logics of modernist design to government branding. The variety of provincial, regional and federal governments urged the Canadian government to rationalize its communication that was compulsorily adopted by all departments in 1978. Issues of transparency and efficiency have been key in the implementation of these house styles (Large 1991: 31–42). Nevertheless, there are symbolic connotations undeniably attached. Arguably, old established, centralized nations have preferred calligraphy and heraldry in their communications above modernity. Their symbols have been fixed along the nineteenth century and have therefore maintained traditional graphic traits. Admittedly, national governments have been rather slow in incorporating modern-looking logos. Is it the same case with subnationalisms? Does the articulation of national symbols differ from established nation-states? Or on the contrary, does it follow them? The next section will analyse a few examples stemming from political devolution in Belgium and in Spain. More specifically, the visual identity programmes for the Catalan government, designed by Josep M. Trias (b. 1948) in 1985, and for the Flemish government, designed by Herman Lampaert (b. 1931) and Antoon De Vijlder (b. 1940) in 1989.

# Political devolution and the negotiation of new symbols

As mentioned in the introduction to this book, Smith traces an historical sociology of nationalisms and national identity. In so doing, he presents an evolution of nationalist theories illustrated with case studies. They include first, the ethnic separatism from old empires in the nineteenth century, and second, the ethnic nationalisms emerging in the overseas territories of European colonial empires in the early to mid-twentieth century. A third wave of demotic ethnic nationalisms is present in industrial societies since the late 1950s and includes the Catalan, Basque, Breton, Scots, Welsh and Flemish movements (Smith 1991: 125). Belgium's and Spain's processes of political devolution started during the last quarter of the twentieth century. On its part, Belgium undertook its first Constitutional reform in December 1970 to create what were named Cultural Parliaments for both the Dutch- and French-speaking communities. Subsequent reforms in 1981 and 1988 expanded regional powers and in 1988 the third Belgian state reformation took place. Then, regional autonomy was strengthened and the maximum allotted powers were transferred to the regions (Dutch *gewesten*/French *régions*). In 1993, the Constitution was reformed and Belgium has been a federal state ever since (Witte et al. 1997: 355–80).

In 1975, the death of General Francisco Franco ended the dictatorship period (1939–1975) in Spain and opened a dual process of democratization and political devolution. The 1978 Constitution laid the groundwork for the subsequent political devolution of the years to come, which materialized in the 'State of the Autonomies'. Between 1979 and 1982, the 17 regional Statutes were approved, which have granted expanded powers through subsequent reforms starting in 1991 (Powell 2001: 391–403).

Remarkably, a great number of the logos for the three Belgian regions (*gewesten/régions*)   and   seventeen   Spanish   Autonomous   Communities (*comunidades autónomas*) followed the example of the house style for the Canadian government. Notably, the re-branding of Belgium and Spain produced a great number of design-led logos. Next to the invocation of their own past, there was a firm attitude on behalf of the regions to construct their future. As Wally Olins explained: 'some nations like Spain and Australia [. . .] very carefully and deliberately adapted the techniques used by corporations in marketing themselves and their products and services in order to help them project a new, or revised, or in some way modified view of themselves' (Olins 2002: 246).

The logos of the Belgian and Spanish regions are examples of Billig's 'banal nationalism' (Billig: 1995). As unnoticeable elements of the everyday landscape, logos may remind us of our belonging to a nation with similar intensity as a flag might. The ways to disseminate them in everyday life can be extremely subtle, yet they nonetheless reinforce the ties that bind the citizens to their territory and government. Logos and coats of arms of local governments make up part of ordinary landscapes. A new public work, garbage containers, or a road-sign reminding drivers of the entrance into a province are good occasions for displaying governmental logos. Unequivocally, they remind the inhabitants of either their belonging to a given nation/region or their presence in a foreign one. Their analysis will show the extent to which they embody notions of tradition and modernity. Indeed, their geneses are generally a product of the reconstruction of a suitable past, joined with the expectations of a promising future. Moreover, politic commissioners play a role in the final aspect of each logo. Political forces have tried to put their stamp onto the institutional logos and thereby link their party forever to the governmental body.

The first two examples to compare will be the visual identity programmes for the Catalan and Flemish governments stemming from political devolution. In both cases, these regions managed to combine nationalist demands by drawing on legitimating, historicist elements with a projection beyond the supranational boundaries towards Europe. On the one hand, the presence of the government for the citizenry sought to anchor the government in traditional traits. On the other hand, modern graphics conveyed a competitive character at European level. The narratives in which both house styles were embedded shifted between tradition and modernity as required by the circumstances. The graphic elements were sufficiently ambiguous and offer one or other face for the new administrative bodies.

# Catalonia's reinterpretation of the past

The 1978 Spanish Constitution started a process of political devolution, which coincided with the widely desired integration of Spain into the European Union.

While the dictatorship evoked centralization and isolation, democracy simultaneously celebrated decentralization and Europeanization. The major Spanish political devolution process of 1979–1984 generated seventeen new autonomous governments, which opted to create their own identity signs in order to manifest their presence among their voters. Apart from the national symbols (flags, costumes, folk-dances, national anthem and coat of arms), the governments felt the need for logos to represent themselves as institutions. During the major part of the 1980s, soon after the new institutions were established, communication tools were developed in order to underpin a new, democratic relationship between governments and voters.

Most scholars have seen the political devolution as the most controversial of all the difficulties derived from the Constitution (Aja 1999: 54; Juliá and Mainer 2000: 50; Powell 2001: 228). The first phase ran between 1977 and 1983, when the future autonomous governments first had an experimental (test) period as pre-autonomous governments. After the approval of their Statutes (1978–1983), the first regional elections took place and the Autonomous Parliaments came into being. Moreover, the Constitutional Court was a central element of this system, as it sought to resolve the conflicts between central and regional governments. The result was a quasi-federalized model officially called the 'State of Autonomies'.

Following Eliseo Aja's comparative study, this model includes all the ingredients of a federal state. But the Constitution, politicians and media did not call it a federal state but rather an autonomic state (Aja 1999: 37). Nevertheless, as Aja points out: 'the more consolidated federal states are based on the absolute constitutional equality among the *Länder* or member states, while the autonomic state presents structural differences among the Autonomous Communities that distance it from those models' (Aja 1999: 155). Remarkably, the seventeen Autonomous Communities have considerable variations. The level of their powers and competencies is different, as rules about language use and financial systems, among others, are specific for some regions. It all derives from an unequal regional self-consciousness and an uneven identification with the central state. Accordingly, while some regions had had previous experience with autonomy, the rest had never included self-government in their political agendas. Related to this fact, the Constitution prepared two denominations for the new entities: nationalities and regions. As Article 2 exposes:

The Constitution is based on the indissoluble unity of the Spanish nation, the common and indivisible homeland of all Spaniards, and recognises and guarantees the right to autonomy of the nationalities and regions which make it up and the solidarity among all of them.

1978 Spanish Constitution, *Título Preliminar, Art. 2*

Whether called a region or a nationality, the status was the same: they were all Autonomous Communities. Through their Statutes, the Autonomies declared themselves a nationality in six cases (Andalusia, the Basque Country, the Canary Islands, Catalonia, Galicia, and the Valencian Community); the rest were either explicitly regions or just avoided defining themselves.[1] This difference remained a symbolic question, an indicator of the will of the different political forces. According to the different approaches, Catalonia's Statute of Autonomy is taken to mean the moment 'when Catalonia regains its freedom' (BOE 1979) while for Murcia's Statute 'the Autonomous Communities [. . .] contribute to reinforcing the unity of Spain' (BOE 1982).

The 1978 Constitution foresaw two speeds at which the Autonomous Communities could obtain the devolved powers. Originally, the three *historical nationalities* – namely the Basque Country, Catalonia and Galicia – might use the fastest route. Indeed, those regions had had their own statutes during the Spanish Second Republic, prior to the moment when the dictatorship invalidated them. As the *historical nationalities* were privileged, the rest of the Autonomous Communities began a tour de force to prove their historical character. The denomination 'historical' made many Autonomous Communities think that this status was attainable by any region with history, which, of course, they all had. Accordingly, regional histories were revived and ancient kingdoms and princedoms began to come to light in an attempt on the part of the Autonomous Communities to document their differences (Aja 1999: 249).

At first, it was intended for only the *historical nationalities* to immediately obtain the highest level of powers foreseen in the 1978 Constitution. The two Autonomous Communities ruled by nationalist parties were Catalonia and the Basque Country. As John Hooper points out: 'They have never been much enamoured of a solution which granted self-government to all seventeen regions, fearing that it was a way of dodging what they regard as the central issue – recognition of the distinctive identities of the three *historical nationalities*' (Hooper 1995: 435). Both autonomies revived the autonomous governments' logotypes from the 1930s, proving that they did not need to go back to the nineteenth or the fourteenth century to find a moment of self-government.

In 1981, the Catalonia Autonomous government revived the emblem designed in 1931 by Bartomeu Llongueras (1906–1994) (DOGC 1981: n.p.) (Figure 5.4). It depicted an oval coat of arms with four red bars on a yellow background. At the four corners, two laurel leaves turned the oval form into a rectangular one. Josep M. Trias' design team developed the implementation guide and variations of the logotype in the visual identity manual published in 1985. Simultaneously, the Generalitat created the Design Board (*Consell de Disseny*) as a permanent consultation body to guide the implementation of the logo. Essentially, this logo reproduced the 1931 emblem, accompanied by the legend 'Generalitat de

# Generalitat de Catalunya

**Figure 5.4** Trias, Josep María (Quod), logo of the Catalan Government (Generalitat de Catalunya, designed originally in 1981), after the modifications of 1996.

Catalunya' in Helvetica typeface. However, even when the designer only adapted the already existing sign and developed the implementations, the outcome was presented as a designer logo (Satué 1997: 25). Paradoxically, this sign joined pictographic features with pictorial ones. As pictograms, it used only one colour; nevertheless the peripheral laurel leaves insinuated an external light source, as they were illuminated in a 'naturalistic way', as reflected the description in Decree 97/1981 (DOGC 1981: n.p.).

In 1996, the same design team updated the manual with no substantial changes (Generalitat de Catalunya 1997[1985]). However, the designers retouched the laurel leaves. Indeed, as their shadows made the logo slightly asymmetrical, external graphic design offices sometimes implemented the logo wrongly and, as a result, it could be seen in the public sphere upside down. The wrong utilization of the logo led to special measures. The update of 1996 depicted the laurel leaves as illuminated in a 'non-naturalistic' way in order to achieve a completely symmetrical logo. This means that all the laurel leaves got the shadows in their outer extreme and, as result, the logo looked exactly the same after being rotated 180 degrees. In addition, according to the Design Board the then completely symmetrical anagram aimed at reflecting 'a more modern and international image' of the Catalan government (Batlle & Rifà 1997: 12).

The Catalan government approached their logo as a communicational element and consequently commissioned a designer to solve it, one who applied the rules of visual and communicational efficacy. Legitimating historicism was found by slightly modifying the original elements of the 1931 symbol that did not seem to affect substantially the 'Catalanness' of the logo. On the contrary, this alteration was welcomed inasmuch as it could contribute to communicational efficiency. The origins of Catalan nationalist doctrine from the late nineteenth century, formulated by Prat de la Riva, experienced a revival during the 1980s. Catalan nationalism was 'founded on cultural, historical bases and mainly on a vocation of modernising Europeanism' (Sepúlveda 1996: 416). As result, the Catalan logo welcomed modernizing graphic values.

# Flanders' problematic lion

In the last quarter of the twentieth century, Belgium underwent a transition from a centralized state to a federal state. The resulting complex federal organization was carried out on two overlapping levels: in cultural communities and economic-administrative regions. As far as the cultural communities are concerned, three were set apart: the French-speaking, the Dutch-speaking, and the German-speaking regions. As far as the administrative was concerned, three regions whose borders did not always coincide exactly with those of the cultural communities came about: Flanders (Dutch-speaking), Brussels (Dutch and French-speaking), and Wallonia (French and German-speaking).

In 1970–1971, the first of up to now five state reforms was carried out, reforms that by 1993 would convert Belgium into a federal state. In 1970, three Cultural Communities were established and the foundations for the three administrative regions were laid out. Ten years later, in 1980, a second state reform took place in which both a government and a parliament were constituted for the two largest administrative regions: Flanders and Wallonia. In 1988–1989, the third state reform began. In this one, the region of Brussels took shape as an administrative region. Simultaneously, new powers were decentralized; first, communities acquired powers in terms of education, and second, the administrative regions did so in transport and public works (Craeybeckx et al. 1997: 371–83). This division into three communities and three regions is typical for Belgian federalism. Both types of entities have their own exclusive competences. Thus, Belgium was to have six parliaments and six governments, apart from the federal parliament (consisting of a House of Representatives and a Senate) and the federal government. However, the Flemish institutions presented a different scenario. Flemish politicians decided in 1980 to merge the Flemish Community with the Flemish Region. As a result, Flanders has one Flemish Parliament and one Flemish Government with powers over community as well as over regional matters.

In the 1980 state reform, the Cultural Council for the Dutch-Speaking Cultural Community was granted powers to create its own government. Its name was the Flemish Executive, and since 1993 the Flemish Government (Goosens 1996: 28).[2] Nevertheless, at the third state reform of 1989, the Flemish Executive got more powers and therefore its public image needed a logo and an implementation manual to mark its public presence. In 1988, the Flemish Executive third legislature had begun as a proportional government presided over by Christian-Democrat Gaston Geens (1931–2002), who had already presided over the government during the two previous legislatures. His cabinet organized an open competition to design the 'Logo of Flanders', in which either professionals or amateurs could participate (Vlaamse Raad 1989). The competition was open from 20 January to 10 March 1989 and the main aim was to 'design a logo that can present Flanders abroad as a progressive, highly qualitative and recognizable region' (Vlaamse Raad 1989: 899). The organizers received 420 logos from 340 participants. Subsequently, the selection commission chose three designs, which the Flemish Executive later assessed. According to minister-president Gaston Geens, they were 'original and of outstanding quality' but failed in their main task, namely 'the visualisation of an internationally recognisable quality label for the Flemish Community' (Vlaamse Raad 1989: 900).

Such a local symbol might, at first sight, be considered to be just an internal task or a communication manoeuvre for domestic viewers; however, it was condensed in major complexity. Indeed, the symbol must serve in the promotion of Flanders abroad and therefore external viewers were included as target viewers as well. In this sense, the words of minister-president Gaston Geens were unambiguous. Moreover, two aspects give an overview of the extent to which this logo, albeit apparently a local question, was actually oriented to an external 'market'. First, the commission that selected the three logos was the Advice Board for the Promotion of Flanders (*Adviescomité Promotie Vlaanderen*) – which decided on the contents of the governmental magazine *Flanders* for external promotion. Second, the intended place to present the logo – a presentation that never took place – was the Flanders Technology trade fair, one of the best-known, internationally oriented initiatives of the Flemish Government (Vlaamse Raad 1989: 900). All this tied the logo to other efforts that sought to boost Flanders as a competitive region at European level. This fact shows how difficult it is to separate the local initiatives from their international vocation and how related the local and the international were in decentralized regions.

Nationalist deputy André De Beul, contested this decision to organize a public competition for such a task. First, he criticized the idea that non-professional designers take part in such a relevant graphic assignment. Second, he stated that the logo should not be enough and that a 'house style' was indispensable. Thirdly, he wondered if the minister had anything against the Flemish lion as a symbol of Flanders, as he attributed to Geens the affirmation that the lion was 'less designated' to represent Flanders abroad. Geens answered that this promotional logo would never change the flag or the coat of arms of Flanders (Vlaamse Raad 1989: 899–900). Presumably, Geens' first idea was not a lion to promote Flanders abroad. However, according to what happened later, his first intentions declined.

The Flemish Executive arranged a supervisory board in order to guide the design of a logo. The General Secretary of the Ministry of the Flemish Community, Willy Juwet, chaired this group, which further included representatives of different governmental departments, specifically those of Fine Arts, Press and Monuments (Ministerie van de Vlaamse Gemeenschap 1989). They commissioned two designers and an artist to approach the project – namely graphic

**Figure 5.5** Lampaert, Herman and Antoon De Vijlder, logo for the Flemish Executive (Vlaamse Overheid), 1989.

designers Herman Lampaert and Antoon De Vijlder, and artist Mark Verstockt (b. 1930). The first two decided to present a common solution and the third one preferred to work separately. Accordingly, their propositions were also very different. De Vijlder and Lampaert proposed a logo which faithfully reproduced the coat of arms (Figure 5.5). They thought that Flanders already had a symbol and that it expressed the qualities sought by the Flemish Government. On the contrary, according to Lampaert and De Vijlder, Verstockt presented an abstract, geometric logo, without any references to the emblems of Flanders (De Vijlder 2005; Lampaert 2005). Mark Verstockt offered a continuance of his own artistic practice, which is distinguishable by the use of elementary, geometric figures – mainly squares and circles – and a limited palette – black, grey and white. The neutral logo objectively reflected a new Flanders, a logo without tradition to reflect a new political entity with a completely new political status.

The commission decided to keep Lampaert and De Vijlder's proposal, which depicted a lion from the coat of arms but synthesized into a pictogram. The Flemish Government had adopted the weapons of the historical county of

Flanders in 1973, which actually differed from the current region of Flanders in its extension. To be precise, the historical county of Flanders was much smaller. It included only two (West Flanders and East Flanders) of the five current Flemish provinces. The black lion on yellow background had been adopted by nationalist Flemish movements since the nineteenth century and had survived until then as a symbol of Flanders. Arguably, this solution was the most reconciliatory of the two. First, it would not trigger critics from those who defended the lion as a valid logo for Flanders. Second, it would fulfil the first intentions of the government to express modernity. The Flemish Government, which appreciated its heraldic suitability and its 'modern and visually attractive' qualities, finally approved the project on 28 July 1989 (Ministerie van de Vlaamse Gemeenschap 1989: 0.2.a). The pictogram rules guided the redrawing of the lion, i.e. no illusion of volume and no detail. The direction of the lines was limited to vertical, horizontal and 45° in the trunk and extremities. Moreover, the rectilinear lines that run through the figure accentuated these parts. These lines made the figure lighter and contrasted with the curves that outlined the head and tail, the two dynamic elements. This contrast confers energy to the overall image.

The work commission considered the redrawing of the lion in a logo as both symbolically and functionally pertinent. Symbolically, because the logo was heraldically correct – i.e. it depicted a lion with red tongue and red claws – and therefore unequivocally symbolized Flanders. It was functional because, unlike the heraldic signs, a pictogram never loses its readability, either amplified or reduced. For example, as heraldic coats of arms, which are generally made up of many figures, get reduced in order to fit onto a letter-paper, then all the elements get squeezed together and become unidentifiable. On the contrary, a pictogram keeps its readability at a minimal size. To achieve this aim, there were two versions of the lion, one with broader yellow lines for reductions under 2 cm high and another with thinner yellow lines if the final size surpassed 2 cm (Ministerie van de Vlaamse Gemeenschap 1989: 1.1–1.2).

The design task involved not only the logo but also the whole house style. The institutional typeface was Galliard, a standard typeface. The designers did not need to design a new type because Galliard mixed perfectly the local and global connotations. Indeed, New York designer Matthew Carter (b. 1937) designed the Galliard font in 1978 on the base of his previous studies at the historical archive of the Plantijn Moretus Museum in Antwerp. More specifically, the work of typographer Robert Granjon (1513–1589), who had worked in the printing-house of Christoffel Plantijn, had inspired the Galliard typeface (Ministerie van de Vlaamse Gemeenschap 1989: 0.2.b). Therefore, according to the implementation manual, this typeface 'underlines the Flemish character of the printed papers and it is cost-effective at the same time' (Ministerie van de Vlaamse Gemeenschap 1989: 0.2.b).

Both the logo and the typeface seem to find a consensus between 'Flemishness' (due to its local, tradition-bounded origin) and international projection (due to its modern-looking style). Consequently, the logo was initially well accepted but later underwent two modifications. In 2000, a redesign of the house style took place, though it did not impinge on the lion (Ministerie van de Vlaamse Gemeenschap 2000). For example, the typeface changed from Galliard to the 'more easily available' Garamond. This change did not trigger any rejection. While the choice of Galliard seemed to fulfil the double intentions of government and designers of conveying Flanders' past, the typeface's capability to transfer symbolic value is more limited. There are some symbols which unequivocally address nationhood (such as the heraldic Flemish lion) and whose presence or absence can raise heated discussions, However, although the Galliard typeface was supposed to convey Flemish tradition and was a substantial component of the Flemish Government house style, its permanence was not essential. In 2014, the logo changed substantially depicting only the head of the lion looking frontally, distancing itself from heraldic references, since the flag depicts the lion full body and from a lateral point of view.

In the period shortly after the acquisition of new powers the debates on symbols were intense. New administrative units sought to validate their existence both among their voters and abroad. Catalonia found historical legitimation in its Statutes during the Second Republic. Flanders drew from the weapons of the historical county of Flanders and its nationalist movement. The result in both cases was a consensual solution, which joined different pairs of antonyms: modernity/tradition, heraldic (high culture)/pictographic (low culture) and local/international. Consequently, divergent perceivers could appreciate it. First, those who were seeking a traditional symbol, and second, those viewers who were searching for the internationally recognizable and progressive Flanders. Hence, Hobsbawm and Ranger's account of the pre-eminence of high culture for representing the national is here present, for example, as the logo displays an important substrate derived from traditional heraldry (Hobsbawm and Ranger 1983: 4). However, symbols can condense diverse layers of meaning and therefore the pre-eminence of high culture elements does not exclude other components. In this case, both logos were rather acting as coats of arms and therefore entered a different logic. As Edensor points out, 'the popular seems to be collapsed into the ceremonial traditions [that Hobsbawm and Ranger] discuss' (Edensor 2002: 5). He argues that the authors do not consider the vernacular and the everyday in their analysis. Though this might be true, the Flemish logo shows that everyday symbols as logos often cannot escape from adopting the external forms and rituals of high cultural elements (as heraldry) in that high culture has indeed guided the national emblems and myths. Even the 2014 version of the Flemish logo did not differ radically from the heraldic symbols of the region.

# Regions as nations

In both Belgium and Spain, processes of political devolution were prompted by subnationalism. Nonetheless, the devolution extended in both cases to all the state. As a result, regions with no nationalist self-conciousness developed similar symbols as did the subnationals, becoming unexpected nations in themselves. In these cases, such as the Comunidad de Madrid and the region of Brussels, symbols were created from scratch – as was the awareness of forming a community equivalent to Catalonia or Flanders. In both cases, both regions had superposing identity levels, since they were articulated around the capitals of Spain and Belgium respectively. If national elements had to hinge upon the historicist and the vernacular, in these cases there was not much that defined either of the regions. In the cases of Catalonia and Flanders, ancient symbols were communicated as 'modern'. In these two cases, the solutions were different. In the case of the Madrid region, objectively new symbols – albeit based on existing identity elements – were manifestly conveyed as novel. In the case of the Brussels region, purely novel symbols were conversely presented as rooted in tradition. The reception of both was also different, but much more problematic in the first case.

## The Madrid Community, five-pointed stars on a red background

Designer José María Cruz Novillo (b. 1936) and art critic Santiago Amón (1927–1988) designed, in 1984, not only the logo but also the flag and the typically heraldic coat of arms of the new Madrid Community, then governed by the Socialist party. The result was extraordinarily controversial. Madrid, as a new Autonomous Community created at the end of the twentieth century, lacked traditional elements of heraldry. The capital and the province, indeed, each had their symbols but an Autonomous Community was something different and the symbols were consciously sought to objectively reflect this. Its new coat of arms became the government's logo, since the original province coat of arms was considered unsuitable. It depicted two castles – representing the two Castiles between which the Madrid region was located – under seven stars derived from the coat of arms of the city of Madrid. Its flag depicted the same seven stars on a red background.

As expected, the result was severely criticized by the right-wing party in opposition. According to them, the red flag with the five-pointed stars appeared subliminally communist, the anthem was 'doubtfully constitutional' and the coat of arms exposed a wrongly conceived crown (Figure 5.6). The Royal Academy of History (*Real Academia de la Historia*) supported this reaction and declared the elements as unrepresentative, proposing a new version, which in the end did not

# Comunidad de Madrid

**Figure 5.6** Cruz Novillo, José María and Santiago Amón, coat of arms and logo for Madrid regional government (Comunidad de Madrid), 1983. First, the coat of arms (left) acted as logo of Madrid Government until 1996 when substituted by a synthetic version of the flag.

prosper. The polemic continued until December 1983, when the Madrid Parliament approved the designed signs. The symbols did not enjoy parliamentary unanimity nor popular acceptance. In January 1984, the flag was hoisted in a ceremony that had few citizens attending, the majority of whom were there to protest (ABC 1983; El País 1983a, 1983b, 1983c, 1983d). The polemic continued locally for fourteen years (see Olaya 1997).

In 1984, the implementation guide was published together with a book seeking to introduce the new symbols to the people of Madrid. During the first few years, the new coat of arms was used as the government logo. It was later substituted by a different, even more synthesized symbol based this time on the flag, which was more easily translated into a graphic sign (Gobierno de la Comunidad de Madrid 1999[1984]). Unlike the logo for the Brussels Region, the sign for Madrid did not seek to validate its newness on a supposed tradition and therefore it triggered both political and popular resistance. Notwithstanding, in 1996, the then Christian-Democrat government, which had ferociously criticized the 1984 signs, continued with the implementation of the logo as originally planned. A new logo – based this time on the flag with the five-pointed stars – was introduced, substituting the logo with the two castles. Paradoxically, the new government did not go back to restore heraldic-looking signs but continued using the pictograms. The logo of Madrid had achieved a close identification with the governmental institutions and therefore its ideological origin seemed blurred. It demonstrates that, although symbols can absorb ideological currents in their origin, they can later achieve legitimization by its continuous use.

## Brussels and the iris flower

The administrative regions of Flanders and Wallonia came out of the 1980 state reform. On the contrary, Brussels was a product of the third state reform of

1988–1989. Making a region out of Brussels was not a clear task, due principally to its complicated symbolic meaning within Belgium and its mixed social composition. Brussels is indeed a (big) city, located just in the middle of Flanders, and officially bilingual but informally French speaking. Moreover, it is an independent region but little bigger than a city and, in addition, the capital of Belgium. Hence, a site of strong symbolic value as engaged in the amalgamated nature of the country but little more than a crossroad point if it were to form an independent entity.

Its own mixed nature presented some difficulties for identifying it with a single symbol. However, shortly after the institutionalization of the Brussels-Capital Region, some parliamentarians submitted new proposals. On 18 October 1989, Stéphane de Lobkowicz (b. 1957), a member of the French-speaking Christian-Democrat party, argued that Brussels-Capital Region had to choose its emblems in order to differentiate it from the other two Belgian regions, Flanders and Wallonia. Paradoxically, Lobkowicz's account did not seek to create a third region but reaffirmed Brussels as a symbolic site for the federation. The main quality of Brussels was its condition as Belgium's leading city and, accordingly, its flag should have the three national colours (i.e. black, yellow and red). Simultaneously, this choice would identify Brussels with the Flemish and Walloon colours – black and yellow for the former, red and yellow for the latter – and, consequently, 'Brussels, as a meeting point for the two communities, could not better express its will for harmony than adopting these colours' (Conseil de la Région de Bruxelles-Capitale 1989a: 1). Moreover, as the capital of Belgium, Brussels 'could only adopt the "Brabant", also called "Belgian" lion on its coat of arms', this is a yellow lion with a crown on black background (Conseil de la Région de Bruxelles-Capitale 1989a: 1). Lobkowicz's idea tried to dilute Brussels' identity into Belgian identity and, at the same time, to conform a nebulous mixture of the defined Flemish and Walloon identities. After considering the rejection of the Madrid case, this proposal would be expected to succeed, as it recognized the dependence of this new region on other national formations. This, however, was not the case, and the brand new region demanded an identity of its own.

Lobkowicz's proposal passed on to the Brussels government but did not go any further (Conseil de la Région de Bruxelles-Capitale 1989b: 174). As a response, the Socialist government of minister-president Charles Picqué (b. 1948) – minister-president of the Brussels-Capital Region during the legislature of 1989–1995 and re-elected for the next legislature of 1995–1999 – launched a public competition to design the emblem of the Brussels-Capital Region. The call got an excellent response from the population, who submitted more than 800 designs. Subsequently, the jury – made up of historians, heraldry specialists, graphic designers and communication professionals – pre-selected seven proposals. However, fellow parliamentarians questioned the procedure of an open contest as well as the quality of the submissions. Deputy De Decker even said, 'none of them could be adopted as a symbol of our region without ridiculing it' (Conseil de la Région de Bruxelles-Capitale 1990a: 878). Besides, even Picqué himself confessed he was not very enamoured with the procedure (Conseil de la Région de Bruxelles-Capitale 1990a: 878–9).

Finally, the organizers declared the contest void in October 1990 (Conseil de la Région de Bruxelles-Capitale 1990b: 1). Nevertheless, the new emblem for Brussels came out of the submissions. An iris flower would be the symbol of the region. On 27 February 1991, the concrete form of the emblem was disclosed in Parliament (Conseil de la Région de Bruxelles-Capitale 1991a: 1–2). It was a design submitted by Jacques Richez (1918–1994) that depicted an iris flower in yellow with a white border on a dark blue background (Figure 5.7). The formal interpretation of the flower recalled art nouveau shapes, a typical Brussels style. Unlike characteristic pictograms, the outline did not follow in a strict grid of directions. Instead, round, fluid contours recreated the natural origin of the motif. However, it displayed the stylization of pictograms, i.e. monochrome, without shadows or illusion of depth.

The meaning of the iris was explained in great length by the work commission. First, a flower that grew on marshland terrain, as the ground Brussels had traditionally been. Second, Brussels art had repeatedly represented this flower. Third, it was unique, as no other symbol from the other Belgian communities and regions resembled it. Fourth, the commissioners invoked Greek mythology. There, the goddess Iris was the messenger of the other gods. Fifth, the iris and other flowers had been widely used in heraldry. Last but not least, the yellow and blue were the colours of the European flag and Brussels was the seat of most European institutions (Conseil de la Région de Bruxelles-Capitale 1991a: 1–2). And so, the emblem appeared to join all the advantages of tradition, high culture (i.e. art, mythology and heraldry) and the international projection towards a European future.

Unlike the previous proposal, all the then chiefs of most of the parliamentary groups signed this proposition. This included principally both the French- and Dutch-speaking fractions of Socialist, Liberal, Green and Christian-Democrat

**REGION DE BRUXELLES-CAPITALE**
**BRUSSELS HOOFDSTEDELIJK GEWEST**

**Figure 5.7** Richez, Jacques, logo for the Brussels Capital-Region (Région de Bruxelles-Capital/Brussels Hoofdstedelijk Gewest), 1991.

parties (Conseil de la Région de Bruxelles-Capitale 1991a: 1–2). Accordingly, the parliamentarian reception of this logo was enthusiastic. The deputies called the author, graphic designer Jacques Richez, an 'artist' even an 'artist of international renown' but never a designer (Conseil de la Région de Bruxelles-Capitale 1991b: 573). The French-speaking Socialist Moureaux described it as a 'collective work', with recollections of Brussels Art-Nouveau and pointed out

> For Brussels, multi-cultural City-Region, with diverse, and often antagonist, sensitivities, this has been a kind of squaring of impossible adventure. What we knew, more or less, from the very beginning is what we might not do: no rooster, or lion, black-yellow-red, yellow and black, yellow and red, red and green, Saint Michel, Atomium, Mannekenpis, no City Hall, twelve, nineteen or twenty-five stars [. . .] As a city with European vocation, Brussels wants to transmit a spirit of openness. Within this symbol, past and present come together.
>
> Conseil de la Région de Bruxelles-Capitale 1991b: 573

French-speaking Christian-Democrats stressed the tradition-bound nature of the symbol, which conveyed Brussels' historical uniqueness (Conseil de la Région de Bruxelles-Capitale 1991b: 574). Conversely, Dutch-speaking Christian-Democrats acclaimed the double nature of Brussels as the capital of Belgium but primarily as the potential capital of Europe, affirming that the new logo was 'not a symbol of a people, but of an international city which has the particular task of being the capital of Belgium, tomorrow perhaps of Europe' (Conseil de la Région de Bruxelles-Capitale 1991b: 573–4). The Dutch-speaking nationalists, the Volksunie as well as the Vlaams Blok, condemned the symbol for different reasons. The former because Flemish and Walloon communities make up Brussels and both already had a symbol. The latter refused the symbol because the party was against the very existence of a Brussels Capital-Region (Conseil de la Région de Bruxelles-Capitale 1991b: 575). Out of the sixty-three present deputies, sixty voted affirmatively, only one voted negatively – namely deputy Van Hauthem from the Vlaams Blok party – and two abstained – namely Stéphane Lobkowicz and Evelyne Huytebroeck. Lobkowicz argued that he was against the division of Belgium and the new emblems only meant a step further in that direction (Conseil de la Région de Bruxelles-Capitale 1991b: 572–6).

After deciding on the symbol, it had to percolate down to the citizenship. To achieve this aim, institutional merchandising popularized this new – if traditional – symbol among the citizenry. In 1991, local radio stations and newspapers distributed ball-point pens, pins, plastic bags and stickers with the blue and yellow iris flower (Conseil de la Région de Bruxelles-Capitale 1992: 2158). Belgian regional symbols condensed a difficult negotiation between their past, their nationalist movements, their current institutions and their political forces. In each case, the antiquity of the symbol had been preferred over its novelty. Even when no symbol existed, as in the case of Brussels, and it had to be newly created, some kind of history was attached to it. However, the recent needs to create an international, modern profile injected the logos with modern features, either pictographic language as in the case of Flanders, or European colours as in the case of Brussels. Thus, their common characteristic was their consensual nature among national/federal, international/local and central/regional, which the parliamentarian composition established in each case. Both the emblems and logos – as visual representations of regional identities – demonstrate how regional identity is not necessarily predictable but rather is forged out of negotiation. Consequently, the symbols overlap layers of meaning, which fulfil the expectations of several currents of opinion by counting on the selective perception of the citizenship.

Symbols of national identity are better seen as biased rather than neutral. In this vein, Billig and Edensor do not explore their connotations and only point to their ubiquity. However, if only studying their ideological connotations, it can be understood how national symbols give rise to acceptance (such as the Brussels' logo) or rejection (such as the Madrid symbols), since that acceptance or rejection is not directed at the nation itself but to the particular interpretation of the nation that those symbols display.

The previous examples show how symbols of national identity tend to appear as high culture elements. Accordingly, design accentuates their dimension as elements of high culture when involved in processes of nation building. Edensor argues that Anderson, Hobsbawm and Smith restrict their survey to elements of high culture and consequently fail to analyse the role of popular culture within the construction of national identity (Edensor 2002: 9). Although this is true, Edensor fails to acknowledge the persistence of high culture schemas in the formation of national identity. Indeed, when entering the list of national references, design does so as high culture products and as such they have to rely upon concepts of authorship, artistic excellence and singularity. Consequently, notions of commodity, mass production or serialization are overlooked. In this process, design fails to impose a different schema to that of high culture.

Finally, the study of design as an element of national identity reveals the prevalence of concepts such as tradition or high culture over modernity and low culture, definitely as far as nation building processes are concerned. This comes to add nuances to the processes of de-differentiation that have taken place during postmodernity. Indeed, within these general processes there is a persistence of hierarchical schemas between high and low culture, tradition and modernity or internationalism and nationalism. This can help understand ongoing historical processes as well as the current status of design in the wider framework of the creative industries.

# Notes

1  The number of 'nationalities' increased later as nationalist parties emerged in other autonomous communities, such as the case of Aragón in 1997.

2  However, it was not until 1995 that the first Flemish elections took place and therefore the Flemish Parliament could be elected directly.

# Chapter 6
# Design as a Matter of State

State and nation are closely related to each other, yet they are clearly distinguishable. According to the philosopher Hannah Arendt, the state predates the nation, since the structure of the state has been pre-configured in monarchies and enlightened despotism. In the form of republics or reformed constitutional monarchies, states inherited the role of acting as a supreme legal institution and of protecting all its inhabitants regardless of their nationality. She continues saying that the increasing national consciousness forced states to recognize only 'nationals' as citizens and 'to grant full civil and political rights only to those who belonged to the national community by right of origin and fact of birth'. Accordingly, she continues, 'the state was partly transformed from an instrument of the law into an instrument of the nation' (Arendt 1973[1951]: 230). This 'conquest of the state by the nation' in Arendt's words, contributes to explain the legitimation of the state in national ideas. States have thereby reproduced the idea of the nation and have spread nationalism. The previous chapter has shown how states have implemented national mechanisms for their legitimation and how the study of design reflects this. In other words, how designing national symbols is underpinned by negotiations between the state and national ideas. The present chapter conversely will discern how the state assists the development of design. Accordingly, the difference between nation and state needs to be acknowledged as much as their interconnection.

The public sphere seems the logical target of state interventions. Architecture, urbanism and public space are all designed according to strict state guidelines. In this, the state plays a double role as supervisory body and active administrator of public works. Studies on the relations between the state and design have focused chiefly on infrastructure and public buildings. A well-known example is Michel Foucault's study of the panopticon (1975), but there have been others in the field of science and technology studies. In *The Whale and the Reactor. A Search for Limits in an Age of High Technology*, for instance, Langdon Winner illustrates the political impact of material objects with his famous example of the low-hanging overpasses on Long Island designed by the architect Robert Moses (Winner 1986: 19–39). The bridges were designed so that only cars, owned by the whites of the upper and middle classes, and not buses, used by racial minorities and low-income groups, could easily get through and access recreation areas. Similarly, Bruno Latour explored in *Aramis or the Love of Technology* the demise of a public transportation project in Paris analysing the role of the different parties involved (Latour 1996[1993]).

State attempts to reach beyond the public domain and invade the private sphere have proved conflictive. Design policies can be seen nonetheless as part of the state's interest in the private sphere and therefore require a particular approach. Ranging from taste education to the promotion of specific products, these policies have had an effect on the private sphere and on the domestic interior. The question then centres on the state's interest in shaping the private sphere and why these actions have remained unquestioned. One could argue that these actions had an effect on the private sphere but served the public interest – or, at least, that they were performed in the name of the public interest. The answer to these questions calls for a conceptualization of the role of the state in design as a legitimizing, pervasive body that is connected to society and materiality in specific ways. The state has intervened in design through different forms, probably the best known being the promotion of 'good design' for the domestic market through advertising campaigns. Although this indoctrinating role has faded since the 1960s, the state has shaped the private sphere through state-related design institutes and the implementation of design policies.

Design policies have aimed at positioning a country as representative of a particular design culture. In defining a country's image abroad, these policies have influenced domestic perceptions as well. These goals have been achieved through the promotion of design through exhibitions; stimulating quality through councils and consultative bodies; advising domestic consumers and manufacturers through design centres; exhibiting selected local production and subsidizing industrialists and designers (Woodham 1999, 2010; Jones 2003; Yagou 2005; McDonald 2008, 2010; Gimeno-Martínez 2010; Thompson 2011).

As Jonathan Woodham explained, design policies are nothing new and can be exemplified by the foundation of the French Royal Manufactories of the Gobelins (tapestry and furniture) and of Sèvres (pottery) under Louis XIV and Louis XV respectively (Woodham 2010: 28). Arguably, a continued design policy has been globally established after the Second World War through the bodies for the promotion of (mostly industrial) design, known as the design councils – which used to have an exhibition space attached, often called Design Centres after the British example (Woodham 2010: 45–6). In the case of dress, state intervention has been less consistent, sometimes but not always included under the umbrella of design. There are however a few examples that have been studied. One has been the British Utility Clothing Scheme during the Second World War (Reynolds 1999) and the present author has studied the economic plans in Belgium and Spain stemming from the textile and clothing crisis in Europe in the 1970s (Gimeno-Martínez 2011). Economic reasons have been behind these councils and plans. Intervention in domestic commercial and industrial sectors has been as important as the increase in exports and the repositioning of the country in external markets. All these actions have had a range of non-economic effects, from the formation of a national design canon to the increased recognition of specific products (McDonald 2008, 2010; Castillo 2010; Gimeno-Martínez et al. 2013; Sparke 2013: 199–216).

The question is then what framework to use when elucidating the role of the state in the spread of nationalism through design. Models on networked relations, such as Actor-Network Theory, might seem useful to map the connections between civic society, the state and materiality (most evidently in Latour 1996[1993]). However, Actor-Network Theory proves to be of little use for this task, since all actors are considered on an equal footing without considering their differences. As Sheila Jasanoff, a professor of Science and Technology Studies, mentioned in her keynote lecture 'Imagined and Invented Worlds: The Three Symmetries of STS' at the 2014 STS Italia conference in Milan, science and technology studies have championed the symmetry between humans and materiality. It is however the clarification of hegemony that this methodology does not explain that well (Jasanoff 2014). Indeed, it is in the imposition of meaning and the privileged position in nations that the state modifies the meaning of design. A proper acknowledgement of this hierarchy might help discern the interaction between the two.

By contrast, this chapter aims at fleshing out the state's role as a privileged actor in giving meaning to materiality, not as one more actor in a flat network. In safeguarding the public interest, the state imprints a stamp of authority on anything it backs. Arguably, this imprint is deemed unbiased and neutral by the citizenry. Max Weber calls this phenomenon the gaining of 'social esteem' (1946: 199–200). He gives the example of the official who achieves a privileged social position by working for the state. Likewise, objects achieve this 'social position' when they come in contact with the state through exhibitions, selections or publications. One example among many is the state-led promotion of aluminium in Italy under Mussolini in the early 1930s. A campaign defending autarchy and condemning the consumption of foreign products valued aluminium among other metals. This campaign gained momentum after the 1935 invasion of Ethiopia in which the League of Nations imposed trade restrictions on Italy (Schnapp 2001: 255–6). The campaign initiated by the government invoked the general interest without making market interests prevail. A similar commercial campaign would have favoured a particular interest, but in this way aluminium got associated with national wellbeing.

State-centric theories derive from those formulated by Karl Marx and Max Weber, who saw the state as a substantial entity separate from society (Marx 1963[1852] and Weber 2006[1968]). Recent theories on the state, however, concur that state and society are analytically distinguishable but cannot be studied separately. For these authors the state is distinct from, yet embedded in, society. For example, Philip Abrams argues that the state should not be studied as a thing, whether concrete or abstract, but as an object of sociological concern (Abrams 2006[1988], 114). For him, the state is a message of domination, an ideological artefact that unites the otherwise disparate actions of the practice of government and legitimizes the institutionalization of power (2006[1988], 125). Abrams also acknowledges that the state's immateriality does not diminish the importance of its study; on the contrary it must be taken 'extremely seriously' (2006[1988], 122). Likewise, Timothy Mitchell argues for a study of the state as embedded within society. He conceptualizes the state as a structural effect generated by daily practices (Mitchell 2006[1999], 180). In sum, these authors see the state as (a) embedded within and not distinct from society, and (b) culturally embedded and discursively constructed instead of as a set of preconstituted institutions performing given functions.

A proper understanding of the state passes through its influence on everyday experiences. Whether material or immaterial, the state is a key element in the comprehension of societies, since the state as a discursive construct reveals the mechanisms behind the creation and implementation of authority. As will be argued below, design participates and gets embedded in this authority. The above authors elaborated rather on the boundaries between society and the state and this chapter adds materiality (more specifically, design) as a third element to this discussion.

# The paradoxical nature of the state

This chapter will therefore first analyse a number of paradoxes tied to design policies that will illustrate the challenges of creating a valid, specific conceptualization model. These paradoxes (A–E) will be discussed in relation to two key aspects: first, the state as connected to both the public and private spheres, and second, the state as related to society and materiality. States – just like nations – move in a dual axis of difference and similarity. As far as they implement one or other policy, have more or less competencies and manage a higher or lower budget, states can be very different from each other. However, to the extent that they are considered as equivalents in status, then they can be considered as similar. This does not mean that all the paradoxes below are applicable to all states. As the examples illustrate, they are applicable to specific cases, yet at the same time elucidate how to study 'the state' as related to design. Or better said, these paradoxes contribute to give a more nuanced conceptualization of the state.

A. – The disconnection between the ideology of design and its instrumentality in the hands of the state

Countless definitions of design have been formulated throughout history, and they have often been subject to much controversy. These discussions are defining for the discipline, since – as John A. Walker states in *Design History and the History of Design* – definitions of design 'are inflected by the different ideological-political positions of those who devise them' (Walker 1989: 32). By instrumentalizing design for different ends – improving economic performance, approaching the public sector for the users, constructing a national image abroad – the state participates in this discussion and even takes a position. An example of this is the injection of ideology to post-war modernism in the Soviet Union. Triin Jerlei describes how modernist design was considered to convey Socialist values. Through the All-Union Scientific Research Institute of Technical Aesthetics (*Vsesoiuznyi nauchno-issledovatel'skii institut tekhnicheskoi estetiki –* VNIITE) founded in 1962, the Soviet state exerted its influence on USSR design. Products were approved by the Art Council before entering production to ensure a homogeneous quality throughout the country (Figure 6.1). Accordingly,

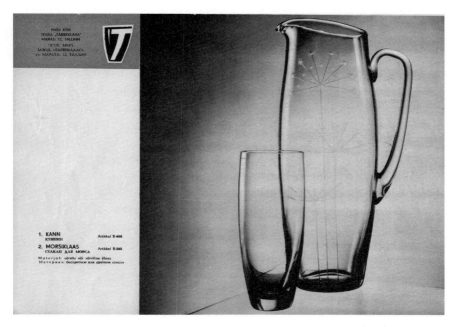

**Figure 6.1** Ingi Vaher. Jug (Article E-608) and a lemonade glass (Article E-265). Coloured or colourless glass. Jug h 283 ø 105 mm; glass h 146 ø 59 mm.

modernism was considered to be a proper communist style. Some ideologists even considered that it clashed with the capitalist system. They appealed to the Bauhaus school and its opposition to the Nazi power and that its origins had to be found in a protest against private property and bourgeois individualism (Jerlei 2014: 589). Nevertheless, it was acknowledged that capitalist countries also promoted modernist aesthetics. Jerlei candidly acknowledges that it is difficult to discern differences between socialist and capitalist aesthetics. As she states, it is as if under Soviet eyes 'in the West, people liked the right things, but for the wrong reasons' (Jerlei 2014: 590). More than visual aspects, it was the method of production and the circulation in a Soviet circuit of distribution and consumption that imbued the products with socialist values.

The position of design policies in the realm of the state influences the way design is promoted, in this case as an ideological element. The relations between state apparatus, design policies and the discipline of design influences the ideology through attachement to a product. The state constructs images and discourses on design by its promotion, conditioning the meaning of design.

B. – The apparent cohesiveness of governmental institutions vs the agency of individuals in public policies

Although states are often seen as separate from society, state-related bodies are run by individuals that may not be aligned with state policies. Consider the activities of the Dutch Institute for Industrial Design (*Instituut voor Industriële Vormgeving* – IIV), established by three employers' federations and subsidized by the Ministry of Economic Affairs and the Ministry of Education, Arts and Sciences. By mediating between manufacturers and designers and by giving aesthetic advice, the IIV would help improve the quality of Dutch products and thereby improve the country's competitiveness. The central message was that attractive products would sell better and firms that paid attention to design could be confident of greater sales. A special 'consultative body' of the IIV gave advice to manufacturers. The agency's first 'aesthetic advisers' – Gerrit Rietveld (1888–1964), Christiaan de Moor (1899–1981) and Arie W. Verbeek (1908–1997) – appraised products in the early 1950s on the basis of technical soundness, serviceability, design and price in relation to these aspects. In practice, many companies mistook the IIV board for some sort of 'taste police' and felt judged against their will, sometimes even disparaged. For the Ministry of Economic Affairs this was sufficient reason to slowly cut off the organization's subsidies. People believed the IIV was beginning to lose sight of the economic importance of industrial design and was apparently more concerned about elevating taste (Simon-Thomas 2008: 123–4).

Without acknowledging the division of competences between the funding bodies and the consultative body, this example could have been interpreted as a top-down indoctrination of manufacturers by government. Aradhana Sharma and Akhil Gupta recall that one of the state's typical attributions is 'a veneer of consistency, systematicity, centralized control, and wholeness' (Sharma & Gupta 2006: 18) that encloses the actual contradictions of exercising government. However, knowing its intricacies and, what is more, conceptualizing the state as contradictory and plural might reveal its complexity. While the funding bodies envisioned this institute as a means to improve the economic performance of the Netherlands, the consultative body saw a means to heighten the quality of products in an idealistic way.

C. – Design policies are implemented from the top down vs democratic governments are elected by the citizenry from the bottom up

If the previous paradox concerns individuals integrated in governmental bodies, this concerns individuals external to them. The participation of the citizenry in state decisions is at times difficult to trace. Once elected, governments have the power to decide on public aspects, in consensus at times with the parliament. Mienke Simon-Thomas, in her analysis of Dutch design after the 1980s, explains that the experimental character of Dutch design has to do partially with the subsidy culture in the Netherlands (see Chapter 3). She affirms that '[n]ew anti-design becomes internationally famous thanks to the generous, progressive subsidy policy pursued by the Dutch government' (Simon Thomas 2008: 10). This affirmation needs clarification. In the Netherlands, the Thorbecke principle governs the allocation of funding for art and science. This principle asserts that the state should not interfere in these fields. Therefore, committees of independent experts decide on the recipients of art and science funding. The final decision to approve the recommendations of those experts is actually of the government department, whose representatives are however not involved in the selection (Ministry of Education, Culture and Science 2013: 4). This might be an extreme case of citizenry's participation in state matters in general and more specifically in the funding of design, yet it prevents an argument against a rigid divide between state and society.

State-centric theories such as those of Marx and Weber viewed 'the state' as a clearly bounded institution distinct from society and often portrayed as a unitary and autonomous actor with the supreme authority to regulate populations within its territory. Conversely, Mitchell argues that the line between state and society is not the perimeter of an intrinsic entity that can be thought of as a freestanding object or actor. He states that 'it is a line drawn internally, within the network of institutional mechanisms through which a certain social and political order is maintained' (Mitchell 2006[1999], 175). The reason why the state's boundary so often seems elusive and unstable, Mitchell adds, is because it never marks a real exterior. In his view, however, this boundary is not illusory. We can see in this example that the boundary between society and state is permeable, yet state and society remain analytically identifiable. This apparently contradictory statement reflects the simultaneous subjugation and hegemony of the state. The imposition of design policies is therefore relative when mechanisms exist for participation in government bodies. Ultimately, however, the state decides on the funding available and accepts or rejects the advice of the above committees.

D. – The creation of a discourse on national design vs the actual material production of a country

State-funded exhibitions aim at being comprehensive. Nevertheless, they are the product of a selection and inevitably include some objects while excluding others. This was the case with the Norwegian participation in the exhibitions *Scandinavian Design* (1954–1957) and the *X Triennale di Milano* (1954). Kjetil Fallan illustrates how these two exhibitions combined contributions from Denmark, Finland, Norway and Sweden. In the case of Norway, both participations were state-funded. The first was intended to show 'craft, industrial art and industrial design' but finally the crafts were dominant. Even when the catalogue displayed a 'typical' Norwegian interior with a settee and easy-chair in organic shapes with steel tubular skeletons, designed by Torbjørn Afdahl (1917–1999) and manufactured by Sandvik & Co., these or similar examples were not represented in the catalogue dominated by the most exclusive range of manufacturers such as Handeland Glassverk. Similarly, the Norwegian section at the 1954 Triennale, equally coordinated by the Norwegian Applied Art Association, limited the display of industrial products to a few lamps when the major part of the objects were craft-based (Fallan 2010: 420–4).

When these strategies are implemented by the state, then the result is a presumably total national image based paradoxically on a selection. These representations of the state then become misleading. Sharma and Gupta (2006) approach the state as a cultural artefact by bringing together the ideological and material aspects of state construction. They distinguish two ways through which the state is culturally constructed: everyday practices and representations. The latter category covers a range of media that represent the government in textual or intertextual ways, e.g. newspapers, reports, radio, television and cinematic representations (Sharma & Gupta 2006: 18). Exhibitions fit in this list. It is through these representations that civil society perceives the state in one way or another. A selection thus offers a biased representation of the state even when pretending to be comprehensive (Greenberg et al. 1996).

E. – The shaping of a national identity as a negotiation between domestic and international aspects

When studying design policies, it is hard to escape the nation-state framework. Although helpful, this framework offers a limited vision. Paradoxically, to understand the instrumentalization of design by the state it is also necessary to look beyond the borders of the national framework and to examine design's transnational and international networks.

An example of a double attitude of national originality and international emulation is the Spanish Plan for the Promotion of Design and Fashion (1985– 1992) that was part of a series of actions already started in the early 1980s and orchestrated by the Ministry of Industry and Energy. The textile crisis of the 1970s put the Spanish textile and clothing sector in a difficult situation. On the one hand, its production was not as technically advanced as the other European countries. On the other hand, its workforce was not as cheap as in other major manufacturers of clothing at that moment, such as South Korea. Consequently, entering the increasingly liberalized market of the European Economic Community (EEC, nowadays European Union) implied choosing one of two directions. The Spanish textile production was dependent in a great way on foreign producers, who licensed the trademarks to local distributors because of market protection and customs duties. Hence, near liberalization would have been catastrophic for the Spanish textile sector, as the foreign producers would be able to directly sell their goods in Spain. To avoid this, a competitive Spanish identity for textile products needed to be found. It was opted to enhance the profile of Spanish fashion, gaining admittance in higher market segments (Gimeno Martínez 2011: 209). The promotion of fashion designers was expected to produce Spanish goods comparable to 'the Italian or French' ones (Alonso 1981).

The Centre for the Promotion of Design and Fashion (CDM) coordinated the plan and acted as intermediary between the Ministry of Industry and Energy and the participants. The CDM began to shape and spread the identity of Spanish fashion both domestically and abroad. María Jesús Escribano, its manager, proclaimed that the major intent was not to sell one or thirty fashion firms, but rather to have a unitary concept. 'A philosophy, a way of understanding life. Spain has something that other European countries lack: the street; we have to transmit the explosion of life – which exists on the street – translated into fashion' (Prades 1987). The centre's agenda included the creation of the brand 'Fashion from Spain' (*Moda de España*), both television and press promotional campaigns, a television slot on Spanish fashion, the advising on television outfits and an exhibition about the history of Spanish fashion.

This example shows how national design policies are connected and interact with transnational networks and that national initiatives depend on foreign examples. This transnational perspective is thus a necessary complement to the nation-state framework to fully understand the creation of design cultures. French philosopher Michel Foucault (1926–1984) coined the concept of 'governmentality' (Burchell et al. 1991: 1–52; Faubion 2001: 201–22; Dean 2010). The short definition of government is the 'conduct of conduct', which roughly means the management of human behaviour. It is important to notice that the notion of 'government' can be understood on different levels. It encompasses a plurality of forms, ranging from self-government to government of others to government of more abstract entities like populations and states.

The concept of 'governmentality' can then be described as the study of the various rationales and technologies involved in the forms of government, i.e. the governance of human conduct. Governance is at once a process that is internal and external to the state (Mitchell 2006 [1999]: 179). Thereby, it bypasses methodological nationalism, moving beyond the traditional convergence of nation and state and elaborating a transnational perspective (Sharma & Gupta 2006: 20–9).

Moreover, transnational networks or organizations such as Oxfam and the International Monetary Fund govern populations outside the realm of the state and are not linked to a territory. This approach has important implications when talking about design policies. By unhinging the state from the nation, and to broaden the discussion from 'state' to 'governance', one can free design policies from the nation-state frame. As such, we need to consider 'non-state' organizations and institutions at supra- and sub-national levels when discussing the creation of design cultures. In 2011, for example, the European Commision launched the European Design Innovation Initiative (EDII) to promote the increased use of design in European industry. These transnational networks can coincide or conflict with or complete national and local policies. Yet, although the state is not the only place where design cultures are created or disseminated, one should not fall back on a flat, horizontal network where the state is just one of many actors. Rather, one should acknowledge the state's coordinating role and its (real or imagined) ability to confer authority on design. As addressed in this last paradox, this transnational approach can describe how national identity is shaped by negotiations between local and international aspects.

# Articulating state, civic society and design: Foucault and Braudel

The above-mentioned paradoxes call for a sophisticated framework to understand the state not as a discourse that is homogeneously created and directed from the top down but as based on co-creation between the state, society and materiality. The concept of 'governmentality' is methodologically useful in the light of this chapter for two reasons. First, it counters the mainstream vision of the state as a well-delineated entity at the apex of society and the highest institution in which power is located (Sharma & Gupta 2006; Bennett & Joyce 2010: 1–22; Lynch 2011; Taylor 2011: 23). Instead, Foucault considers the state not in itself an autonomous source of power. Power is considered here not as a quality, or a property, nor as something that can be located or can originate in a certain place such as the state. Rather, it is something omnipresent, which is exercised but not possessed, and emerges in relations and interactions. As regards the state apparatuses and institutions, power is a dense web that passes through them, rather than being localized in them. Thus, following Foucault the state has no essence, but is, in his famous definition, nothing but 'the mobile effect of a regime of multiple governmentalities'. Using this conceptual framework as a backdrop enables us to tackle the problems illustrated by paradoxes A and B. By seeing the state not as a unique and coherent actor but as a heterogeneous collection of government practices, we can address the role of individuals in creating design policies, describe the position of design bodies in the realm of the state, and better analyse the representations of the state by design.

The second reason why this concept of 'governmentality' is methodologically useful is because it enables us to move beyond the traditional convergence of the nation and state (Sharma & Gupta 2006, 20–9). The state is often approached as a unitary actor that regulates the territory of the nation-state and the people who inhabit that territory. Yet, by disentangling governance of the territory and governance of the population, one can address the role that 'non-state' actors play in mundane processes of governance and the transnational regimes that govern populations. For example, neo-liberal governments unload public services onto communities and private organizations, thereby shrinking the state's boundaries. This process gets different names, ranging from the degovernmentalization of the state to the de-statization of government to the governmentalization of society.

Concerning the link between governance and materiality, in an interview in 1982 Foucault considered design as one of the techniques used to shape human conduct. He stated that from the eighteenth century, with the beginnings of liberalism, architecture became a concern of politicians as a technique regarding the government of societies. From then on, design became politicized, or political. When Foucault himself talked about design and politics and how they were intertwined, he focused mainly on the organization of cities and issues of urbanization such as collective infrastructure, public facilities and housing (Faubion 2001: 349–64). He elaborated in particular on the relation between power and spatial arrangements, studying railroads and electricity. Thus, he discussed the material or spatial dimension mostly in the context of the public sphere, where the state's intervention is deemed more natural. However, this leaves the question open as to how state authority and government operate in the material fabric of people's daily lives. This is where Fernand Braudel's theoretical insights come in.

A member of the Annales School of historiography, the historian Fernand Braudel (1902–1985) elaborated on this relationship between state, society and materiality. His work regards history as composed of short-, medium- and long-term events which all influence one another. This approach was already explored in *The Mediterranean in the Age of Philip* II (1949), but his interest in materiality is most evident in his three-volume major work *Civilization and Capitalism, 15th–18th Centuries*, more specifically in the first volume, *The Structures of Everyday*

*Life* (1967). In this book he defines material civilization as a first level of short-term events connected to everyday life, discussing, e.g. the evolution of food habits, fashion and cities. The everyday routines of this first volume are later linked to economic processes in the second volume, *The Wheels of Commerce* (1979), to later explain the evolution and success of capitalism in his third volume, *The Perspective of the World* (1979). The everyday aspects of life are seen as the foundations of macro-historic events.

Braudel's interweaving of state, society and materiality connects the poles of production and consumption. He states that routine, everyday activities of ordinary people amounted to the production of economic wealth and to the consumption of goods. Traditional economics had focused on the institutions of the market, companies, banks, the state and developing forms of capitalist investment such as the joint stock company (Dant 2005: 27). His interest in the evolution of capitalism is of little relevance to this chapter but his methodology, when elevated to an abstract level, can help discern the interaction between materiality and the state. When discussing the relevance of fashion, for example, he states that everything in this field depends on everything else and that participants have less freedom than they imagine. He wonders whether fashion might be an interpretation of 'deeper phenomena – of the energies, possibilities, demands and *joie de vivre* of a given society, economy and civilization' (Braudel 1979 [1981]: 323). Paradox D elaborates on the power of materiality to represent the state, which might affect the economy and politics. It might attract foreign investors or decide political bonds with similarly represented countries. The capacity of materiality might be easily perceptible in short-term processes yet affects long-term ones.

Braudel turns his attention to economic relations and how material life underpins them (Dant 2005: 30). He does not prioritize the sphere of material civilization but argues that it must be recognized as contributing to the economic history of societies. Braudel proposes a dialectical approach that will consider the market economy, the actions of key economic actors and the materiality. The mechanisms of capitalism are not to be found at any one level of economic processes but need to be understood as flowing through them (Dant 2005: 27). In sum, Braudel provides a methodological framework that recognizes the importance of materiality in historical accounts while maintaining a hierarchy between state and society as well as a distinction between the private and public spheres. The state is not just one more actor in a historical account, but one that exerts power and can be identified, or not, with economic developments. Moreover, private and public spheres are distinguishable, yet interconnected. This model offers perspectives on the interaction between state and design, providing tools for assessing the state's intrusion in the private sphere. In this sense, Paradox C develops this discussion, showing that civil society, the state and materiality are connected in multiple ways. The interconnection does not imply an absence of hierarchy. Participative state models still give a dominant role to the state, which in turn decides what the available means are and the autonomy and decision-making power of each participating agent, as also shown in Paradox B.

# Conclusion

As related to the double question regarding the interest of the state in intervening in the private sphere and why these actions remain uncontested, a tentative answer considering the above can be formulated. First, the state exists and is disseminated among the citizenry through representations. Interventions in the private sphere confer identity and recognition for the state and make it present in daily life – even through partial representations of the nation yet conveying a sense of comprehensiveness. In this case, Braudel's interrelation between materiality and long-term historical processes offers the model to link everyday life with history. These representations contribute to a legitimation of the state and its persistence. On the other hand, Foucault's concept of 'governmentality' as an attitude shared by the state but based on human conduct explains why these interventions remain uncontested since, arguably, they are seen as the normal unfolding of events.

Illustrated by the different paradoxes, the problematization that arises when studying design policies demands a proper conceptualization of the state. While state theoreticians have already discussed the connections between society and the state exhaustively, the issue of materiality needs acknowledgement. The exploration of state theories through the Foucauldian concept of governmentality vis-à-vis Braudel's theory allows this chapter to relate state, civic society and materiality. The state is not seen as the ultimate seat of power, but as a unifying factor of different practices of governance. Although the state cannot be studied separately from society and materiality, the analytical distinction is maintained in order to characterize the state and not minimize it as one of many actors in a horizontal network. Rather, it is approached as a privileged actor in loading authority on design and giving meaning to the material fabric of the private everyday life, including design and by extension also the domestic interior.

Design represents the state not only in the form of brochures, logos and graphics in general but also in exhibitions, the selection of best-designed products, and taste education. Thereby, the state is made tangible for the citizenry and acquires presence in everyday life. In their turn, the visual and material artefacts participating in these actions get endowed with what Weber called 'social esteem' and partake of the state's authoritative power. The conscious perception of this authoritative power is relative as it is embedded in routines and everyday activities that reproduce this system of 'governmentality'.

However, the analysis and critique of these mechanisms is necessary to discern the state's role in the interaction between society and materiality. Only following a given (cultural) product from its conception to its consumption can reveal which national values it conveys.

National symbols have been governed by high cultural elements or folk elements, based either on international prestige or on ethnic roots, to such an extent that even newly created national symbols are based on an aura of the past, as Hobsbawm and Ranger have demonstrated. As such, the symbolic production of the state mobilizes deliberated symbols of nationhood (flags, national anthem, national emblem or folk costumes), and other more ordinary symbols which reproduce the nation in the everyday. As a result, both public and private spaces are embedded in a sense of familiarity, which is perceived only unconsciously, as it fits in the national 'habitus'. As Edensor affirms, the distance given by experiencing other cultures evidences the 'national' character of our everyday environment.

# PART THREE

# Nationalism from Below: Bottom-up Approaches to National Identity

After Michael Billig's *Banal Nationalism*, some theorists stressed the importance of the citizenry in the creation of national identity. Modernist scholars had prioritized a top-down approach in which the state was the major force behind the creation of nationalism. The new bottom-up approaches share the constructivist methodology for the study of national identity but not their top-down perspective. The geographer Tim Edensor has been one of the theorists whose research can be best applied to the field of design. His connection between the nation and the familiar opens new avenues in defining how design can convey national identity.

The role of the citizens as far as design is concerned can be divided into two main groups, producers and consumers of national discourse. Citizens engage in the production of a national discourse as designers, for example. On the other hand, consumers can interpret messages in multifarious ways. Messages are not always interpreted as originally intended but can be missed and subverted, creating possibilities for creative consumption.

The familiar as an element of the nation is contested in the realm of both individual and collective identities. One can decide what element is more familiar than others but negotiations occur in the public sphere. Multiculturalism has been seen as one of the threats to national identity. The decision of what elements get assimilated within a specific national identity is subject to everyday negotiations in which the citizenry also has a voice.

# Chapter 7
# The Nation and the Familiar

*We cannot properly appreciate the variable meaning and salience of nationhood in everyday life by only studying its state-sponsored construction, modern industrial context or elite manipulation. This is not to suggest that everyday nationhood should be studied independently of these phenomena. But this is where our study begins; not where it ends.*

FOX & MILLER-IDRISS 2008: 553–4

The previous two parts of this book have traced the national character of design when connecting with the public sphere. The chapters composing this third part will focus conversely on the interconnections between design and the nation emanating from the private sphere. Modernist theories of national identity have explored the nation as a cultural construction and have traced its dissemination through cultural representation. Their major contribution has been the identification of symbols and discourses related to national identity. But is nationalism only constructed from above? Is civic society not also responsible for its construction? And is the appropriation of nationalism always univocal? What is at stake is what role does society play in nationalism, not only as a passive receptor but also as a conveyor of nationalist ideas and as an active contributor to the creation, modulation and dissemination of nationalism.

Notwithstanding the important role of the state in the process of nation building, the contributions of society cannot be overlooked. Nationalism is most visible when emanating from the state, but the state cannot be considered as the only source of nationalist ideas. As described in Chapter 2, the ideals of the Mingei movement were first developed by Yanagi Sōetsu and his circle to later be incorporated by the Japanese state as a mechanism of nation building. The equation of crafts with authentic Japaneseness that Yanagi had formulated dovetailed with the cultural policy of Prime Minister Konoe Fumimaro

(1891–1945). Since the start of the second Sino-Japanese War in 1937, the 'revitalitation of locality' was one of the ideological messages of the government New Order plan for mobilization for the war. The government, Yanagi and the Japan Folk Crafts Association, jointly undertook several initiatives including symposia and programmes to invigorate local crafts. Probably, the most evident appropriation of Mingei ideals by the Japanese state was the recommendation of Yanagi's book *Kōgei* by the Ministry of Education, which became synonymous of wartime propaganda (Kikuchi 2004: 113–15).

The constructed nature of national identity is an established and well-accepted issue and has not been contested by later authors. Main critiques to modernist approaches consider, nonetheless, the nature of the symbols of national identity and their reception. Edensor argues for the expansion of the symbols of national identity from the most obvious 'high', 'official' and 'traditional' culture towards elements of popular culture at large (Edensor 2002: 2 and 12). Similarly, the sociologist Michael Skey acknowledges Billig's study of the capability of marking a shift in focus in the canonical perception of nationalism 'moving away from the macro-scale theorising to more empirical-based studies, focusing on issues of representation, contestation and localised meaning-making as well as more contextualized studies' (Skey 2009: 333). He reckons Billig, however, inattentive to the practices of the everyday (Skey 2009: 332–3). Skey underlines how pivotal is the exploration of the everyday production and reproduction of national identity when analysing banal signifiers, and he considers it fundamental to keep the focus on daily forms of life, 'lived and understood in relation to a world of nations' (Skey 2009: 334).

A second line of critique towards Billig refers to the assumption that citizenry interprets discourses of national identity homogeneously. For example, the sociologists Jon E. Fox and Cynthia Miller-Idriss argue that – as any other symbol – national symbols are not decoded univocally. On the contrary, symbols can say different things to different people at different times. They even point out that symbols can just miss their mark and are incapable of communicating their message (Fox & Miller-Idriss 2008: 546–9). Likewise, Skey argues that top-down approaches ignore the variety of receptions of the banal flagging of the nation (Skey 2009: 337).

The historians Maarten Van Ginderachter and Marnix Beyen, in *Nationhood from Below: Europe in the Long Nineteenth Century* (2012) recognize a trend within nationalist theories to contemplate the phenomenon from a bottom-up perspective, giving attention to a spread of nationalist ideas not initiated by the elites or the state. They called this 'nationhood from below' or 'nationalism from below', localizing its beginnings in the '*histoire d'en bas*' a term coined by French historian Lucien Febvre, one of the founders of the Annales School. This interest in writing the history of the masses found an echo in the British 'history from below' represented by E.P. Thompson, the German *Alltagsgeschichte* ('history of the everyday') – developing in the mid-1970s – and the Italian *microstoria* (Van Ginderachter & Beyen 2012: 4). According to these authors, this trend studied the role of the masses but did not pay much attention to questions of nationalism. On the other hand, modernist approaches to nationalism insisted in the creation of national identity in a top-down perspective. Consequently, the omnipresence of elites and the state as uniquely responsible for the creation and dissemination of nationalism left little room for the people's agency. This tension however did not prevent some authors from claiming for an investigation of national histories through a perspective from below, invoked prominently by Hobsbawm in his *Nations and Nationalism since 1780: Programme, Myth, Reality* (1991). He acknowledged that nationalism is constructed essentially from above but is only understood when analysed from below, in terms of the 'assumptions, hopes, needs, longings and interests of ordinary people, which are not necessarily national and still less nationalist' (Hobsbawm 1991: 10).

Scholars of nationalism have approached these questions differently. Van Ginderachter and Beyen reconstruct the evolution of the theories of nationalism tracing its origins from a top-down to a bottom-up approach. The three stages of development are centred on the 1970–1980s, the 1990s and the early 2000s. The first period represents the modernist era, during which common people were generally excluded from nationalism research (Van Ginderachter & Beyen 2012: 124). As Hobsbawm also stated, at that time still very little was known about what national consciousness meant to the mass of the nationalities concerned (Hobsbawm 1991: 130). The second stage concentrates on an 'awakening' happening in the 1990s in nationalism studies (Van Ginderachter & Beyen 2012: 127). Although the top-down paradigm was still strongly present, several scholars began to question it and started to look elsewhere for better accounts including region, class and gender questioning the efficacy of nationalizing institutions (Van Ginderachter & Beyen 2012: 127–9). The last period analysed, the 2000s, saw a more systematic and broadly based qualitative source investigation of how individuals construct national identity, underlining how an approach from below became crucial for a thorough investigation of nationalism (Van Ginderachter & Beyen 2012: 130).

Van Ginderachter and Beyen acknowledge the pivotal role of Billig's *Banal Nationalism*, reminding us, however, that his approach follows a top-down socialization. His major contribution was the attention given to everyday manifestations of national identity (Van Ginderachter & Beyen 2012: 13). Nevertheless, Billig investigates the everyday representation of nationalism from above, its impact being the continuous reminder to the nation and the nourishing of nationalism as 'habitus'. He refers to 'banal nationalism' as something that can hardly be innocent for it reproduces institutions and all the empowerment they epitomize (Billig 1995: 6–7). Drawing on Hannah Arendt, Billig refers to 'banality' as not necessarily harmless or benign. In fact, banal stands for the part of imposed nationalism people tend to overlook, to ignore as such, and that becomes more subliminal than real, highlighting how nationalism could easily be both obvious and obscure or hidden (Billig 1995: 8 and 14).

# The nation as home

Several authors have similarly acknowledged Billig's contribution to the study of nationalism from below but have pinpointed its limitations. The authors mentioned below have been influential for different reasons in defining how design can convey notions of national identity. Most remarkably, geographer Edensor in his book *National Identity, Popular Culture and Everyday Life* (2002), acknowledges Billig's theories as one of the most prominent attempts to redirect the traditional investigation of national identity towards popular culture and the everyday (Edensor 2002: 11). Their main differences are twofold. First, Edensor expands the category of national symbols beyond state representation, departing from Billig's study of state symbolism and expanding national symbols to popular culture. He includes places, rituals and material culture as conveyors of nationalism. Second, he compares national identity to the feeling of home. In doing so, he provides the individual with agency in defining what is national. Thereby, Edensor does not deny the importance of state-led nationalism but acknowledges a multiplicity of possible interpretations. In his account, the connection and dependence between collective and individual identities become salient.

Regarding the expansion of national symbolism, Edensor's contribution has already been briefly illustrated in Chapter 4 against the backdrop of modernist scholarship. It is, however, decisive to see how he expands the repertoire of national symbols to include everyday places, practices and artefacts as national symbols (Edensor 2002: 39–48). He considers rural landscapes as the most natural expression of symbolic values and national virtues and, moreover, as emblems of cultural genuineness and continuity, places where people can return to their roots. National landscapes are recirculated in popular culture for example through touristic campaigns for foreigners, which transform cultural local references in sites of pilgrimage and part of an economy of national identity marketed by the state itself (Edensor 2002: 40). Countryside and rural sites, which are normally the bigger part of national touristic efforts, show little or no sign of modernity but rather reproduce the ideal of purified and traditional spaces, recalling nostalgia and historicism (Edensor 2002: 42–3). Edensor argues that pristine landscapes become functional for political agendas aiming at promoting the purity of the nation through the untouchable myth of national splendour (Edensor 2002: 42–4). Likewise, iconic sites also contribute to the building of a national image, providing individuals with sacred centres, spiritual and historical sites and reveal the uniqueness of a nation moral geography – Edensor uses the examples of the Great Pyramids and the Taj Mahal. He opposes these established common places to popular sites (parks, stadia, promenades, quarters), which are frequently questioned about their relevance in nation building values, being seemingly irrelevant at an historical level (Edensor 2002: 45–9). Likewise, domestic architecture and namely gardens, fencing, home *décor*, can be considered part of a fundamental vernacular symbolism capable of stitching the local and the national together through serial reproductions across nations (Edensor 2002: 51 and 53).

Furthermore, Edensor asserts that the performance of mundane tasks and duties are identified in common-sense understanding as national, and mentions three forms of quotidian performances that consolidate the sense of belonging to the nations: popular competencies, embodied habits and synchronized enactions. 'Popular competencies' are derived from state regulations with the aim of coordinating the performance of citizenship, such as what side of the road to drive on. Additionally, there are other everyday competences, like knowing where to buy theatre tickets, for example. 'Embodied habits' refer to etiquette and conventions on how to behave in certain situations – that Edensor relate to Bourdieau's 'habitus' – and are defined as 'culturally located unreflexive enactions' that constitute a sense of belonging. He puts the example of how loud to laugh in a certain situation or gestures used to convey irritations. Finally, the 'synchronized enactions' refer to the repetition of daily, monthly and annual activities. Some of these are subject to state regulation and some not. He puts the example of attending school between particular hours or having lunch at a certain time (Edensor 2002: 92–6).

Edensor finally investigates the relation between national identity and material culture, analysing objects that thanks to their ubiquitous presence, provide material proof of shared ways of living and common habits, besides partly enabling mundane transactions between people in their everyday lives (Edensor 2002: 103). He examines the cultural systems of objects in relation to their use and the meanings they achieve through it and observes that certain objects have become representative of certain communities because they have been produced in a specific region. He established the relation between the objects and the community in terms of production and mentions as examples everyday domestic objects, especially food, garments, crafts and other objects for the home (and garden) (Edensor 2002: 104–5). His account of material culture is much more conventional than the previous two, since it is based on the 'typical' products of a region, meanwhile the landscapes and performances made reference to less conventional examples. Moreover, this limited account contrasts with his exposure on the mechanisms that make things national. If he later elaborates that the nationalization of products resides in the individual consumer, his examples in this section seem to suggest that the national character of material culture needs to have been negotiated collectively.

His article 'Automobility and National Identity' is much more explicit as long as material culture is concerned. He acknowledges that objects can be domesticated in foreign places and become signifiers of the nation by affirming that 'objects from elsewhere are apt to acquire symbolic significance in local and national contexts' (Edensor 2004: 118). He describes national identity as a matrix of relational cultural elements that include the practices, representations and spaces gathered around them (Edensor 2004: 103). As soon as an object, whatever its origin, gets involved in this matrix, then it contributes to a sense of national identity. He mentions the MacDonalds' logos that define the English landscape (Edensor 2004: 109) and more extensively analyses the domestication of the Ford Cortina as a distinctive feature of the British roads (Figure 7.1.). Its entrance into British popular culture transformed it into a national symbol acquiring meanings that were distinctively British. Regarding this, he mentions how the Cortina was included in popular songs by the singer Ian Dury (Edensor 2004: 106).

Edensor defends that the nation is performed everyday. However, are all daily activities performed related to the nation? According to Edensor, objects in familiar environments do not disclose their second nature, grounded in the habitual experience. The irruption of unfamiliar sites, habits and artefacts alter our sense of

**Figure 7.1** A Ford Cortina de Luxe parked outside a house. Photo: 1965.

the familiar (Edensor 2002: 106–7). Nevertheless, these alterations cannot always be translated into national terms. At times, there is a chronological aspect involved with no national implications. For example, sites change through time, habits can evolve and new artefacts can substitute old ones, but people need not think that the nation has changed, too.

Similarly, the anthropologist Nigel Rapport, in his research on Scottish hospitals, noted that nationality was less important for the members of the staff on a daily basis. It was rather when engaged in some practices or events, such as watching football on television or having an argument with a colleague who one supposed was born somewhere else, that their nationality was at stake (Rapport 2007: 3). He concludes that the confrontation with difference activates national identity. When related to design, being surrounded by an unfamiliar environment injects an object with a sense of nationhood. As accidental national symbols, they are capable of evoking the nation only under certain circumstances. Reading Edensor, we can conclude that discourses and artefacts mostly travel separately. As long as the consumer can connect the two, then the message is received and the consumer can decide how to internalize it. If the object is apprehended independently of an additional discourse, then the consumer is free to give meaning to objects. The agency of the artefact is in this case considerably reduced and its interpretation open.

# The changing face of familiarity

The consideration of the familiar as the national challenges the dominance of National Romanticism as a dominant discourse for the nation. In this sense, Edensor draws on Doreen Massey and her concept of 'a progressive sense of place' (Edensor 2002: 68 and 114). There, she argues for a non-essentialist sense of place that is not grounded on traditions and static identities, but that evolves and is in constant change. Massey refuses the conceptualization of places and localities as forms of romanticized escapism involving retrograde nationalisms or introverted obsession with heritage (Massey 1994a: 151). In her search for the adequate adjustment to a progressive sense of place, reactionary notions prove unsuitable for two reasons: first, they hint of places as bearers of single and essential identities and second, they suggest a sense of place that is merely inward-looking and history biased, delving into the past instead of into the present (Massey 1994a: 152). Massey supports the idea of places as holders of multiple identities, as people are, and as extroverted, indicating a connection to the wider world that positively includes the global and local (Massey 1994a: 155). By so declaring, the author fights the tendency to construct fixed and static identities for places and demolishes the definition of spaces in opposition against the 'other' and the outside (Massey 1994b: 168–9).

Massey dismantles the persistent identification of a specific place with a specific community pleading that social relations work in and across space creating a social place, a space that takes its form from a simultaneous coexistence of human interrelations at all geographical scales, from the intimacy of the household and from the transglobal connections (Massey 1994b: 168). She affirms that places can be home but not because they are connected to nostalgia. Massey adds that one 'may indeed have many of them. And what is more, each of these home places is itself an equally complex product of the ever-shifting geography of social relations present and past' (Massey 1994b: 172).

This has clear consequences to define what is 'national design'. Chapter 3 discussed the recurring permanence of national design as 'indigenous design'. In the example of the 2012 exhibition 'British Design from 1948: Innovation in the Modern Age' at the Victoria and Albert Museum, the criterion to define 'British Design' was the work of designers 'born, trained or working in the UK' (Breward & Wood 2012: 8 and 16). One can wonder if this design truly configures a sense of home and familiarity for British people. Probably, both local and foreign products furnish British homes and fill British wardrobes. One can argue that from Massey's perspective foreign products can be included as markers of national design, since both the public and the private sphere are defined by both local and foreign products. As an example, Massey's account would allow something as logic as categorizing the Statue of Liberty as American, even when it was designed by a French sculptor, fabricated in France and shipped to New York in 1885. The fact that it has fabricated in France would be of less importance than the fact that this statue has shaped the image of New York and by extension of the United States.

Along these lines, Michael Skey's biggest concern about Billig's thesis – besides not being inclusive of the important part represented by the everyday dynamics – is the lack of investigation about contemporary globalization and the missed opportunity to relate the national to the global (Skey 2009: 338). Skey is dissatisfied with Billig's rejection of the possible concepts of nation-state in an era of global flows and post-modern identities (Skey 2009: 334). Billig's rather simplistic description of globalization is equal to Americanization, narrowing and regressing the vision of nations as part of the globalized process (Skey 2009: 333). Edensor for instance argues:

> Globalisation and nation identity should not be conceived of in binary terms but as two inextricably linked processes. As global cultural flows become more extensive, they may facilitate the expansion of national identities and also provide cultural resources which can be domesticated, enfolded within popular and everyday national cultures. Therefore global processes may diminish a sense of national identity or reinforce it.
>
> EDENSOR 2002: 29

Skey similarly stresses the necessity of nationalism and globalization to be reconstructed as co-original and in co-evolution rather than two opposing forces (Skey 2009: 340; see also Chernilo 2007) affirming that national or even regional culture *can* no longer be conceived as reflecting a coherent and distinct identity (Skey 2009: 339). At the same time he fosters Hutchinson's thesis that sees nation formation as a dynamic and potentially 'reversible process that in particular periods and places may become stabilized and naturalized' (Hutchinson 2006: 295).

# National capital

Arguably then, as long as artefacts define a sense of home, then they belong to the category of 'national design'. In the first place, canonical national design does not always respond to strict national design and manufacturing processes but can in fact be embedded in a transnational system of production. Deciding what country a product represents then becomes a difficult task. Moreover, it is the civil society and not the product itself that decides what constitutes 'home' and 'the familiar'. Consumers do not need to know the country of origin of a product. In some cases it might be known, but not in all cases. Some campaigns use the country of origin as a selling argument, some consumers can deem this important. Nevertheless, the creation of a feeling of home goes beyond the origin of the products themselves. The visual and material culture typical of a nation can stem from, as Massey says, transglobal connections as much as it can be defined through locally produced products. As mentioned in Chapter 4, Edensor similarly points out that national symbols do not need to be peculiar to a concrete nation, but to achieve this status 'is not to imply that they are unfamiliar in other contexts' (Edensor 2002: 108).

According to this, the uniqueness of nations that Herder announced can be nuanced. Every nation can be unique through a specific combination of its characteristics, but this does not mean that all its characteristics need to be unique. Herder defended this idea regarding the stimuli that creates a national character, but not the cultural products stemming from a national culture. A German designer creating French-inspired design, according to Herder, is not creating German design. Emphasizing the consumption side of the national, not only French-inspired German design but also imported design from France could be considered German as long as it was consumed in Germany. What defines a nation is not only its exclusive traits but also those that it shares with others. When this is translated into 'national design', both indigenous and foreign design can define the national design landscape.

These 'progressive' visions of the national will need to be confronted to its most essentialist versions. Thus, even when the national is defined as the 'home' and 'the familiar', there will be some discourses that will say what is more or less 'familiar' as far as the nation is concerned. Drawing on the sociologist Ghassan Hage from his study on multiculturalism in Australia, it could be said that some artefacts possess more 'national capital' than others. With this term, Hage refers to the fact that some groups of the population are perceived as and made to feel more or less national than others, according to their ethnic background (Hage 1998: 52). He cites the example of a hijab (Islamic headscarf) as representing an Australian (Hage 2006: 10). The hijab, for example, will be considered as having a little 'national capital' in countries where 'Muslim' is seen as a foreign religion – regardless of how well represented the Muslim community is. It is in this tension between national stereotypes and actual configuration of a country's reality that the notion of the national as 'familiar' is forged.

Hage distinguishes between citizenship and practical nationality. The former implies a *de facto* condition, a formal indicator of national belonging, and the latter a widely recognized status as a national. Citizenship is absolute – one has a given nationality or not – but practical nationality is cumulative – one can be considered as more or less national. This leads on to Anderson's third characteristic on how nations are imagined, namely as a 'deep, horizontal comradeship' (Anderson 1991[1983]: 7). Anderson says, regardless of the inequality and exploitation that may prevail in each, all national members have the same status as nationals. Hage specifies that equal citizenship can be fulfilled in theory but in practice there are inequalities in the level of national recognition. He defines practical nationality as 'the sum of accumulated nationally sanctified and valued social and physical cultural styles and dispositions (national culture) adopted by individuals and groups, as well as valued characteristics (national types and national character) within a national field: looks, accent, demeanour, taste, nationally valued social and cultural preferences and behaviour' (Hage 1998: 53). So, there are some skills that define who is more national than others. Drawing on Bourdieu's concept of 'cultural capital', Hage situates 'national capital' as the cultural capital that one can achieve within the field of the nation. Once this capital is gathered, the recognition of the national community converts it in symbolic capital, i.e. national belonging.

Nevertheless, if the agency of civil society is to be fully acknowledged, it is their interpretation of the national that counts. Evidently this interpretation will not change dramatically from individual to individual, since it is heavily conditioned by dominant discourses. This tension between sterotypes and personal interpretations of the nation is salient in Skey's work, who engages in answering the unsolved question Billig left pending: how does banal nationalism work on ordinary people? (Skey 2011: 1–8). To resolve this enigma, Skey focuses on a group of Britons (twenty-one respondents born and raised in England) with whom he engages in conversations trying to define what represents their country, what it is like to live there and what has changed their community throughout the years (Skey 2011: 38). Skey asked them to come up with two or three 'things' they associated with the country. The answers to the question 'What do you associate with this country?' combined mainstream with unconventional answers. The majority of responses mentioned monarchy, the Queen, cricket, rain, red buses and pubs as the most common national icons. There were however answers such as 'curry' or 'diversity of population' that could be considered initially as possessing little 'national capital' but that got attached to the nation (Skey 2011: 40–1).

# Everyday negotiation of nationhood

Like Van Ginderachter and Beyen at the beginning of this review, Jon E. Fox and Cynthia Miller-Idriss engage in taking Hobsbawm's call to investigate nationalism from below in a substantial way, aiming at observing and elaborating the ways people act, create and legitimate the nation in the multiple contexts of their everyday lives (Fox & Miller-Idriss 2008: 554). Their focus is strictly on the people and how they assimilate and mediate the nation and its standardizations (language, education, taxation to name a few) and how nation and people are made one with their state (Fox & Miller-Idriss 2008: 537). Summing up, these authors criticize the contradictory positions that render nationalism as a popular phenomenon, but at the same time neglect the study of the masses (Fox & Miller-Idriss 2008: 536).

Fox and Miller-Idriss propose four different ways in which nationhood is reproduced in everyday life: talking the nation, choosing the nation, performing the nation and consuming the nation. The first part, talking the nation, tackles the way in which the nation is constructed by people as a discourse, considering the way they choose to talk about it. In this way, these authors shed a light on the importance of focusing on ordinary people as active producers of national discourse connecting the construction of nationhood to the routine contexts of everyday life (Fox & Miller-Idriss 2008: 539). The second part, choosing the nation, investigates the ways in which nationhood frames the choices people make and what effect people's agency can have on nationhood through their choices. Choosing or agreeing a school, friends or marriage, people opt for a specific national trajectory of following choices that reinforce and determine their belonging to a given nation (Fox & Miller-Idriss 2008: 542). By making daily choices people confirm (or reconfirm) ethno-nationality, in a frame where nationhood both shapes and is shaped by everyday choices (Fox & Miller-Idriss 2008: 544–5).

In the section dedicated to performing the nation, Fox and Miller-Idriss concentrate on rituals and festivals (Fox & Miller-Idriss 2008: 545). Common and shared experiences, such as national festivals or sports events, have an impact on the national sensibility of each person and create a sort of concert of values among people who decide to take part in the collective act of performing nationhood (Fox & Miller-Idriss 2008: 546). In the last part, centred on the national connotations of the mundane taste of people, nationhood is interpreted through the analysis of everyday acts of consumption. Thus, consumers do not simply purchase national commodities; they rather build a national taste and constitute national sensibility and pride through their consumption (Fox & Miller-Idriss 2008: 550).

These different ways of reproducing the nation appear to range from a more active role (talking and choosing) to a more passive one (performing and consuming). The authors however make clear that, despite their marked receptive character, the last two can also be generative of national symbols. Anyhow, these four ways seem to be quite limited in scope. The two first, for example, do not contemplate the capacity of individuals of having an impact beyond their own immediate environment. Talking to friends or choosing a school does not seem to have a major repercussion for others. The ways of generating a nationalist discourse also include engaging with, for example, design activities, such as designing an advertisement or a poster that reproduces a nationalist discourse.

Arguably, 'talking the nation' can be stretched towards the creation of any discourse on the nation, but the examples given by Fox and Miller-Idriss do not go beyond conventional conversations. If this is the author's intention and that we should apply the same rule to the other two categories, then 'choosing the nation' and 'consuming the nation' might overlap. To choose a nation goes beyond the selection or a school for your children in territories with competing nationalities. The selection of a product that reflects a specific vision of the nation can be considered also as 'choosing the nation' and therefore seems too much the same as the fourth category. The third category, 'performing the nation' has exclusively to do with holidays, festivals and sport celebrations. It is therefore much limited to a category of national manifestation and not so much to a general way of reproducing the nation. Lastly, the 'consumption of the nation' implies that consuming products with a national discourse implies accepting it. The myriad of possibilities to appropriate a product is in this case ignored.

These categories offer few possibilities for design historians to reflect on how people produce and reproduce national design. More revealing are the observations made in the section 'performing the nation' when Fox and Miller-Idriss elaborate on 'mixed and missed messages'. People can interpret symbols differently and therefore they label this kind as 'mixed messages'. Examples are the celebrations around the Fourth of July in the USA or Bastille Day in France. Even when they are intended to reproduce a sense of belonging to the nation, for some people these can be opportunities just for family outings or public spending. Likewise, symbols can be completely ignored and work then as 'missed messages'. One can think of monuments or street names that celebrate the heroes of the nation. If these cannot be identified, then their intended nation-building character fades (Fox & Miller-Idriss 2008: 546–9). Even when the 'mixed and missed messages' are only related to the performing category, they could play a role in any of the other three. They reveal how individuals can position themselves as creators and interpreters of national symbols. In other parts of their article, Fox and Miller-Idriss expand on this, albeit briefly, pointing out that national symbols can be not only consumed and imbibed but also subverted and deflected (Fox & Miller-Idriss 2008: 551).

Similarly, Van Ginderachter and Beyen divide their case studies among 'appropriation', 'rejection' and 'competition' of elite and non-elite notions of the nation. They acknowledge that these categories are intimately interconnected and that they cannot be disentangled (Van Ginderachter & Beyen 2012: 18). Indeed, processes of rejection of a given national symbol results in the creation of an alternative vision of the nation. Based on these two studies, and taking into account the interconnection of these processes, the next chapter will illustrate with design examples how people can act as producers and consumers of national discourses and the possibilities to ignore, miss, deflect and contest national symbols.

# De/sedimenting

Most of the authors dealing with nationalism use Bourdieu's 'habitus' as a framework. The ubiquity and inconspicuousness of the habitus reflect well how nationalism has become a widespread ideology. Furthermore, its capacity to reflect and shape life at the same time corresponds to 'structured and structuring structure' that defines the 'habitus'. Notwithstanding the validity of this concept, it does not define in detail how national symbols are interpreted. Skey (2011) proposes the concept of 'sedimentation' as used by the philosopher Ernesto Laclau. Skey sees Billig's idea of nationalism as static and incapable of reflecting change and the agency of civic society. Similar to Billig, Laclau's sedimentation refers to discourses that become routinized and taken for granted, such as nationalism. Sedimented discourses are not perceived as just a vision of the world but present themselves as the only alternative (Skey 2009: 342–3). Of the concept of sedimentation, Skey values its capacity to present nations as processes and not 'things'. Sedimentation becomes counteracted by de-sedimentation, the opposite process that runs parallel with the first. Thereby, he presents nationalism as in constant negotiation in which both institutions and civic society possess agency to modelling it.

Laclau, in his turn, takes this definition from the philosopher Edmund Husserl that confronts 'sedimentation' with 'reactivation'. Sedimented discourses conceal the acts of their original institution, meanwhile their reactivation makes them visible again (Laclau & Mouffe 2001[1985]: viii). Laclau's interest in sedimentation is directed towards a re-foundation of Marxism, by going to its origins, instead of accepting the Marxist-Leninist interpretation as the only valid one. Laclau's implementation to dominant discourses, such as nationalism, does not argue for a reactivation in Husserl's terms. For him, going back to the institution is less important than demonstrating the contingency of a hegemonic discourse. This goal is achieved by putting into question the apparent invariability of the specific discourse. This duality between contingency and invariability reflects on the one hand the perception of the nation as if it was an essentialist given, that society performs daily, and on the other hand makes possible a de-automatizing lecture of it.

Skey appreciates that sedimentation accounts for both continuity and change in relation to the everyday practices of social actors (Skey 2011: 12). He wonders how these processes of de/sedimentation take place in practice. First, from a macro-perspective, wider structural transformations may de-sediment dominant discourses. Examples include the modernizing processes of industrialization, urbanization or mass communication. They have fractured dynastic/feudal societies and underpinned the growth of nationalism. Furthermore, he wonders how these established social foundations are maintained (Skey 2011: 35). The answer combines a macro- and a micro-perspective, involving both social structures and individual actions. Social structures and new institutional forms created to underpin the modern state are important as long as their framework becomes validated through social, economic and political domains (Skey 2011: 13). Yet, there are also those everyday activities that maintain and reproduce a national logic 'through routine habits, taken-for-granted symbolic systems and familiar material environments' (Skey 2011: 35). He proposes the insights of the studies of everyday life to disentangle the ways in which a 'complex matrix of knowledge, social practices and institutional settings contribute to the (re)production of a relatively consistent and meaningful sense of "reality" for disparate individuals' (Skey 2011: 14). By acknowledging the part that everyday actions take in this process, Skey opens the possibility for individual agency to not only sediment, but also de-sediment those hegemonic discourses.

Glenn Bowman lists monuments and rituals among those 'sediments' that allude to the nation and make its presence irrefutable (Bowman 1994: 143). Next to monuments, the previous chapters add a number of design examples that can be considered as national sediments. There is also design that can contribute to de-sedimentation. An example is the fabrication of lace 'stringi' in the Polish village of Koniaków that has been studied by Nicolette Makovicki (2011) (Figure 7.2). Gorale tradition had been the inspiration for the revival of Zakopane vernacular at the end of the nineteenth century described in Chapter 2. Equally the home of Gorale and proudly displaying its Gorale tradition, Koniaków has known a crochet

**Figure 7.2** Malgorzata Sanaszek, presents a hand made frilly string, Photo: 18 January 2007 in Koniaków.

lace tradition at least since the late nineteenth century (Makovicki 2011: 164). Products that have spread the fame of this local craft have been doilies, tablecloths, collars and blouses, as well as ecclesiastical textiles and vestments, a typical feature being its floral patterns. Since 2003, a major convulsion unsettled the community, since also feminine underwear was made with this technique and became successful. Its reception was ambivalent and the National Artistic and Ethnographic Commission declined to certify this product as 'folk art' (Makovicki 2011: 161). The main argument its functional character, even though tablecloths and vestments had got this label before. Moreover there was a clear precedent. In the 1950s, the Institute of Industrial Design (*Institut Wzornictwa Przemysłowego*) asked peasants to develop prototype designs to be later developed for production by trained designers and the Koniaków lace maker Lidia Buczek reinterpreted lace designs to create templates for decorative lingerie (Makovicki 2011: 165). Even then, Koniaków folk craft at the beginning of the twenty-first century evidenced a sedimented form that excluded lingerie from it. The production and subsequent success of the 'stringi' came to de-sediment this established vision. The National Artistic and Ethnographic Commission, as the gatekeeper of 'folk art,' decided however to re-sediment these practices. Nevertheless, more recent research on this phenomenon has proved that 'stringi' are now better accepted by lace makers in Koniaków and it has even expanded its product range to include men's underwear (Makovicki 2011: 167).

Thus, the 'stringi' can be seen as a de-sedimenting practice that has transformed the discourse of Polish folk art offering an alternative to a hegemonic discourse. With it, the discourse of the nation has been equally de-sedimented along with one of its symbols. Skey notes that in the debates on inmigration that formed part of his research, established notions of the nation were at stake. These included a bounded space in which those who belonged could assess the presence and behaviour of different out-groups. Even when these discussions impinged upon abstract issues of control and agency, they were experienced in banal settings or incidents such as 'the shop owner couldn't speak English, the presence of "other" people in local spaces, public signs written in foreign languages, people celebrating the achievements of other national teams, media debates concerning the banning of words, events or objects thought to offend minorities' (Skey 2011: 156). This proves how taken-for-granted objects, practices or symbols remain paramount in generating a sense of nationhood. A way to protect hegemonic discourses from de-sedimenting practices is by isolating them. In the case of the 'stringi', for example, one of the lace makers proposed to call them 'Koniaków G-strings, not Koniaków lace' (Makovicki 2011: 158). Its mere existence was not as problematic as the destabilization of the discourse of traditional lace. Even when the 'stringi' might be made in Koniaków using traditional techniques and patterns, the category 'Koniaków lace' is essentialized and new variations on the theme put it in danger.

# Chapter 8
# Trafficking the National

The previous chapter has explored how symbols of the nation can be created at the moment of perception. In this vein, deliberated or accidental, symbols generate national meaning when interpreted as such. This chapter explores the generation of national symbols outside the realm of the state, both through production and through consumption. The ways in which the citizenry generates national symbols can be multiple and the engagement of citizenry in cultural production in general and design in particular is an example. Moreover, this chapter investigates the ways in which citizenry can interpret national symbols of any kind. It will look at how meanings are the products of negotiations between the symbol and the perceiver.

The role of civic society as creators of national symbols goes beyond 'talking or choosing the nation' as Fox and Miller-Idriss have pointed out. Corporations have clearly presented a decisive alternative to states as symbols of the nation. States have appropriated strategies of corporations when branding themselves, adopting programmes of visual identity or launching more or less orchestrated programmes to shape their identity to both a domestic and a foreign audience. Corporations, too, have adopted strategies that align them to states. In many cases corporations have conveyed the values of a nation and have offered similar identity tools for nations to identify. Sara Kristoffersson has explored how IKEA has represented Sweden. Selling knock-down, flat-packed furniture since the 1950s, the firm has promoted ideals of functionality and democracy beneath a blue and yellow logo. The Swedish Institute, in charge of promoting the image of Sweden abroad, recognized in 2011 that 'IKEA is doing more to disseminate the image of Sweden than all governmental efforts put together' (Olle Wästberg quoted in Kristoffersson 2014: 79). Kristoffersson acknowledges that the branding of the country and of IKEA have been based on similar concepts of solidarity, security and equality. Probably, this might be the recipe for a long-term branding of a corporation, that it is distinctive enough to differentiate it from competitors and coincide with the stereotypical vision of the represented nation.

In this case a win-win situation emerges in which the stereotypes on the national community contribute to reaffirm the virtues of the corporation and the corporation acts as a herald of the national community. The communion of the two has prompted the Swedish Institute to declare that 'to visit IKEA is to visit Sweden' (Kristoffersson 2014: 85).

Corporations define their communication strategies carefully and their connections with the nation mainly result from them. We can affirm then that designers are generators of national symbology, too. To discern the ways in which designers act as creators of national symbols, the following section focuses on advertisements. Their potential to reproduce the nation is twofold. First, advertisements can reproduce a nationalist discourse and are therefore appealing to a national audience. In this case, the advert in itself reproduces and maintains the nationalist logic. Second, advertisements can imbue the announced product with national connotations. Then, it is the product that potentially reproduces the nation. Accounts on the nationalist character of advertisements have run in two directions. First, advertisements have been studied in their ability to recall the national community in the way that printed material does, according to Benedict Anderson. Second, advertisements have reproduced the nation in particular ways and constructed discourses that can reproduce hegemonic discourses or on the contrary alternative visions.

The anthropologist Robert J. Foster has studied national identity in regard to print advertising published in Papua New Guinea in the late 1980s. In considering this relationship between advertisements and the nation, or how do the adverts construct 'Papua New Guinea' and 'Papua New Guineaness', he used two approaches (Foster 1995: 151–2). The first approach emphasizes the sociocultural linkages brought about by mass-consumption practices. The second approach focuses on the rhetorical form common to all advertisements. On this note, Foster is not concerned with the particular messages of particular adverts. Moreover, he does not consider the intentions of the advertiser, nor the effects of adverts on individual purchasing decisions (Foster 1995: 154). These are characteristics of all adverts that reproduce the national community through their mere dissemination and rhetoric.

The first approach, as the author expresses, recalls the 'mass ceremony' of newspaper reading advanced by Anderson in regard to the creation of 'imagined communities'. Viewing the same adverts can create a shared frame of reference. Foster states namely that advertisements have become important vehicles for the 'imagination' of a community of consumers whose shared consumption practices and ideals connect them with each other (Foster 1995: 152). Different places are brought into relationship with each other through a single object of consumption, displayed in the adverts (Foster 1995: 169–70). When staring at the advert, the viewer is conscious that fellow nationals are performing the same activity, reinforcing the belonging to a national community.

The second approach has more to do with the rhetoric of advertisements *per se*. Foster argues that advertisements presuppose and naturalize a general structure of social relations, 'a structure of social relations characteristic of commodity consumption in capitalist societies' (Foster 1995: 153). The nation takes the form of a collection of people united by the commodities they jointly possess and consume in common. It predicates relations among such individuals by categorizing them as fellow consumers, and thus alike (Foster 1995: 170). Symbolic citizenship is acquired through acts of consumption so qualified, by participation in the 'life-style' represented in the advert (Foster 1995: 155). In this way, shared mass-consumption practices anchor an imagined national community in ordinary, everyday practice (Foster 1995: 153).

# Advertising the nation: who and how

The political scientist Jillian Prideaux has looked more specifically at how company advertising reproduces a national discourse. She states that it is expected to see the symbols and language of nationalism used in public, political and national events, however much less so in relation to everyday commodities. In extension of Billig's (1995) and Edensor's (2002) literature, Prideaux's starting point is how commercial expressions of nationalism constitute a 'daily reminder' of a person's belonging to a particular nation (Prideaux 2009: 617). Prideaux criticizes homogenic approaches towards nationalism in company advertising since in this literature 'companies are not considered as actors that have to make choices as to how they portray nationalism, and are not seen as being capable of distinct political agendas apart from the need to sell more products' (Prideaux 2009: 633). Therefore, she argues for in-depth studies of how particular companies engage with nationalist discourses. Her goal is illustrating the varying ways of companies on engaging, shaping and impacting wider nationalistic discourses (Prideaux 2009: 616).

In order to address this gap in the literature, Prideaux has developed a categorization of how companies use nationalism in advertising depending on two variables. First, to what extent the product is already identified as quintessentially national, this means if it is considered to be a marker of a national identity (Prideaux 2009: 622). Here, she distinguishes between products 'achieving nationalist credentials' or with 'established nationalist credentials'. Second, she looks at if the advert is merely linking the product to the nation or goes beyond that and identifies the act of purchase with a nationalist action. Then she distinguishes between 'ordinary marketing' and 'activist marketing'. The resulting types are (1) 'ordinary marketing/achieving nationalist credentials', (2) 'ordinary marketing/established nationalist credentials' and (3) 'activist marketing/ achieving nationalist credentials'. Using Australian adverts as case studies, she could not find any belonging to type (4) 'activist marketing/established nationalist credentials'. Through this classification system, the role and extent of companies as nationalist actors can be examined, and how advertisements can engage with and impact on wider national discourses (Prideaux 2009: 620).

Regarding the first and second types, she observes that products that are not yet established as national icons tend to use explicit nationalist discourses and imagery. The company in question aims at establishing nationalist credentials, therefore participating more explicitly in current nationalist discourses. In contrast, in cases where companies already have established their nationalist credentials, they no longer need to attempt to establish themselves within the national discourse. Previous marketing has already achieved this goal and therefore these companies tend to invoke heritage and nostalgia (Prideaux 2009: 623 and 627). It is questionable if this always happens like this, as Prideaux seems to suggest, or if this rule can be disputed.

An example of the first type is a 2007 advert from an Australian telecommunications provider announcing its free broadband service. It starts with a map of the USA overlain with a national flag stating, 'We've got cheap broadband in the US', followed by a map of the United Kingdom with its flag and the message, 'We've got free broadband in the UK'. The advert ends with an Australian map and flag and the Dodo mascot flying over it saying 'now, thanks to Dodo, we have free broadband in Australia!' The advert finishes with a woman wearing an Australian flag string bikini stating the conditions of this offer (Prideaux 2009: 623–4; a similar version of the advert described by Prideaux can be accessed through www.youtube.com/watch?v=B6JDX3ELQgE). An example of the second case is Vegemite, a yeast-based sandwich spread popular in Australia (Figure 8.1). She refers to the website of the product, rich in references to the product heritage but with no depiction of Australian flags or emblems (www.vegemite.com.au). She points to a printed advert dating back to the 1940s' wartime era depicting a small child wearing an oversized Australian army slouch hat, clearly belonging to an adult. The advert legend states 'He's doing his bit for Dad' and 'Vegemite is with the troops!' This brings Prideaux to assert that established brands have passed through a period of iconization using the same strategies as contemporary products 'achieving national credentials' (Prideaux 2009: 628).

Prideaux's account is useful to see that companies embark on similar nationalistic campaigns as governments can do. The use and dissemination of national symbols is not an exclusive task of the state. Less convincing is that products achieve a status of national icons only through a manifest nationalistic campaign. There are other mechanisms to achieve that aim. Products can become national symbols, for example through the intensive consumption of a product in a territory during a long period of time. Products do not need to be explicitly marketed as national to achieve their status as national icons. In the

**Figure 8.1** Jars of Vegemite are seen during a press call to celebrate the Vegemite brand's 90th year at the Vegemite factory on 24 October 2013 in Melbourne, Australia.

case of Vegemite, Prideaux seems to suggest that the product was systematically advertised as intermingled with nationalist symbols in its 'achieving national credentials' phase. However, when looking at other old adverts displayed on the same website, one can see that the advert with the army hat is rather the exception than the rule. Adverts predominate where the nutritional value of the product is enhanced, but references to Australian symbolism are difficult to find. The achievement of national value in this case has been established in the realm of consumption independently of the marketing campaigns. Therefore, the association of a product with the nation can emerge spontaneously through its linkage with tradition or through a longstanding presence in the national market. Adverts can at times reinforce this status and sometimes create it from scratch, but success is not guaranteed.

The third type is also revealing of how companies can resemble states when intertwined in nationalist discourse. Prideaux defines 'activist marketing' when the viewers are urged to help the company achieve nationalistic goals through diverse actions, such as 'buying goods produced in the nation and lobbying the Government' (Prideaux 2009: 621–2). An example of this type is an advert announcing a threat to the nation or to a national icon, and to promote itself as a solution to the problem (Prideaux 2009: 629). Prideaux puts the example of Dick Smith Foods, a food company that mobilizes its consumers to buy Australian products, made fully in Australia, in order to keep jobs in the country. In this advertisement, Vegemite for example is straightforwardly attacked, since part of its production process is outsourced to China. The advert shows newspaper clippings at the top of the page featuring headlines such as 'Vegemite maker exports jobs to China' and 'That's the way the Kraft cookie crumbles'. Underneath the newspaper clippings appears the caption, 'Who's next? Buy Australian while you still can'. The centre of the page displays a variety of Dick Smith Food products. All products feature the Dick Smith label with the entrepreneur's face as well as Australian flag motifs (Prideaux 2009: 630).

These products associate themselves not only with their country of origin but with the act of defending the Australian economy. This patriotic call is more typical of a state-related institution or of political parties than of a profit-making company. Invoking the general interest is normally a task of the state. Needless to say, this call in the name of general interest is at the same time beneficial for this company. In this sense, the nationalist rhetoric is as useful here as it can be when mobilizing the population to defend the country. Regardless of the reasons, as a result the products get connected not only to a specific consumption habit but also with the safeguard of the national economy and national jobs.

After having studied the effect of advertisements in general and how companies engage with a nationalist discourse, it is necessary to have a closer look and discern what strategies have been used to link products to a nationalist discourse. In his study, Foster located discursive strategies similar to those examined by Billig. Specific terms as 'we', 'this', 'here' work as elements of a deixis that proves fundamental to attain national consensus and to absorb the effects of invisible nationalism once flagged (Billig 1995: 94–5). Such flagging, argues Billig, is an inescapable part of the habitual condition of contemporary state politics (Billig 1995: 98). The use of 'our' and 'everybody' as referring to the national community is detected in adverts pertaining to both state-run and private companies. An example of the former is the 1982 advert for the Papua New Guinea Credit Corporation, a 100 per cent nationally owned company. The advert runs the heading 'Keep our money in our country'. Beneath this there is a picture of the national flag and a logo of the Credit Corporation (Foster 1995: 159). Readers are then connected to a larger community, reminded of its existence and of their belonging to the nation. The advert presupposes that readers are national, using a specific and direct language targeting both their specific and common features of individuals belonging to the same group. The same applies to Dick Smith Foods' ultra-patriotic communication style explained above, which shows that state-driven and company adverts can both use the same nationalist language to appeal to consumers.

Along with the verbal strategies, there are also visual strategies. Artemis Yagou has studied a selection of twentieth-century Greek advertisements covering a range of locally produced products, such as cigarettes, beer, furniture and electrical equipment, intended to be used by the Greek public (Yagou 2012: 111). She argues that the products have become significant in the shaping of Greek national identity and especially in the representation and reproduction of the idea of 'Greekness'. Central to this concept is the role and influence of ancient Greek culture (Yagou 2012: 109). In order to better understand the visual expression of nationalist ideas, Yagou has grouped the adverts into four dominant themes: (1) evocation of antiquity, (2) patriotic production and consumption, (3) craft versus industry, and lastly (4) attractions of modernity (Yagou 2012: 112).

Historical references to a Hellenic past have been used to stress the beauty of the products and traditional references have been used to reproduce an essentialized Greek identity and to mobilize patriotic consumption. Craft tradition, for its part, has transferred the high quality typical of the handicrafts to industrially manufactured commodities. Recurrent themes are therefore history, tradition and the vernacular, those that have been studied in Part One and that refer to a primordialist understanding of the nation. Modernity has also been a reference, either combined with traditional traits or on its own. Yagou stresses the inconvenience of tradition and history mostly in technical products, oriented to what she calls a technocratic audience. It is therefore the target public and the product's category which decides how to communicate its national origin. Yagou also points to contextual parameters such as historical circumstances. She notes that after the Second World War, a wave of patriotic consumption made nationalist rhetoric proliferate (Yagou 2012: 119). In this sense, modernity can be a communicator of nationhood, albeit one that draws on the changing face of the nation, as Massey advocates, instead of one reproducing a static interpretation of it.

The value and impact of consumerism in relation to national identity has also been explored by the historian Charles McGovern in *Sold American: Consumption and Citizenship* (2009), an analysis of American advertisement of the late nineteenth and early twentieth century. McGovern has coined this strategy of linking products to political and historical symbols as 'material nationalism'. He opposes this variant to civic and racial nationalism. If the former emphasizes the power of the state in reuniting diverse ethnicities and is therefore inclusive, the latter stresses the nation as dependent on blood and ancestry, and is therefore exclusionary. He argues that material nationalism blended the inclusionary spirit of the civic and the essentialism of the racial. Advertisements developed a promise of equalitarian, and therefore civic, pursuit of happiness that nevertheless was represented by a restricted portion of the American population, and therefore racial (McGovern 2009: 104). The invocation of national symbols injected the act of buying with powerful cultural authority (McGovern 2009: 105). In their references to history, tradition, heritage and self-sacrifice, these adverts recreated the idea of a nation as primordialist, beyond ongoing contingencies, furthering ideals of patriotism.

This meant that the act of becoming American was realized through purchasing and consuming these advertised commodities (McGovern 2009: 96). In extension, McGovern compares this phenomenon to America's most valued ideals, arguing that by 'equating the market with society, advertisers portrayed consumption as a political exercise in resonant accord with the rituals of American freedom' (McGovern 2009: 67). That is, the associations of suffrage, democracy and independence connected with some of the most important and cherished ideals in American life such as individual liberty, independence, equality and sovereignty, were identified with the sales messages and consumption advocated in the adverts (McGovern 2009: 80, 95 and 103). To promote this nationalist attitude of consumption among the American consumers, advertisers relied on national images and emblems.

McGovern convincingly analyses the patriotic messages included in these adverts, referring to deixical appellations to the community or the representation of national symbols. What is open to scrutiny is his assumption that these patriotic messages would unleash patriotic consumption. He says for example that 'by purchasing goods that expressed American values and ideals, consumers asserted their own American nationality, vesting it in the things they purchased' (McGovern 2009: 120). While the possibility was there and the products were indeed introduced in a nationalist logic, the agency of the consumer must be taken into account. It is not that because a product was advertised as national that the consumer needed to perform a nationalist action. On the contrary, this must be observed as one of a myriad of possibilities. The following sections deal with the negotiation of meanings by the consumer beyond the intentions of the advertisers. Global products can de consumed as national and patriotic products can be subverted in meaning and integrated in an anti-patriotic discourse.

# Indigenizing foreign products

Besides the creation of national symbols, there is the appropriation and reaction towards them through acts of consumption. First, there is the appropriation of products that were not intended to represent the nation. There are a number of studies that have explored the indigenization of foreign products. Independently of their marketing strategies, the circulation and consumption of those objects have conferred them specific national meaning. The anthropologist Daniel Miller's well known study of Coca-Cola in Trinidad is a good example. He illustrates how Coca-Cola generates new localized meanings that despite the commodity in question cannot be labelled as 'global'. Similarly to Massey, Miller avows that the local is in constant change. The idea that only a primeval Trinidanian identity existed until globalization arrived, is too simplistic and does not reflect the sophisticated connection between the local and the global (Miller 1998: 176). Trinidad's national drink is rum and Coke and was created only after the American beverage entered the island in 1939 (Miller 1998: 172). Moreover, because Coca-Cola was bottled in Trinidad, it fell under the market protection of the government – in a policy that paradoxically banned 'foreign' beverages – and its price was under government control (Miller 1998: 178). These facts are salient enough to demonstrate the domestication of Coca-Cola in Trinidad. Nevertheless, Miller continues explaining the meaning of this brand within the production and consumption of soft drinks – there called 'sweet drinks' – on the island. As a result, Trinidadian Coca-Cola becomes intertwined in different levels of identification with the Black African majority, as opposed to the Indian minority.

Coke and other 'black sweet drinks' are related to Black African Trinidadians, the majority of the population. Meanwhile, the sweeter 'red sweet drinks' are related to the Indian minority (Miller 1998: 179). This connection happens in the sphere of production, but in the sphere of consumption it is estimated to be the other way around, Indians being the main consumers of black drinks and Black Africans of the red variant (Miller 1998: 180). Thus, Africans drink red sweet drinks as a representation of Indian identity, which is conceived as the 'other' in opposition to themselves and as an element of their identity as Trinidadians. In that way, Coca-Cola's meaning in Trinidad impinges upon the whole of beverages present in the national market and reflects local demographic aspects. The complex identifications of Coca-Cola integrate in the culture of the island and percolate to reach the identification of ethnic groups. The meanings generated through the networks of production and consumption are unique to the island and reflect its peculiarities. Miller's concluding point is the local embeddedness of global products such as Coke.

A second way of incorporating foreign products as national is offered in the study of Miller and Sophie Woodward on jeans. Their research results in the conclusion that especially immigrants in London attach jeans a sense of ordinariness related to Britishness. In the eyes of the respondents, jeans are not homogeneous but differences can be made between American, Italian or British jeans (Miller & Woodward 2012: 108). The will of integration brings immigrants to wear jeans, since this garment allows them to pass unnoticed in the streets (Miller & Woodward 2012: 110). The ordinariness of a global product in this case does not translate in an absence of national identity. The respondents associate this quality with Britishness and consciously opt for it.

A third example comes again from Foster's study. He comments on a humorous calendar illustration by Bob Browne entitled 'What All the Young Village Kids are Getting Educated to Become: the Yuppies' (ca. 1989) parodying middle-class consumption practices in Papua-New Guinea (Figure 8.2). The illustration depicts two boys and one girl sitting at a table while waiting for their mother to serve their meal. The mother stands next to the table ready to serve instant noodles on their plates. They all watch TV except for the youngest brother

**Figure 8.2** Browne, Bob (1989) 'What All the Young Village Kids are Getting Educated to Become: the Yuppies', in Bob Browne, Gima Segore, John Atep, *The Grass Roots Offisel Kalenda: The People of Papua New Guinea*, Port Moresby: Grass Roots Comic Company.

who listens to the radio. Most of the objects depicted are accompanied of a short explanation and their symbolic value in this interior. Thus for example, a souvenir from Fiji hanging on the wall is interpreted as 'Souveniers [sic] of overseas travel. Been there, done that' denoting tourism as the access to free time and expenditure. The noodles are described as 'Indo-Mie noodles. Fastest food in town, fast to eat – good to cook!' implying the little time that modern women enjoy to prepare traditional, elaborated meals. Foster refers to the mixture of local and transnational products in the illustration. There is local tinned meat on the table but the family eats Indonesian food and a Walkman hangs on the chair of the girl. Nevertheless, Foster argues it is this mixture that 'transcends local particularity, but which also potentially effaces national particularity' (Foster 1995: 176). Accordingly, it is not the presence of regional products what makes the whole image national but actually the indigenization of foreign products. Their presence supersedes regional particularism to make reference to a truly national community (Foster 1991: 251). The nation as a crossroads between the regional and the global needs to be a sum of the regional vernacular and the global cosmopolitan. If the regional is too tied to traditions and to locality, foreign products add a less particular dimension that better reflects the national.

The three examples offer different views of how foreign products can configure a sense of home and shape a sense of the national. The first example achieves this aim through the integration of Coca-Cola in national symbolism and as a conveyor of ethnic relations. The second refers to the establishment of a national identity beyond individual specificity. The third concerns the opposition between regions and nations, considering the latter as a collective reality that reunites regional differences. The configuration of national symbols do not take place in the idealization of the nation, but in the everyday reality composed as it is of artefacts from different origins. It is in the configuration of that immediate reality that the nation takes shape. This is not to deny that nations are constructed discourses, but to add that the interpretation of that discourse cannot be eradicated from the experience of the nation.

# Contesting the nation

The agency of the consumer can be so decisive that even national symbols can get an opposed meaning when being interpreted by the citizenry. Consumers can be mobilized to take activist positions towards consumption – such as in Dick Smith Food – and yet ignoring it. Equally, they can take an activist position by subverting the meaning of symbols. A good example can be found in late nineteenth-century Finland, when the Russian Empire's control rocketed. Many Finns subverted the official nationalism of the state by placing Russian stamps upside down on the envelope, protesting against cultural imposition. The stamp was originally intended to celebrate the Russian Empire, to which Finland belonged, and as a token of banal nationalism. It became however a means to put the authority into question and a means for activist subnationalism instead. Banal nationalism, intended to pass unnoticed, can be the target of inner cultural attacks by those seeing nations as symbols of oppression (Raento & Brunn 2005: 147). The top-down connotation of stamps and their mundane omnipresence make them a perfect tool of banal nationalism but as any symbol, they are also 'a potential tool for resistance' (Raento & Brunn 2005: 145).

After Billig coined the concept of banal nationalism, John Hutchinson discussed its relative uniformity putting into relevance its multiple shades. Meanwhile, for some people nationalism can be a banal phenomenon, some others can be deeply engaged. Hutchinson seeks to depolarize the conceptions 'hot' and 'banal' showing the interconnections between the two. He refers to 'hot' as a feeling that springs from a sense of crises and to 'banal' as a compendium of everything that people culturally consume as a part of their everyday life (Hutchinson 2006: 295). According to Hutchinson, this would determine the existence of two types of nationalism. The hot one promotes the idea of the nation as a sacred and transcendent object of worship and sacrifice. The banal one is typical of populations that approach nationalism in a rather unconscious way as a guide to the conduct of everyday life as expressed in popular songs, political posters, stamps, banknotes, coinage and brand names of staple products (Hutchinson 2006: 299). Unlike Billig, Hutchinson analyses both hot and banal nationalism as two concepts that operate together. The question that he raises is whether hot and banal nationalism have any relationship, admitting that both act together as two parts of a totality. He contests that both operate linearly, one after the other, and defends, on the contrary, their simultaneity (Hutchinson 2006: 303).

In relation to this, Rhys Jones and Peter Merriman equally refuse Billig's division between hot and banal. Accordingly, they stress the need to move beyond these categories and examine how nationalist discourses and practices are reproduced in everyday contexts (Jones & Merriman 2009: 164). They suggest instead replacing these two categories with the term 'everyday nationalism', which would combine hot and banal elements (Jones & Merriman 2009: 164). According to them, the term 'everyday' combines how people consume different kinds of 'knowledges, rationalities and nationalisms that emanate from the state' with the possibility of individuals to oppose projects imposed from above (Jones & Merriman 2009: 166–7).

To illustrate this, Jones and Merriman analyse the turmoil generated around the campaign in favour of bilingual road signs in Wales between 1967 and 1975. Despite the protests of Welsh people, the government never responded positively to their request for bilingual signs, a fact that led opponents of the use of English on a rather confrontational tone and reached the point of vandalism against the signs. Finally, in the late 1970s the central government and the Welsh authorities agreed on the use of bilingual signs (Jones & Merriman 2009: 168). Although the violence used by Welsh people and official organizations to promote the use of bilingual signs was long demonized, 'monolingual road signs were viewed as state-supported acts of vandalism in their own right' (Jones & Merriman 2009: 169). Promoted by the Welsh authorities to assure road safety, monolingual signs were considered an abstraction of the state, a 'symbol of injustice', a landscape cultural oppression, clearly based on the politics of the everyday that needed to be fought from below (Jones 2006: 168–70).

# Chapter 9
# Is Multiculturalism the New Vernacular?

The definition of the nation as home can change from theory to theory. If primordialist thinking would defend perennial, continuist ideas; theories based in Massey's 'progressive change of place' would accept change and evolution. What is or is not home can be decided both individually and collectively. Likewise, the material culture defining home is also a contested terrain. One of the examples might be Aaron Betsky's description of Dutch architecture landscape. He points out that 'within the next few decades, non-native Dutch will become a majority of the population. Minarets are appearing on the skylines of most Dutch cities, and their design has little to do with Dutch traditions' (Betsky 2008: 334). This quote shows how some things are condemned to remain foreign even when being present in the national landscape. This attitude is not an isolated example from the Netherlands but echoes the decision by a majority of voters in Switzerland in 2009 to ban the building of minarets (Skey 2011: 3). Dominant discourses on the nation produce dominant and peripheral ethnicities. If the former are legitimated by tradition, the latter are relegated to a second-range status. Regarding design, these conflicts between the real and the ideal imply the prevalence of some design above others as defining factors of the nation. Dominant discourses shape an image of the nation as home and consequently design objects are labelled either as exotic or as native.

Dominant discourses can nevertheless be challenged bottom-up, putting their hegemonic vision into question. Confrontations can emerge, for example in the rights to wear certain clothing. The case of the hijab in French schools is illustrative, also known in French as *l'affaire du foulard*. It first surfaced in September 1989 when three Muslim girls wore hijab to their ethnically mixed school in Creil, some sixty kilometers north of Paris (Figure 9.1). The headmaster objected to the Muslim girls wearing the hijab in the classroom on the grounds that it went against the secular character of the French state schools. Since the girls refused to comply, he barred them from attending the school. The matter acquired national importance when many Muslim girls throughout France began

**Figure 9.1** Demonstration to support the Muslim Creil school girls wearing headscarves in Paris on 22 October 1989.

to wear hijabs to school as a gesture of solidarity. The Education Minister, Lionel Jospin, consulted the Conseil d'Etat which ruled that the hijab did not violate the principle of secularity, provided that the girls did not engage in 'pressure, provocation, proselytism or propaganda', the decision on which was to be made by the local education authority on a case-by-case basis. The situation was finally resolved when one of the girls voluntarily, and the other two under pressure from King Hassan of Morocco, agreed to drop the scarves to the shoulders in the classroom (Parekh 1998: 402–3).

As the political theorist Bhikhu Parekh points out, the national debate on the hijab 'went to the heart of the French conceptions of citizenship and national identity, and divided the country' (Parekh 1998: 403). If the case might be intricate in itself, the reactions unleashed were sometimes unexpected, even more so when it distanced positions that *a priori* seemed close, such as multiculturalism and feminism. Both concerned with the questioning of hegemonic discourses, their positions collided in this case. In her essay *Is Multiculturalism Bad for Women?* Susan Moller Okin remembers how feminists were aligned with those defenders of secular education and unexpectedly also with far-right nationalists against the use of the hijab, which feminists understood as a token of oppression. Left-wing sympathizers conversely supported the claim for flexibility accusing their opponents of racism and cultural imperialism (Okin 1999: 9). Okin argues that women might be oppressed by minority cultures and that minority rights can conflict with individual rights. Nevertheless, positions within feminism can be confronted, too. The feminist philosopher Aziza Y. Al-Hibri rejected Okin's statements suggesting that her viewpoint is condescending, even patriarchal, to consider from an outside point of view just how women from these religious backgrounds should lead their lives. She asks, 'why is it oppressive to wear a head scarf but liberating to wear a miniskirt?' challenging Okin's self-allocated superior positioning (Al-Hibri 1999: 46). She wonders how can Okin be sure that women are wearing headscarves out of force? It is not unreasonable to suggest that women may wear them out of personal choice.

Within the framework of Ghassan Hage's national capital, this case would exemplify how dress can be a signifier of possessing more or less national capital and how the struggle between majoritarian and minoritarian concepts of the nation takes place. Hage recognizes that, '[t]he aim of accumulating national capital is precisely to convert it into national belonging; to have your accumulated national capital recognised as legitimately national by the dominant cultural grouping within the field' (Hage 1998: 53). Individuals might have their own interpretation of the nation as home. Nevertheless, collective recognition conditions how individual conceptions of the national can be developed in the public sphere. If citizenship *per se* might be less open to discussion, it is in the terrain of practical nationality where dominant ideas become conflictive.

# Multiculturalism

The negotiation between national majorities and minorities is discussed in multiculturalism, a frame of thought most actively discussed in political theory, philosophy and anthropology. Also coined the 'politics of difference', or the 'politics of recognition', theorists have defined multiculturalism differently. Multiculturalism 'condemns intolerance of other ways of life, find the human what might seem Other, and encourages cultural diversity' (Cohen et al. 1999: 4). Christopher Crowder defines 'multiculturalism proper' as 'the active state recognition and promotion of minority cultures within a society' (Crowder 2013: viii). Anne Phillips wrote that, 'Multiculturalism recognizes itself the route to a more tolerant and inclusive society, because it recognizes that there *is* a diversity of cultures, and rejects the assimilation of these into the cultural traditions of the dominant group' (Phillips 2007: 14). It is therefore not enough to recognize the existence of different cultures to be involved in a multiculturalist debate; a pro-active way of thinking is required when adopting a multiculturalist point of view.

The broadest and most accepted definition of the term, according to the sociologist Tariq Modood, who echoes a definition made by Will Kymlicka, it is 'the political accommodation of difference'. He prefers to use 'difference' to 'culture' because difference is constituted relationally, as a product of the interaction between majorities and minorities. More specifically, he claims that '[t]o speak of "difference" rather than "culture" as the sociological starting point is to recognize that the difference in question is not just constituted from the "inside", from the side of a minority culture, but also from the outside, from the representations and treatment of the minorities in question' (Modood 2013[2007]: 36). He refers to negative difference based on race, ethnicity, cultural heritage and religious community. These characteristics are negativized and constitute, on the other hand, the basis for identity formation of those groups. Therefore, the differences at issue constitute both a form of distinctness and a form of alienness or inferiority that 'diminishes or makes difficult equal membership in the wider society or polity' (Modood 2013[2007]: 34).

Kymlicka is a pivotal author of multiculturalism, towards whom other theories get shaped either in favour or in opposition. He notes that the introduction of basic human rights policies by the United Nations after the Second World War was an attempt to protect national minorities through the consensus of human equality, though this re-justification does not satisfactorily accommodate minority rights or resolve issues surrounding all minority cultures. Rather than granting every religious group individual rights, states took on a neutral approach to their policies in religion, where there was guaranteed 'individual freedom of worship' neither advocating nor prohibiting the worship of any particular religious group (Kymlicka 1995a: 3). Though this seems to be the fairest way to allow for differing religious groups to exist, Kymlicka notes that in recent years it has become exceedingly tough to place such a diverse collective under the single category of 'human rights'. Each cultural minority has different needs, and the basic principles of human right cannot answer all questions, 'should each ethnic or national group have publicly funded education in its mother tongue? [. . .] Should political office be distributed in accordance with a principle of nation or ethnic proportionality? [. . .] What are the responsibilities of minorities to integrate?' (Kymlicka 1995a: 5). These are just a few of the matters that must to be addressed and all cannot be simply answered by everyone 'having the right . . .'

Kymlicka's theory is based on liberalism. This political doctrine is roughly based on four principles, i.e. the value of individual liberty, the capability of humans of deciding how to live, a limited government and private property (Crowder 2013: 39–40). Kymlicka's account nonetheless prioritizes individual liberty and decision capability above a limited government, since his re-interpretation of individual freedom is defined as 'the capacity of people to choose their own plan of life'. To achieve this aim, he defends state interventionism to guarantee individual rights. What could seem incongruent becomes justified by the disadvantaged position of some groups in respect of others and the beneficial character of these groups for individuals. The state then acts as a corrective for undeserved disadvantage by securing 'group rights' for minorities (Kymlicka 1995a: 80).

Kymlicka believes that societal cultures greatly contribute to following a meaningful way of life by sharing memories or values and, in a liberal society, individuals should have the freedom to choose to partake in these societal cultures. A way of life that is feasible and appealing to individuals should be by way of choosing, rather than following the only path available. Therefore, a liberal state, as outlined previously, is actually dependent on different societal cultures for liberal values to thrive. Access to information from other pursuits of life provides people with the choice and encouragement to reflect on their own and hence lead better lives, as well as affirming a sense of common identity and solidarity to those also involved. For this, the conditions must be created. He advocates for specific 'group rights' for groups that, due to unchosen circumstances for which they are not responsible, live in a culture in which they form a minority (Kymlicka 1995a: 109).

Defending multiculturalism, Kymlicka is not defending that there is a value in cultural diversity itself. It is not that the presence of multiple cultures in a society adds to the richness of people's life. He says that there is some truth in this argument but 'it is a mistake to put much weight on it as a defence of national rights' (Kymlicka 1995a: 121). On the contrary, his quest for minority rights is the valuation of one's culture as the framework providing a context for choice and a basis for self-respect. As such, it is essential for individuals' good life. He opposes the acceptance of cultural minorities to disintegrate, which in turn leads to cultural assimilation (Kymlicka 1995b: 5). It is in Kymlicka's philosophy that the cultural minorities need special rights to preserve their cultural traditions. This seems constructive; to have a minority culture assimilate to the majority would destroy the terms on which *multiculturalism* is grounded upon.

To ensure that minority cultures survive, Kymlicka's theory is not solely based on the sense of cultural membership but proposes that groups are provided with three types of group-differentiated rights to guarantee their preservation and external protection, should they seek it. These fall under self-government – the delegation of powers to national minorities, often through some form of federalism – polyethnic rights – financial support and legal protection for certain practices associated with particular ethnic or religious groups – and special representation rights – guaranteed seats for ethnic or national groups within the central institutions of the larger state (Kymlicka 1995a: 6–7). It is necessary to provide different forms of rights, as different groups, whether aboriginal or immigrants, demand different forms of protection. By granting these rights, minority groups are able to preserve and continue religious and cultural practices without the threat of extinction.

The minority groups he has in mind are aboriginal groups, sub-nationalisms and immigrants. As he admits 'there is no simple formula for deciding exactly which rights should be accorded to which groups' (Kymlicka 1995a: 131). Nevertheless, Kymlicka admits then that in general 'national minorities have societal cultures, and immigrant groups do not' (Kymlicka 1995a: 101). He considers that immigrants are expected to integrate and that they cannot expect to become a national minority, unlike aboriginal and sub-nationalisms. As a general rule, he argues that immigrants have chosen to move to a different country, unlike refugees, and therefore their group-rights must be polyethnic, guaranteeing the continuation of their cultures but not of the other two kinds (Kymlicka 1995a: 97). This divide might seem too simplistic. Kymlicka recognizes, nevertheless, that the divide between voluntary immigrants and involuntary refugees is at times difficult to trace. Under conditions of involuntariness, he is keener to concede national rights to these minority groups. He reckons that rich countries have obligations of international justice to redistribute resources to poor countries. If this was true, probably less involuntary emigration would take place. A way of compensating this failure might be to concede these national rights (Kymlicka 1995a: 99).

One of the examples of group rights to minorities is the exemption to wear helmets to turban-wearing Sikhs in the UK (Figure 9.2). Practicing Sikh males do not cut their hair. Their hair is drawn forward, twisted tightly along its length and wound into a knot on top of the head. The turban material is usually light cotton gauze and its dimensions are approximately 4.5 m long and 1 m wide. The Road Traffic Act of 1972 made it compulsory for motorcyclists to wear protective headgear. Despite claims by Sikh groups to the Ministry of Transport, the minister refused to make an exception. Following this legislation, some Sikhs deliberately flouted the law by riding motorcycles without helmets and campaigned against the law with considerable popular support. Their main arguments were that the turban was as safe as the crash helmet and that, if they had fought for the British in two World Wars without anyone considering their turbans unsafe, they could surely ride motorcycles (Parekh 1998: 401). After social and political mobilization, the exemption was conceded when the Labour government decided to support a Private Members' Bill introduced by Sidney Bidwell, the Member of Parliament for Southall. The Motor-Cycle Crash Helmets (Religious Exemption) Act (1976) modified the Road Traffic Act by declaring that it 'shall not apply to followers of the Sikh religion while he is wearing a turban'. In giving support to this measure, the government was quite clear that it was moved by considerations of religious tolerance (Singh 2005: 160–1).

Kymlicka's agenda for group rights is where most other theorists raise questions. Brian Barry, for example, opines that legal exemptions are unjustified if the law has public goals. If there are reasons for minorities for not complying with the law, then the law was probably not well conceived and deserves rethinking (Barry 2001: 39). If the law conversely is necessary, then it should be applicable to all. He says that crash-helmet laws aim at preventing serious

**Figure 9.2** A Sikh man rides a motorcycle in the streets of New Delhi on 11 April 2012.

injuries and that the law does not prevent Sikhs from practicing their religion. To avoid wearing helmets, they just do not have to ride motorbikes (Barry 2001: 44–5).

# Redundant culture and state

Multiculturalism argues, then, for the respect for minority cultures and not for their eradication. Recalling Hannah Arendt's definition discussed in Chapter 6 can be useful to stress this point. She wrote about the 'conquest of the state by the nation', since states have increasingly prioritized a nation among others, meanwhile its task has been the protection of all its inhabitants regardless of their nationality (Arendt 1973[1951]: 230). In this sense, multiculturalism reverses this situation and seeks to diminish the nationalization of the state by recognizing the existence of both dominant and minority cultures but does not aim for full denationalization. National communities and cultures are considered important and worth preserving.

Some authors depart from this position and have considered the very concept of culture as the main problem within the debates of multiculturalism. The opening pages of Anne Phillips' *Multiculturalism without Culture* respond directly to Okin's essay, concerned that it contributed to a false perception of minority cultures and their maltreatment of women. The purpose of her book is to support multiculturalism, gender equality and women's rights suggesting that Okin's essay behaves as a scapegoat for other feminists to place blame, and unduly stygmatize cultures (Phillips 2007: 2). To achieve this goal, she endorses a multiculturalism *without* culture, under the conception that culture only feeds stereotypes (Phillips 2007: 8). Phillips argues that a more delicate understanding of how cultures operate is needed, rather than essentialized understanding of culture that merely stereotypes and limits groups and their individual freedoms. She points out that in recent years, and as a consequence of radicalized Islamic groups and terrorist attacks, Western liberal societies have become increasingly more hostile towards ethnic minority groups. Her utmost concern following such events is the tendency to construct cultural stereotypes between Western and non-Western values (Phillips 2007: 23). 'Differences of culture and religion are seen as suggestive of profound differences of value, and these are being mapped onto opposing sides of a liberal/illiberal divide' (Phillips 2007: 23). She argues that the reason for this categorizing of radical difference between East and West, liberal and illiberal is due to the failure to problematize culture, encouraging multicultural critics to the misrepresentation of cultural difference as a source of instability (Phillips 2007: 23). Therefore, she places value in autonomy and human agency that will essentially free individuals from restricted conceptions of culture, concluding that '[t]he perception of people as products of their culture, and culture as the all-encompassing explanation of what people do, is worryingly prevalent as a way of understanding people from minority or non-western cultures' and it behaves as an impetus for formulating the distinction between 'us' and 'them' (Phillips 2007: 31). Multiculturalism calls up these stereotypes, bringing forth a way of imagining different cultures as a whole.

According to Phillips, multiculturalism, a principle that is intended to accommodate cultural diversity, has been criticized for pigeonholing minority ethnic and cultural groups. As a consequence, their differences are exaggerated, making it difficult for these groups to cross cultural borders and redefine themselves as they should be free to do; essentially placing them into a 'cultural straitjacket' (Phillips 2007: 14). If culture were to be considered a fluid entity, something that does not rest upon categorization and essentialism, then there would be no need for multicultural policy altogether. Culture, a series of traditions, discourses and assumptions would have no role in impinging particular groups into categories. People would no longer criticize individuals to conform or retract from cultural tendencies and traditions (Phillips 2007: 14). In a way that is not too dissimilar from Kymlicka's suggestions, Phillips argues that so long as culture is understood as fluid and malleable, liberated from restrictions, then multiculturalism as political thought and in practice may thrive. She does question, nevertheless, Kymlicka's understanding of the accommodation and promotion of cultures as a way of increasing autonomy, again returning to the foundations of her argument maintaining that culture ultimately constrains groups.

The questioning of Kymlicka's multiculturalism as nurturing difference is equally criticized by the political theorist Chandran Kukathas. His book *The Liberal Archipelago: A Theory of Diversity and Freedom* (2003) attempts to answer how a liberal society, by his definition, can exist freely in peace without conflict. His theory of minority rights suggests that a free society should not be constituted by the majority giving the minorities group rights, but a society in which hierarchies are eliminated to form an 'archipelago of overlapping and competing jurisdictions' (Kukathas 2003: 75), the community accepting the 'free association' between differing members that honour this societal arrangement. The regulatory role of the state has been explored in depth within multiculturalism and has defined different currents within it. Though both stemming from liberal political positions, Kukathas sees Kymlicka as his ultimate opposition; totally countering Kymlicka's insistence on cultural membership and social unity.

Crowder distinguishes the two theorists' approaches to their liberal theory of multiculturalism as Kymlicka promoting autonomy, and Kukathas championing toleration; both fundamental views on liberalism, but both conflicting (Crowder 2013: 55). If for Kymlicka, both individual liberty and capability of decision are prioritized above a limited state, for Kukathas a limited state would facilitate the first two. Overall, Kukathas is critical of Kymlicka's theory of 'group differentiated rights'. Legitimating the power of the nation-state by providing smaller groups with special recognition only reinforces cultural differences. Kukathas sees Kymlicka's group rights as unnecessarily interfering and irrelevant for the accommodation of cultural minorities. Kukathas defends *laissez-faire*, suggesting that cultures, whether minority or majority, should be left alone. Kukathas suggests making these advancements in a true free society based on freedom of association, which will culminate in a world where communities who have disparate beliefs coexist alongside one another. He promotes equal treatment meaning equal toleration for all groups, regardless of their internal practices. The state would only secure that individuals cannot only associate but also dissociate with any community at their convenience. A good society is a free society, 'because it upholds liberty of conscience. This is a society in which difference and dissent are tolerated' (Kukathas 2003: 76).

To some extent, Kukathas makes agreeable points, cultures and religions have their own discrepancies between them, and to assign special rights to an entire group is to assume that the entire group equally requires this special treatment and are all the same, which goes against the principle of internal diversity. Moreover, Kukathas opposes Kymlicka in his theoretical definition of what a society consists of. Where Kymlicka defines societal cultures as being predominantly territorialized, whilst sharing the same language, but also defining the national minorities of a specific place; Kukathas opposes his strict definition between different groups. He proposes that societies are the source of social mutability; people variably change their habits and customs in the different circumstances, making it difficult to distinguish the minorities, since they 'are internally diverse and turn out to be political alliances rather than cultural communities' (Kukathas 2003: 84).

# On chopsticks and forks

According to Crowder, 'multiculturalism proper' needs to both recognize and promote minority cultures. Nonetheless, how to defend minorities is also open to discussion. Theories of multiculturalism have debated about the appropriate ways of carrying out this accommodation of difference. Either distilling common traits among different cultural groups or enhancing their particularities are only two extremes through which the wide range of multiculturalist positions are situated. Parekh summarizes this debate in his definition of a multicultural society. He says that '[l]ike any other society, a multicultural society needs a broadly shared culture to sustain it. Since it involves several cultures, the shared culture can only grow out of their interaction and should both respect and nurture their diversity and unite them around a common way of life' (Parekh 2000: 220). The tension between the interaction of different cultures and the formulation of a shared culture is a challenge for multiculturalist thinking. The respect for diversity and the risk for homogeneization are two poles that delimit multiculturalist thought. In this tension, issues debated in previous chapters such as the definition of a national character, its symbolism and its interpretation are at stake.

The different strategies through which design has reflected multiculturalism illustrate this debate. A classic example is the pictograms that Otl Aicher (1922–1991) designed in 1967 for the 1972 Munich Olympic Games (Figure 9.3). His work was characterized by a rational approach to design, typical of the Ulm Institute of Design (*Hochschule für Gestaltung*) that he founded in 1953 along with Inge Scholl (1917–1998) and Max Bill (1908–1994). Aicher's rational approach to visual communication is chiefly concerned with its social dimension

**Figure 9.3** Aicher, Otl, pictograms for the 1972 Olympic Games in Munich. From left to right: boxing, weightlifting, handball and gymnastics.

(Betts 1998). He led the team that developed the graphic programme of the Munich Olympic Games, which aimed to communicate with multilingual and multicultural groups through simple, universally understandable symbols. For this project, local characteristics were considered an obstacle for an efficient communication with an international public. Accordingly, verbal communication was substituted when possible with visual symbols. A thorough study on perception and interpretation was carried out to achieve something close to universal symbols that if not everybody at least a great majority could understand. In this sense, the report published by the German Olympic Committee is revealing when stating that '[in] practice there are no actual barriers because civilization provides a general sort of consensus. Even those who are accustomed to eating with chop sticks [*sic*] at least know what a "knife and fork" means' (NOC Germany 1972: 272).

The Munich Olympics graphic programme made use of pictograms. A pictogram can be described as the reduction of complex figures to an elementary shape. Moreover, the polychromy of the original is reduced to one colour, generally black. Pictograms have been used as trademarks and in any graphic element that needs to be easily perceived by a wide range of people. For example, traffic signs depict objects such as bridges, animals and ruins as pictograms. The use of pictograms intends to create such univocal graphic signs that can easily substitute written language. Therefore, they are extremely suitable for universally-oriented events. Aicher's pictograms to depict each sport category have been most celebrated and were the fourth in a series of attempts to create sport pictograms for the Olympic Games (Dormer 1993: 95). They followed the 1956 Olympic Games in Melbourne, the 1964 Olympic Games in Tokyo and the 1968 Olympic Games in Mexico City.

Similar observations had been considered when designing the pictograms for the 1964 Tokyo Olympic Games by its designer Kamekura Yasaku (1915–1997). As Jilly Traganou has noted, these preoccupations to reach a universal audience recall those by Austrian philosopher and sociologist Otto Neurath (1882–1945), who devised the isotype. He said that, '[a] man coming into a strange country without a knowledge of the language is uncertain where to get his ticket at the station or the harbour, where to put his boxes, how to make use of the telephone in the telephone box, where to go in the post office. But if he sees pictures by the side of the strange words they will put him on the right way' (Neurath quoted in Traganou 2011a: 470). The search of a common denominator of comprehensibility was the goal of these initiatives. Universal values and modes of perception were at the basis of this understanding of multicultural design.

Aicher's pictograms closest precedent was indeed the Tokyo body postures. Yet, while the Olympic Committee in Tokyo limited itself to the simplified abstraction of posture, the Olympic Committee in Munich based its symbols on a geometrical basic structure, a formal syntax, which would give coherence to the whole collection. The individual symbol responded to a common grammar and thus became an element of a definable, unitary system. To achieve this aim, strict compositional rules guided the construction of all the different characters. The square delimited the area of the figures and vertical and horizontal lines dominated the composition. In addition, 45° and 135° diagonals accompanied the verticals and horizontal, creating an underlying grid, which conditioned the disposition of the elements and their relative positions. Moreover, few analogous elements formed the figures: lines with round ends, rectangles and points, which codified arms and legs, torsos and heads. A thin, simplified line depicted significant sports equipment – such as the ball or the weights – which accompanied the characters in a few cases (NOC Germany 1972: 272).

In this strict compositional framework, the main challenge was to combine great expressiveness with a simple construction. Take for example the boxer, which despite its strict graphic grammar at first sight it offers a very natural stance. The boxer's position is particularly recognizable, in its bearing of legs and arms that seek to defend the body and attack the opponent simultaneously. Particularly expressive is the head, which seeks protection behind the arms. Only with a slight displacement of the head from the vertical – not exactly on the shoulders but 'ahead' of them – the figure achieves dynamism and expressiveness. Having a close look at its two legs, we observe that two segments compose the leg forwards, i.e. a vertical line from the foot to the knee and a 45° line from the knee upwards. This last fragment is parallel to the boxer's left arm (shoulder to elbow). Still in its left arm, its left forearm is parallel to its back leg (fragment from foot to knee). This economy of elements and directions makes an easy-to-perceive shape, which – in spite of its abstraction of the human body – displays easily recognizable figures. Therefore, these strict compositional rules make for great dynamism, which is especially convenient when, as in this case, the shapes represent sports.

These symbols stressed the common features of different cultures beyond their differences. This posture would be, for example, applauded by Modood, since he defends multiculturalism as highlighting commonalities between majority and minority cultures. His goal is not only to defend differences but also to foster common traits. Hence, social mixing and interaction would be facilitated and minority segregation avoided (Modood 2013[2007]: 59). He argues that difference has to be related 'to things we have in common' and that is citizenship (Modood 2013[2007]: 135). His position concurs with Phillips to a certain extent, but it actually proclaims completely the opposite. In Modood's opinion the strengthening of a national identity will make a success of the multicultural project. This evidently implies the redefinition of a national identity not based in strong nationalisms but in its multiculturalist character (Modood 2013[2007]: 140). Admittedly, Modood's multiculturalism urges nationalism to move from primordialism in the direction of Doreen Massey's 'sense of place', by accepting that national identity is a changing phenomenon, not restricted to atavist essences. Likewise, the strengthening of commonalities as represented in Aicher's pictograms promotes interaction among cultural groups through cultural artefacts not rooted in any tradition but conceived as *tabula rasa*.

The question is, are these commonalities legitimate or just depict an apparent neutrality? In other words, are Aicher's pictograms actually reflecting universalism proper or on the contrary a hegemonic, Western vision of it? In this sense, the quote of the above-mentioned report about the widespread familiarity of 'knife and fork' is significant. The consensus sought by the pictograms does not rethink universalism at the margins of any culture. On the contrary, it seeks consensus by acknowledging that there is a dominant culture familiar to many. Likewise, Kymlicka questions if the neutral state actually exists, a state that does not privilege any national group above any other. This idea of the 'civic state' is according to him rather fictional. He does not believe that states do not privilege any culture and define citizenship according to principles of democracy and justice. On the contrary, states are 'ethnic states' based on values of a specific culture (Kymlicka 2001: 24). Similarly, the political scientist Iris Marion Young proclaims that when there are privileged and oppressed groups, the standpoint of the privileged is constructed as neutral and standard (Young 1990: 116). Thus, the doubt is if the common traits are indeed common and represent the different groups or are falsely neutral and disguise discrimination.

The debate can complicate even more if we consider that the praise for commonality supresses on the other hand the expression of particularities. Therefore, this conception clashes with the claim for recognition made by the philosopher Charles Taylor. He claims that 'all should enjoy the presumption that their traditional culture has value' (Taylor 1994[1992]: 68). He draws from George Herbert Mead's concept of the 'significant others' to argue that our identity is formed dialogically through the valuation that others have of ourselves (Taylor 1994[1992]: 32). This happens as much in the private sphere as in the public sphere. In the latter case, groups are constructed and self perceived through their recognition in society. Accordingly, denying the existence of a group is a form of oppression, too.

An alternative for Aicher's universal language can be found in the 'chork', a hybrid piece of cutlery between chopstick and fork (www.thechork.com) (Figure 9.4). This utensil gives the user the choice to eat sushi using the tool as a Western-style fork, or alternatively break the fork into two, enabling the user to eat sushi in the traditional 'oriental' style as a sushi stick. The sticks have the malleability to accommodate both traditional eating practices which is neither obstructive nor exclusive of one of the two habitual practices. This kind of product negotiates the terms between two different cultures, not through the search for a common denominator but through fusion. Though eating sushi immediately entails the consumer into an Eastern cultural habit, the tradition can prove difficult for users

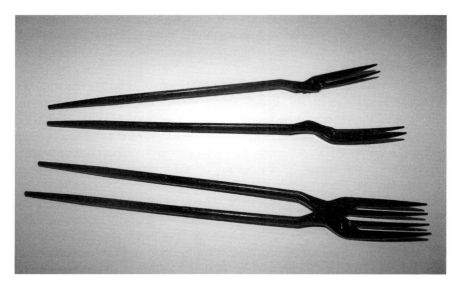

**Figure 9.4** The 'chork', produced in Food Grade Hi Impact Polystyrene by the Brown Innovation Group, Incorporated (B.I.G. Inc) founded in March 2008 and located in Salt Lake City, Utah (USA). https://www.thechork.com/

unfamiliar with using sushi sticks. One possible interpretation is that the 'chork' has recognized this dilemma and come up with a piece of cutlery that is mutually respectful with both Eastern and Western traditional eating habits.

Hybrid designs like the 'chork' might be seen as a product of recent globalization, but one can find many other examples in earlier periods. An example is *Delftware* porcelain, which today is perceived as being quintessentially, and traditionally, Dutch. When visiting souvenir shops in the Netherlands, all kinds of objects are decorated as Delftware, recreating a national imaginary in white and blue. Yet it actually has origins in the Far East, first popularized in the sixteenth century when traders of the Dutch East India Company returned to the Netherlands with Chinese porcelain formerly unbeknown to the Dutch. Its popularity led potters and painters to deploy the same techniques so as not to lose a place in the trade altogether. Alan Caiger-Smith notes in *Tin-Glaze Pottery in Europe and the Islamic World* that it took the Dutch years of imitation to perfect their rendition of porcelain and its glazed finish. The demand for Chinese porcelain was so great that the Dutch began to derive border patterns from Wan-Li originals, making pieces taken directly from the Chinese conventions, gradually 'assimilating Chinese design ideas' (Caiger-Smith 1973: 129). This hybridization or cross-fertilization as Caiger-Smith coined it, of Eastern tradition and Western forms exemplifies a unity of cultural and national motifs (Caiger-Smith 1973: 127). Potters and painters attempted to imitate the Oriental style, the Chinese and Japanese motifs upon white porcelain, appropriating the style and technique to depict traditional, local Dutch scenes; windmills, landscapes and seascapes of fishing boats and more elaborate ports, large ships at sea, all representations of a colonizing, successful nation.

This example makes us think of Parekh's comment on Chinese cuisine. Once imported from the East to the West as exotic, it has evolved to influence Western cuisine lending methods of cooking, ingredients and transforming and being transformed by the other (Parekh 2000: 220–1). He considers this the most legitimate way towards the creation of a multicultural identity. It is not based on the common denominator of the existing cultures, like Aicher's pictograms, but on a new culture resulting in the interaction of the different cultures. In Parekh's *Rethinking Multiculturalism* he considers that cultures, beside totally primitive ones, are internally and externally plural in that they are shaped by other cultures surrounding them. He is against the idea that cultures are a self-contained whole, echoing a familiar judgement made by Anne Phillips, that of the 'us' and 'them' discourse, which only alienates and distinguishes different cultures more so. He asks therefore that we rethink the modern state, to explore new kinds of political structures which may be better suited to contemporary multicultural societies (Parekh 2000: 12). Accordingly, Parekh does not identify himself with any political doctrine or ideology, arguing that they are all culturally embedded (Parekh 2000: 338). To be truly accommodating of multicultural societies, political doctrines should be reassessed (i.e liberal, conservative, nationalist) as each of these have a specific vision which in some way neglects a particular culture, or some culture does not accept it (Parekh 2000: 340). He disagrees with the liberal endorsement of personal autonomy by arguing that it is wholly ethnocentric to consider autonomy as a preferable, culturally developed and advanced position to be in. Some cultures have traditions that truly will never value a liberal, self-determining life, and will always value dictation and structure. Human beings are different and simply cannot be culturally homogeneous. Parekh's unique view of multiculturalism rejects the thought that it is mainly concerned with cultural minorities, and sees multiculturalism as more about the intricate relationships between different cultural communities (Parekh 2000: 13).

All questions over multicultural societies are based around culture, and for a multicultural society to be stable, Parekh argues that a 'common culture' (Parekh 2000: 219) needs be shared amongst citizens, that is accessible beyond the limits of religious or ethnic beliefs, one that is based upon a way of life, music, arts, literature and so on. Parekh believes this is integral for a multicultural community to thrive. As much as the government should encourage this, and ensure these are being pursued with equality in mind, this also should be happening organically, and genuinely (Parekh 2000: 222). Therefore, Parekh suggests to rethink the way that the political structure of our state (this being a Western state) is made up, so rather than abiding by the laws of one ruling sovereignty, there be a number of authorities who reach conclusions through compromise and negotiation (Parekh 2000: 194). In this way, Parekh is similar to Kukathas in his wish for a 'liberal archipelago', which essentially is comprised of a similar structure. However, unlike Kukathas, he posits that the political structure of a multicultural society must *not* ignore the demands of diversity, acknowledging differences.

One last question is, under which circumstances are these hybrids respectful with the cultures they represent? One inalienable condition is that these cultures coexist in equality. For this to happen, a proper climate needs to be created and for this the state needs to play a major role. A policy of hands-off, underestimating the important regulatory role of the state, is what Kymlicka calls the 'benign neglect'. This would leave vulnerable groups alone in their circumstances of disadvantage. Minority cultural groups cannot compete in equal conditions with dominant cultures. Members of dominant cultures are represented and recognized in the public sphere. Minorities conversely need the state to guarantee their cultural rights (Kymlicka 1989: 189). He argues that Kukathas' solution of granting citizens the right to exit their cultural groups represents this 'benign neglect'. Coercion can condition the free will of leaving a group (Kymlicka 1995a: 168–9). His conclusion is that a *laissez faire* attitude will not facilitate equality *per se*.

# Immigrant design

But how has design history dealt with difference? What has been the place allocated to national minorities in design historiography? In general, we see that immigrant designers with successful trajectories have been included in national histories of design. For example, Cuban-born Clara Porset (1895–1981) has been considered as a Mexican designer and Indonesian-born Dutch/Swiss Hans Gugelot (1920–1965) has been considered a German designer (Salinas 2006, Wichmann 1987).

The inclusion of aboriginal design has been acknowledged in Pat Kirkham and Susan Weber's book (2013), where the chapters on the Americas include sections on Indigenous America North and South. Inuits, Native Americans or Pueblo cultures are thereby represented, offering an account that complements the dominant, colonizing cultures. These objects, traditionally studied within anthropology, come to relativize the difference between the crafts and decorative arts and between the crafts and industrial design. The conception of design goes beyond more or less industrialized production to focus on the categorization of the objects as such. Thereby, indigenous design gets its own recognition not only subsumed to its impact on colonial design, but as developing its own discourse.

Regarding racial minorities, Victor Margolin has revised the exclusion of African-American designers from the surveys on graphic design in Chicago. He notes that this history has been dominated by 'middle-class white men and a few middle-class white women' (Margolin 2001: 11). After offering evidence of an important involvement of African-Americans in Chicago graphic arts, he wonders why their contribution has not received adequate recognition. He points out that the history of Chicago has been bifurcated in accounts dealing with either white or black accounts, but not both together. Therefore, many designers working for journals distributed among the black population all throughout the United States have not entered narratives of the white-dominated graphic world. A second reason is the lack of opportunities that African-American designers had in the 1940s and even in the 1960s, which made them less visible. Despite having studied in well-known schools, in their jobs only white designers got in touch with the white clients. Margolin claims that black struggle and accomplishment are elements of the history of graphic design in Chicago, but probably will not be reflected in a history of design purely recording aesthetic quality. Conversely, a social history of design would need to include these narratives of minorities, with as a result a more realistic historical context (Margolin 2001: 15).

The role of émigrés has been little theorized but a special issue in the *Journal of Design History* edited by Henning Engelke and Tobias Hochscherf has explored the phenomenon. Mostly based on migrations caused by the rise of Nazism in Germany and Austria, the authors claim that their discussion is not limited to mid-twentieth-century European émigrés (Engelke and Hochscherf 2015: 2). They see an evolution in the study of émigrés from an early interest in their biography to their interest in elucidating the constructedness of culture and national identity (Engelke and Hochscherf 2015: 5). One can argue that the incorporation or not of émigrés delivers evidence about the limits of national histories of design as a format. Not only about their incorporation but how exactly it has been justified. Possible justifications mentioned in this book have enumerated training and residence in one country. These manoeuvres to include designers in adoptive countries evidence both the flexibility and the rigidness of methodological nationalism. It is flexible in as much as its limits can be stretched to embrace foreign designers in virtue of their contribution of national design or because they share a common approach to design. Its malleability also evidences its rigidness as a method. If its boundaries need to be often justified and rethought, then there must be something artificial in its formulation.

The above-mentioned examples reflect how the elasticity of methodological nationalism has only been implemented to authorship, which shows how much national histories of design are related to the biographical approach. Designers have been classified as either ethnic nationals or émigrés. In as much as they have contributed to define national design, then the definition of the national has been relativized. The challenge of national histories of design is superseding the biographical approach to focus on design artefacts straightforwardly. If designers can either be or become nationals, why not granting this possibility to objects, too? Cannot objects be nationals – as creations of national designers or produced by national manufacturers – or become national – as adopted in a given national context? Then, national design would not only be defined by native design but also by immigrant design. As with humans, we can talk about citizenship or practical nationality of designed objects (Hage 1998). Design can shape *de facto* a national reality but not be recognized as such in this task. Reconsidering the limits of national histories of design can contribute to this recognition. If design history is departing from a designer-bounded history, then its formats will need to adapt in this direction.

Possible objections towards a renovated approach to national histories of design along these lines are manifold. First, a vast amount of objects will come into consideration as national. This is indeed a fact but only a problem if we consider the existing national histories of design as comprehensive, something that revisionist approaches refute by constantly evidencing lacunae of previous historiography. In this sense, their shortcomings in representing national reality are nothing new. Opening up the spectrum towards immigrant design would contribute to point out the limited range of national histories of design. Second, national design icons will need to compete with foreign creations. Publications and exhibitions on national design would need to be rethought, not to recreate the glory and character of a nation, as Smith proclaimed, but to reflect its reality properly. One of the possible consequences will be the realization that the impact of objects designed and produced locally has probably been less salient than one can expect. Thirdly, it will collapse with previous surveys based on national designers instead of national design. This will be a problem only if forthcoming national histories of design are expected to be continuistic. On the contrary, immigrant design opens up possibilities for revisionistic accounts. Fourthly, national histories of design will lose national specificity, since the same objects will be present in different accounts. As long as the consideration of national cultures as isolated from each other is fictive, the combination of native and immigrant design will be positively critical with these fictive visions of the nation. Moreover, existing national histories are already little nationally distinctive, since they tend to be based on very similar style periodization across countries. Accordingly, the lack of specificity is already a fact.

The advantages of including immigrant design are equally manifold. First, they would offer a more accurate vision of national design, regardless of the nationality of the designer or producer. The selection of national design will be based on artefacts and not on the humans involved. The nationalization or not of creators and producers will not be an obstacle to acknowledge the relevance of an object in a specific national context. Second, it would show transnational influences more evidently. The current definition of native objects shows a very partial vision of the nation. For example, the use of so-called foreign artefacts might have inspired national objects. Actual separations of what is foreign and what is national obscure these connections. In other words, the inter-national is not the only valid framework to discern transnational traffic of influences. The national contains transnational characteristics, too. Thirdly, the selection will be more consumer-oriented than designer-oriented, what offers a more appropriate framework for the definition of the national. If consumers fulfil active roles in defining the national, then it is acceptable that they will condition the framework to work on. A focus on consumption fits in better with a proper conceptualization of the national than a focus on production, as we have seen in this Part Three. Fourthly, essentialist definitions of national design will be contested more efficiently. National design will not be based on any component such as the descent or character of the presumed designer/consumer. Affirming that there is something of a national character in national design will be easily rebuttable.

National histories of design are representations of the national and explicitly or implicitly sustain a definition of the nation. To construct a more or less essentialist vision is a choice that depends on the theoretical framework that design historians select. Recognizing immigrant design as part of national design will open possibilities to see the multicultural as an ongoing condition of national design, and not one that has been introduced by globalization. The concept of the vernacular as the pristine loses ground to be conversely redefined through the multicultural. Consequently, a more realistic vision of national material culture results from this change of perspective. Including immigrant design opens up possibilities for defining nations as hybrid products of transnational influences. Exclusionary definitions of the nation then become unsubstantiated.

# Diaspora or immigration

Foreign products contribute to create a national landscape; this seems evident. As discussed in this book and depending on the theoretical framework selected, these objects can be considered as 'national design'. The next step would then be to grant recognition to this reality and to rethink national histories of design. Partly, this has been done by Daniel Miller in his account of Coca-Cola in Trinidad (Miller 1998). At first sight a foreign product, the emergence of situated meanings reflects national dynamics that paradoxically escape current conceptualizations of national design. Positioning Coca-Cola as an American product would not incorporate its Trinidadian narrative. An account of Trinidadian design would not consider foreign products such as Coca-Cola.

The main difference between immigrant design and diaspora design is the implicit field in to which it is related. Diaspora refers to the expansion of population beyond its home country. Becoming diasporic is only possible through settling in a foreign country but prioritizes dynamics related to the home country; the connection with the host country is only relative. On the contrary, immigrant design would change focus and consider the settled element precisely in relation to the host country. For example, a diaspora point of view would conceptualize Coca-Cola as an American beverage in Trinidad. Immigrant design would conversely conceptualize Coca-Cola as a Trinidadian beverage from the United States. Worth noticing is that diaspora conveys a connotation of minority ethnic groups and in this case also their designed material culture. Talking of immigrant is technically more straightforward – albeit not free of connotations – indicating the assimilation of a foreign element by a host country. The term immigrant is therefore most appropriated when considering the impact of foreign design in the host country, since it includes imported products used in a given country at large.

Following this rationale, I have mapped with my students the design culture of Amsterdam South East – a multicultural neighbourhood that today is home to some 100,000 people of more than 150 nationalities. Through this case, the dynamics of national design was studied through this neighbourhood. Students were asked to select one artefact from that environment and research how that artefact relates to canonized Dutch design. Chosen artefacts have included boxing gloves, Ghanaian dresses, garden gnomes, food crates, fences, skating parks, handmade music drums, the 'I love Surinam' t-shirt and bird cages, among others. Students are asked to conduct a thorough research of these objects in terms of production, mediation and consumption. This entails combining literature research, archival and ethnographic research methods. In the final essay, all of these aspects come together as students present their alternative versions by positioning them in relation to the Dutch Design canon and considering how their case contests or complements canonical history.

The example of the 'I love SU' t-shirt – an ideogram of 'I love Surinam', based on Milton Glasser's 'I love NY' logo from 1977 – refers to the country of Suriname instead of the North American city. Since its official introduction in 2010 by the clothing store Dresscode, this t-shirt has promoted patriotism among the Surinamese youth. Its connection to national pride was stressed by the date of its launch on 25 November, the day commemorating Surinamese Independence from the Netherlands. The communication of the values attached to this t-shirt has been supported by a wide-reach campaign, involving Surinamese celebrities, and promoting certain values such as working towards the development of the nation's economy, keeping your country clean or helping all those in need including the poor, the sick and the disabled.

The use of the t-shirt in the Netherlands was mostly confined to Surinamese immigrants but not exclusively. This case explored a foreign product, mostly used by foreign users and making explicit reference to a foreign nationality. Arguably, this could be a reason to consider this garment as non-Dutch. Nevertheless, as nearly all Surinamese in the Netherlands possess the Dutch nationality (98 per cent) and are therefore Dutch citizens, their material culture should also be considered as Dutch material culture. Moreover, the use of the 'I love SU' t-shirt in the Netherlands presented some particularities, starting with the fact that a t-shirt with short sleeves became in Netherlands a seasonal garment because of the climate; meanwhile in Suriname the same t-shirt could be used the whole year round. Moreover, Dutch users were largely unaware of the campaign attached to the t-shirt, so omnipresent in Suriname, and on the contrary wore this garment for different reasons. Most respondents claimed national pride or patriotism (58 per cent), fondness of the design (38 per cent), souvenir (13 per cent) and collecting purposes (4 per cent). Reading these results in national terms shows how the display of other nationalities makes part of the Dutch material landscape. Considering this object as Dutch reflects a society that is plural, in which an ethnic Dutch identity is both complemented and contested by other identities. It adds the dimension of the souvenir and the collectible to a garment that is for the rest ubiquitous and inconspicuous in Suriname. In sum, it opens up new interpretations for an object that are not only limited to the expansion of the Surinamese identity but to the articulation of the Dutch identity through designed material culture.

In conclusion, these methods allow to re-examine and to call into question national histories by positioning them in larger transnational contexts. Doing so does not so much entail exposing existing national histories of design as unreal, but rather both engaging with them and moving beyond. Along these lines, Grever and Stuurman state that '[t]he implication of these new developments in historical research and writing is not that nations are not important or deserve no place in the writing of history' (Stuurman & Grever 2007: 6). They add that '[t]he formation of nations, as we now see it, cannot be understood apart from the global networks and imperial connections in which they evolved' (Stuurman & Grever 2007: 7). Consequently, through this approach the 'national' is composed not only by the 'vernacular' and the 'local' but also by concepts that might seem to be in stark opposition, such as the 'peripheral', the 'cosmopolitan' and the 'international'.

# Conclusion

There are two major outcomes springing from the last three chapters. The first one concerns the relevance of a bottom-up approach when dealing with nationalism, nationhood and a sense of belonging to a community. When people and their experiences are involved a state-driven nationalism is not sufficient. Citizens are able to create a national discourse through design in multifarious ways; states are not the only artifices of a national discourse. If we consider nationalism as a pervasive logic – or as a matrix, as Edensor puts it – then the role of the citizenry needs to be acknowledged. The second point, which might sound at first sight slightly contradictory with the first, concerns the importance of not excluding completely, or *a priori,* top-down approaches. Although the importance of an analysis from below is indisputable, excluding analysis from above will again miss a substantial element of the mechanism. It might signify to refuse the existence of dominance dynamics and to invalidate relations of power. The role of the state is still key to give validity and recognition to initiatives stemming from the civic society. This last chapter has shown how the degree of national familiarity of artefacts is claimed and contested by the citizenry, yet state recognition contributes to its consolidation. The dynamics of de/sedimentation illustrate how these processes take shape.

Another aspect is the dichotomy between the creation and the reception of national messages. We can reconstruct how a message on the nation has been created – what delivers details on how a given nation is intended to be experienced or how a product gets related to a nation. As such, this is an important exercise, since it sheds light on mechanisms of nation building. Another aspect is how these messages are interpreted and consumed. Design might be intended to communicate the nation in a specific way, but its interpretation does not need to coincide with its intended meaning. In this vein, the philosopher Michel de Certeau said that use 'must thus be analyzed in itself', making reference precisely to the open interpretation of cultural products (Certeau 1984: 32). There is no lack of modalities and examples on how users have subverted the meaning of objects. From entire obliviousness to radical subversion, consumers contribute to the creation of national meaning.

The role of the citizenry is definitely key when defining the nation as the familiar or as home. In that sense, the nation is defined in the realm of individual identities. Nevertheless, the tension between individual and collective identities when defining what is national design corresponds to the tension between the circulation of objects in everyday life and their recognition as belonging to the nation. The permeability between civic society and the state is then at stake. One's own definition of the familiar can differ from other national fellows; nevertheless, the level of normativity or eccentricity of each choice depends of its public recognition. Analysing the intricacies of multiculturalism shows how important recognition is. The reality of a multicultural society is not necessarily acknowledged in the public domain and national histories of design can contribute to this. Elaborating on Modood's definition of 'multiculturalism', the difference can exist, but it is not neccesarily accommodated. National histories of design have focused on the oeuvre of national designers, how elastic this category can be. This book proposes an alternative approach, focusing on the designed visual and material landscape of a nation.

# Conclusion

When thinking of design as related to national identity, its instrumentalization by the state – perhaps more salient in dictatorial regimes – might be one of the first examples that comes to mind. There are however more subtle ways in which design can be related to national identity. This book contributes to the debate about the nation-state as an analytical unit to study design. Far from being uniform, positions around this question remain divided. Traganou has proposed to shift from the orthodox focus of the nation-state to consider both internal diversity and transnational forces within the nation (Traganou 2011b: 166). Her account considers how national architecture is shaped both by the presence of foreign architects and by international networks of production and manufacture. On the other hand, Fallan and Lees-Maffei argue that 'a move to discard national frameworks is premature and unwise' (Fallan & Lees-Maffei 2013: 2) arguing that the national has been a tried-and-tested unit of analysis and that it has had repercussions on the ways design has been produced, mediated and consumed. This book concurs with Traganou that national frameworks need revision and with Fallan and Lees-Maffei that – once revised – the national is still a valuable analytical unit. A proper understanding of national design passes through its reconceptualization. The remaining question is what aspects need revision and what is the use of national histories of design? The studied theoretical platforms shed some light on their advantages and disadvantages.

One of the issues that deserve scrutiny is the difference between how the nation has been conceptualized and how it has been reproduced, performed and experienced. A proper understanding of nationalism is necessary, chiefly because its academic definition differs from its customary use. In academia, nationalism is a widespread ideology that makes a world divided into nations appear as natural. In everyday language, nationalism is conversely related to subnationalisms claiming from a greater autonomy or self-government. Therefore, not only subnationalisms, but also established nations reproduce the logic of nationalism, yet they get other denominations such as 'chauvinism' or 'patriotism'. The reproduction of nationalism through design therefore expands beyond its most strident examples to embrace mundane manifestations that can range from a governmental logo, to a fashion contest inspired in folklore or any association of design with the own nation.

This complexity is made more intricate with the spread of nationalism as a universal ideology. Its ubiquity and inconspicuousness makes that the production and consumption of the nation through design combines conscious and unconscious acts. Therefore, Bourdieu's notion of 'habitus' has been a recurrent reference when defining the mechanisms behind nationalism. Its ubiquity makes nationalism imperceptible. Nevertheless, its presence is reiterated and flagged daily through designed objects: whether a chair or an advert design, either using or embedded within a national rhetoric, is a potential conveyor of nationalist messages. These messages however are not univocal and the perception of the consumer needs a separate analysis.

A second aspect is the survival and relative validity of, at first sight, contradictory theoretical approaches. The three theoretical platforms structuring this book have built successively upon each other, yet they remain valid; shedding light on different aspects of national identity. Primordialism offers an answer of how national identity is dominantly communicated and understood. Conversely, modernism explores how it has been constructed top-down. Finally, nationhood from below reflects on the role of the citizens in its construction and reception. They all reveal useful perspectives in their own ways for the study of design as related to national identity. First, primordialism elucidates why historicism and the vernacular have been privileged means of communicating the nation. Their evocation of a perennial nation dovetails national pretensions of continuity. Second, modernism discusses how design has served the state to create an own identity both through the creation of its symbols and through state patronage. It evidences how design has been a matter of state in multiple ways. Thirdly, debates on nationhood from below reveal the agency of citizens for the creation and interpretation of nation-related symbols.

Ideas of a national character emerging at the end of the eighteenth century have had a continuous influence up to the present. The resonance of Herder's culture-based nationalism is still salient today in, first, how design exhibitions and publications hinge upon the presupposition of a national canon and in, second, the consideration of native design as both a product and a mirror of the national character. Traditional conceptions of the nation might be contested but still underpin definitions of national design. While essentialist positions have ebbed away progressively, there is still some work to make them disappear completely. Moreover, the definition of what is a native designer has been elastically adapted to the demands of design historians, putting this category into discussion. Nevertheless, national designers or manufacturers still define what is national design.

To disentangle this intricacy, identifying the different active participants is pivotal. Parts Two and Three have discussed the interconnection between the state and civic society. Even when the limit between the two is blurry, they respond to different categories. The hegemony of the state cannot be underestimated. On the other hand, its permeability with civic society must be equally acknowledged. Foucault proposes the term 'governmentality' to articulate this complex relationship. The parallel between state, society and materiality reveals the interconnection between the everyday and major historical cycles, as announced by Braudel. As a result, the agency of society and design in the production and reproduction of nationalism appears distinctively defined.

Resulting from these considerations, this book proposes to rethink national histories of design to make them illustrative of sophisticated national dynamics. It proposes to shift the national focus from manufacturers and designers towards the object themselves. National design would then be the objects that configure a national visual and material landscape. The contribution of those design objects to configure this landscape might then be more decisive in deciding their nationality than the nationality of their designers or manufacturers. Therefore, this book introduces the term 'immigrant design' as similar yet different from diaspora design. As with people, the tension between citizenship and practical nationality is applicable to design. Recognizing either a person or an object as national makes the difference between a formal and a practical attribution of belonging. In this, the role of national histories of design is key. Rethinking national design in terms of a national visual and material landscape implies reconsidering its integrative objects. National histories of design both create and reproduce dominant notions of the nation and as such have a responsibility.

The mobility and ubiquity of design makes of it an ideal tool to rethink the relationship within materiality and the nation. Their mobility relates design in sophisticated ways to nations. Their ubiquity confers them a central position when defining a national landscape in visual and material terms. Traganou admits that architecture for example is inescapably localized (Traganou 2011b: 169). Even then, the conception and construction of buildings can be located far away from its building site. This book has focused on mobile design, which allows it to furnish different national visual and material landscapes. Its lack of a physical connection with the soil makes them especially adequate to discuss current conditions of the nation. The ties between design and the nation are then more flexible, subject to processes of increasing mobility similar to those affecting the flux of people between nations.

In his influential chapter 'The Cultural Biography of Things: Commoditization as Process', anthropologist Igor Kopytoff elaborates on the Durkhemian notion that a society orders the world of things on the pattern of structure that prevails in the social world of its people. Kopytoff adds that 'societies constrain both these worlds simultaneously and in the same way, constructing objects as they construct people' (Kopytoff 1986: 90). In this sense, considerations towards immigrant people can be extrapolated to immigrant objects; alongside the tensions surrounding processes of assimilation and national recognition. Recognizing 'immigrant design' as part of national design would then prevent national histories of design from attributing a stereotypical character to nations and second, would extend the concept of nationals from people to objects. Design history has advanced in general towards constructivist approaches and towards relativizing the importance of the biographical approach. Accordingly, considering 'immigrant design' as part of national design is coherent with the advances of design history as a discipline. At the same time, national recognition participates of wider social processes of inclusion and differentiation. When translated to the field of design, these are recognizable in what objects to include in national histories of design.

# Bibliography

ABC (1983) 'La oposición cree que el himno de Madrid puede ser inconstitucional', in *ABC*, 6 October.

Abitare (1985) *Abitare. Olanda, Natura e Cultura del Territorio/Holland, Nature and Culture of the Land* 236, July–August.

Abitare (2002) *Abitare. Speciale Olanda* 417, May.

Abramovicz, Manuel and sixty-four others (1998) 'Gedaan met nationalistische dwaasheid. Intellectuelen en kunstenaars willen niet langer dat België het mikpunt blijft van spot in Europa door wat ze noemen, "de nationalistische obsessies van een minderheid"', *De Standaard*, 6 March.

Abrams, Philip (2006[1988]) 'Notes on the Difficulty of Studying the State', in Aradhana Sharma and Akhil Gupta (eds) *The Antropology of the State. A Reader*, Oxford: Blackwell Publishing.

Al-Hibri, Azizah (1999) 'Is Western Patriarchal Feminism Good For Third World/Minority Women?', in Joshua Cohen, Matthew Howard and Martha C. Nussbaum (eds) *Is Multiculturalism Bad For Women?*, Princeton/Chichester: Princeton University Press.

Aja, Eliseo (1999) *El Estado Autonómico. Federalismo y Hechos Diferenciales*, Madrid: Alianza.

Alonso, Nacho (1981) 'La creación de moda, salida inmediata a la crisis de la Industria Textil', *El País*, 6 February.

Anderson, Benedict (1991[1983]) *Imagined Communities*, London: Verso.

Arendt, Hannah (1973[1951]) *The Origins of Totalitarism*, Orlando: Houghton Mifflin Honcourt.

Arscott, Caroline (2006) 'William Morris: Decoration and Materialism', in Andrew Hemingway (ed.), *Marxism and the History of Art. From William Morris to the New Left*, London: Pluto.

Ashby, Charlotte (2010) 'Nation Building and Design: Finnish Textiles and the Work of the Friends of Finnish Handicrafts', *Journal of Design History* 23(4): 351–65.

Aynsley, Jeremy (1993), *Nationalism and Internationalism. Design in the 20th Century*, London: Victoria and Albert Museum.

Aynsley, Jeremy (2009), *Designing Modern Germany*, London: Reaktion.

Bakker, Wibo (2011) *Droom van helderheid. Huisstijlen, ontwerpbureaus en modernisme in Nederland, 1960–1975*, Rotterdam: 010.

Bakker, Gijs and Evert Rodrigo (1980) *Design from the Netherlands/Design aus den Niederlande* [exhibition catalogue], Amsterdam: Bureau Beeldende Kunst Buitenland [Visual Arts Office for Abroad], Ministerie CRM [Ministry of Culture, Recreation and Social Welfare].

Barnard, Frederick M. (1983) 'National Culture and Political Legitimacy: Herder and Rousseau', *Journal of the History of Ideas* 44(2): 231–53.

Barry, Brian (1997) 'Liberalism & Multiculturalism', *Ethical Perspectives* 4(2): 3–14.

Barry, Brian (2001) *Culture & Equality: An Egalitarian Critique of Multiculturalism,* London: Polity Press.

Bártolo, Carlos (2014) 'The Good Taste of an authoritarian regime: the Good Taste Campaign in Portuguese magazine Panorama', in Priscilla Farias and Paul Atkinson (eds), *Design Frontiers. Territories, Concepts, Technologies*, Mexico: Designio.

Batlle, Mercè and Santi Rifà (1997) 'Apunts sobre la actualització i l'ampliació del Programa d'Identificació Visual (PIV) de la Generalitat de Catalunya', *Llengua i Ús. Revista técnica de normalització lingüística* 8(2), Barcelona: Generalitat de Catalunya. Departament de Cultura.

Bavelaar, Hestia (ed.) (2010) *The Style of the State – The Visual Style of the Dutch Government*, The Hague: Stichting Design.

Bennett, Tony (2001) *Differing Diversities. Transversal Study on the Theme of Cultural Policy and Cultural Diversity*, Strasbourg: Council of Europe. Available at http://www.coe.int/t/dg4/cultureheritage/culture/completed/diversity/EN_Diversity_Bennett.pdf [Accessed November 2013].

Bennett, Tony, and Patrick Joyce (2010) *Material Powers. Cultural Studies, History and the Material Turn*, New York: Routledge.

Betsky, Aaron (2008) *False Flat. Why Dutch Design Is So Good*, London/New York: Phaidon.

Betts, Paul (1998) 'Science, Semiotics and Society: The Ulm Hochschule für Gestaltung in Retrospect', *Design Issues* 14(2): 67–82.

Billig, Michael (1995) *Banal Nationalism*, London: Sage.

Boletín Oficial del Estado (BOE) (1979) 'Ley Orgánica 4/1979, 18 December, Estatuto de Autonomía de Cataluña', in *BOE* 306, 22 December, Preámbulo.

Boletín Oficial del Estado (BOE) (1982) 'Ley Orgánica 4/1982, 10 August, Estatuto de Autonomía para la Región de Murcia', in *BOE* 146, 19 June, Preámbulo.

Bourdieu, Pierre (1977) *Outline of a Theory of Practice*, Cambridge: Cambridge University Press.

Bourdieu, Pierre (2002[1979]), *Distinction. A Social Critique of the Judgement of Taste*, London: Routledge.

Bowe, Nicola Gordon (1991) 'The Irish Arts and Crafts Movement (1886–1925), *Irish Arts Review*, 1990/1991, pp. 172–85.

Bowe, Nicola Gordon (ed.) (1993) *Art and the National Dream: The Search for Vernacular Expression in Turn-of-the-Century Design*, Dublin: Irish Academic Press.

Bowman, Glenn (1994) '"A Country of Words": Conceiving the Palestinian Nation from the Position of Exile', in Ernesto Laclau (ed.), *The Making of Political Identities*, London: Verso.

Branzi, Andrea (ed.) (1991) *Neues europäisches Design: Barcelona, Paris, Mailand, Budapest, London, Berlin, Wien, Neapel, Köln-Düsseldorf* [New European Design. Barcelona, Paris, Milan, Budapest, London, Berlin, Naples, Cologne-Dusseldorf], Berlin: Ernst.

Braudel, Fernand (1981 [1967]) *Civilization and Capitalism 15th–18th Century*. Volume I. *The Structures of Everyday Life,* London: Collins.

Braudel, Fernand (1982 [1979]) *Civilization and Capitalism 15th–18th Century*. Volume II. *The Wheels of Commerce*, London: Collins.

Braudel, Fernand (1984 [1979]) *Civilization and Capitalism 15th–18th Century*. Volume III. *The Perspective of the World*, London: Collins.

Braudel, Fernand (1996 [1949]) *The Mediterranean in the Age of Philip II,* Berkeley: University of California Press.

Breward, Christopher and Ghislaine Wood (2012) *British Design from 1948: Innovation in the Modern Age* [exhibition catalogue] London: V&A Publications.

Brubaker, Rogers (1996) *Nationalism Reframed: Nationhood and the National Question in the New Europe*, Cambridge: Cambridge University Press.

Brubaker, Rogers (2002) 'Ethnicity without Groups', *Archives Européenes de Sociologie*, XLIII(2): 163–89.

Bruinsma, Max (1996) 'Beheerste avant-garde. De invloed van Studio Dumbar', *Items* 2(15), March.

Buckley, Cheryl (2007), *Designing Modern Britain*, London: Reaktion.

Buitrago Trujillo, Juan Camilo (2012) *Creatividad Social. La profesionalización del diseño industrial en Colombia*, Cali: Universidad del Valle.

Burchell, Graham, Colin Gordon, and Peter Miller (1991) *The Foucault Effect. Studies in Governmentality*, Chicago: University of Chicago Press.

Caiger-Smith, Alan (1973) *Tin-Glaze Pottery in Europe and the Islamic World: The Tradition of 1000 Years in Maiolica, Faience and Delftware,* London: Faber & Faber.

Camille, Michael (1996) 'Prophets, Canons, and Promising Monsters', *The Art Bulletin* 78(2): 198–201.

Castiglione, Baldassare (1903[1528]) *The Book of the Courtier*, New York: Charles Scribner's Sons.

Castillo, Greg (2010) *Cold War on the Home Front: The Soft Power of Midcentury Design*, Minneapolis: University of Minnesota Press.

Certeau, Michel de (1984) *The Practice of Everyday Life*, Berkeley/Los Angeles: University of California Press.

Chernilo, Daniel (2007) *A Social Theory of the Nation State. The Political Forms of Modernity Beyond Methodological Nationalism*, London/New York: Routledge.

Choi, Jungwon (2014) 'K-Design: the New Design Vision for the New Korean Government', in Helena Barbosa and Anna Calvera (eds), *Tradition, Transition, Trajectories: Major or Minor Influences? Proceedings*, Aveiro: University of Aveiro.

Cohen, Joshua, Matthew Howard and Martha C. Nussbaum (eds) (1999) *Is Multiculturalism Bad for Women?,* New Jersey: Princeton University Press.

Conseil de la Région de Bruxelles-Capitale (1989a) *Session ordinaire 1989–1990. Proposition d'ordonnance relative aux symbols de la Région de Bruxelles-Capitale (A 11-1–89–90)*, Brussels, Conseil de la Région de Bruxelles-Capitale, 18 October.

Conseil de la Région de Bruxelles-Capitale (1989b) *Séance plénière du vendredi 20 octobre 1989. Séance de l'aprés-midi. Sommaire*, no 5, Brussels, Conseil de la Région de Bruxelles-Capitale, 20 October.

Conseil de la Région de Bruxelles-Capitale (1990a) *Séance plénière du jeudi 28 juin 1990. Sommaire*, no 26, Brussels, Conseil de la Région de Bruxelles-Capitale, 28 June.

Conseil de la Région de Bruxelles-Capitale (1990b) *Session ordinaire 1990–1991. Proposition de resolution relative au symbole de la Région de Bruxelles-Capitale (A-70/1–90–91)*, Brussels, Conseil de la Région de Bruxelles-Capitale, 17 October.

Conseil de la Région de Bruxelles-Capitale (1991a) *Session ordinaire 1990–1991. Proposition d'ordonnance portant fixation de l'emblème et du drapeau de la Région de Bruxelles-Capitale (A-106/1–90–91)*, Brussels, Conseil de la Région de Bruxelles-Capitale, 27 February.

Conseil de la Région de Bruxelles-Capitale (1991b) *Séance plénière du mardi 5 mars 1991. Sommaire*, no 17, Brussels, Conseil de la Région de Bruxelles-Capitale, 5 March.

Conseil de la Région de Bruxelles-Capitale (1992) *Session ordinaire. 6 juin 1992. Questions et Réponses*, Brussels, Conseil de la Région de Bruxelles-Capitale, 6 June.

Craeybeckx, Jan, Alain Meynen and Els Witte (1997) *Politieke geschiedenis van België. Van 1830 tot heden*, Antwerp: Standaard.

Crowder, George (2013) *Theories of Multiculturalism. An Introduction*, Cambridge/ Malden: Polity Press.

Crowley, David (1992) *National Style and Nation-State. Design in Poland from the Vernacular Revival to the International Style*, Manchester/New York: Manchester University Press.

Crowley, David (2001) 'Finding Poland in the Margins: The Case of the Zakopane Style', *Journal of Design History* 14(2): 105–116.

Daly, Steven (1998) '*Belgique c'est chic*. Translation: Belgian Style Rocks', *Rolling Stone*, 17 September.

Dant, Tim (2005) *Materiality and Society*, Maidenhead: Open University Press.

Dean, Mitchell (2010) *Governmentality. Power and Rule in Modern Society*. 2nd ed. London: Sage.

De Rijk, Timo (2010) 'So-called Craft: The Formative Years of Droog Design, 1992–1998', *Journal of Modern Craft* 3(2): 161–78.

Devalle, Verónica (2009) *La travesía de la forma. Emergencia y consolidación del diseño gráfico (1948–1984)*, Buenos Aires/Barcelona/México: Paidós.

De Vijlder, Antoon (2005) interview with the author, 17 October.

Diario Oficial de la Generalitat de Catalunya (DOGC) (1981) 'Decree 97/1981, 2 April, Signo de la Generalitat', *DOGC* 123, 29 April. [Corrected in *DOGC* (1981), 141, 10 July.]

Dormer, Peter (1993) *Design since 1945*, London: Thames and Hudson.

Edensor, Tim (2002) *National Identity, Popular Culture and Everyday Life*, Oxford/New York: Berg.

Edensor, Tim (2004) 'Automobility and National Identity Representation, Geography and Driving Practice', *Theory, Culture & Society* 21(4/5): 101–20.

Eller, Jack David and Reed M. Goughlan (1993) 'The Poverty of Primordialism: The Demystification of Ethnic Attachments', *Ethnic and Racial Studies*, 16(2): 183–201.

El País (1983a) 'El himno de la comunidad autónoma se perfila como objeto de polémica', *El País*, 3 October.

El País (1983b) 'El Grupo Popular considera de dudosa constitucionalidad el himno de Madrid', *El País*, 6 October.

El País (1983c) 'Siete estrellas polémicas', *El País*, 10 October.

El País (1983d) 'Bandera, escudo e himno', *El País*, 19 October, 1983.

El País (1987) 'El Ministerio de Industria crea los Premios Nacionales de la Moda', *El País*, 13 December.

Engelke, Henning and Tobias Hochscherf (2015) 'Between Avant-Garde and Commercialism: Reconsidering Émigrés and Design', *Journal of Design History* 28(1): 1–14.

Eriksen, Thomas Hylland (2007) 'Nationalism and the Internet', *Nations and Nationalism* 13(1): 1–17.

Evrigenis, Ioannis D. and Daniel Pellerin (2004) 'Introduction', in Johann Gottfried Herder (ed.), *Another Philosophy of History and Selected Political Writings*, Indianapolis/ Cambridge: Hackett.

Fallan, Kjetil & Grace Lees-Maffei (2013) 'Introduction', in Grace Lees-Maffei and Kjetil Fallan (eds), *Made in Italy. Rethinking a Century of Italian Design*, New York: Bloomsbury Academic.

Fallan, Kjetil (2012) 'Introduction', in Kjetil Fallan (ed.) *Scandinavian Design. Alternative Histories*, London: Bloomsbury Academic.

Fallan, Kjetil (2010) 'Crafting Scandinavian Design: Craft vs. Industrial Design in the Norwegian Contributions to the "Design in Scandinavia" & the "X Triennale di Milano" exhibitions', in Javier Gimeno-Martínez and Fredie Floré (eds), *Design and Craft: A History of Convergences and Divergences. 7th Conference of the International Committee of Design History and Design Studies (ICDHS) 20–22 September 2010*, Brussels: Koninklijke Vlaamse Academie van België voor Wetenschappen en Kunsten.

Fanon, Frantz and Jean-Paul Sartre (foreword) (1961) *Les damnés de la terre*, Paris: Maspero.

Faubion, James (2001) *Power*. Edited by Paul Rabinow. Vol. 3, *The Essential Works of Foucault 1954–1984*, New York: The New Press.

Fleming, John and Hugh Honour (1977) *The Penguin Dictionary of Decorative Arts*, Harmondsworth: Penguin.

Foster, Robert J. (1991) 'Making National Cultures in the Global Ecumene', *Annual Review of Anthropology* 20: 235–60.

Foster, Robert J. (1995) 'Print Advertisements and Nation Making in Metropolitan Papua New Guinea', in Robert J. Foster (ed.), *Nation Making: Emergent Identities in Postcolonial Melanesia*, Michigan: University of Michigan Press.

Fox, Jon E. and Cynthia Miller-Idriss (2008) 'Everyday Nationhood', *Ethnicities* 8(4): 536–63.

Fry, Tony (1988) *Design History Australia*, Sidney: Hale & Iremonger.

Fuss, Diana (1989) *Essentially Speaking. Feminism, Nature and Difference*. New York/London: Routledge.

Gadamer, Hans-Georg (1960) *Wahrheit und Methode I*, Tübingen: JCB Mohr.

Gellner, Ernest (1983) *Nations and Nationalism*, Oxford: Basil Blackwell.

Generalitat de Catalunya (1997[1985]) *Programa d'Identificació Visual*, Barcelona: Generalitat de Catalunya.

Gieben-Gamal, Emma (2005) 'Diversifying the Design History Curriculum. A Review of Recent Resources', *Journal of Design History* 18(3): 293–8.

Gilbert, Emily (1999) 'Forging a National Currency: Money, State-Making and Nation-Building in Canada', in Emily Gilbert and Eric Helleiner (eds), *Nation-States and Money: The Past, Present and Future of National Currencies*, New York: Routledge.

Gille, Szusza (2012) 'Global Ethnography 2.0. From Methodological Nationalism to Methodological Materialism', in Anna Amelina et al. (eds), *Beyond Methodological Nationalism: Research Methodologies for Cross-border Studies*, London: Routledge.

Gimeno-Martínez, Javier (2010) 'The Signe d'Or Award Scheme from 1956 to 1960: The Economic Reasons for "Good Design"', *Konsthistorisk Tikskrift/Journal of Art History* 79(3): 127–45.

Gimeno-Martínez, Javier (2011) 'Restructuring Plans for the Textile and Clothing Sector in Belgium and Spain', *Fashion Practice* 3(2): 197–224.

Gimeno-Martínez, Javier, Joana Ozorio de Almeida Meroz, and Katarina Serulus (2013) 'Localizing Design/Desiging Location: Creative Cities in the Low Countries', *Dutch Crossing* 37(3): 274–92.

Glancey, John (1985) *National Characteristics in Design* [exhibition catalogue], London: Boilerhouse/Victoria and Albert Museum.

Gobierno de la Comunidad de Madrid (1999[1984]) *Manual de Identidad Corporativa*, Madrid: Comunidad de Madrid.

Gombrich, Ernst (1996[1979]) 'The Primitive and Its Value in Art', in Richard Woodfield (ed.), *The Essential Gombrich*, London: Phaidon.

Goodrum, Alison (2005) *The National Fabric. Fashion, Britishness, Globalization*, Oxford/ New York: Berg.

Goossens, Martine (1996) *Het Vlaams Parlement*, Tielt: Lannoo.

Greenberg, Reesa, Bruce Ferguson and Sandy Nairne (1996) *Thinking About Exhibitions*, London: Routledge.

Greenhalgh, Paul (ed.) (2000) *Art Nouveau 1890–1914* [exhibition catalogue], London: V&A Publications.

Grever, Maria and Kees Ribbens (2004) 'De historische canon onder de loep', *Kleio*, XLV(7): 2–7.

Guffey, Elizabeth E. (2006) *Retro. The Culture of Revival*, London: Reaktion.

Hage, Ghassan (1998) *White nation: Fantasies of White Supremacy in a Multi-cultural Society*, Annadale: Pluto Press.

Hage, Ghassan (2006) 'The Doubts Down Under', *Catalyst: Journal of the British Commission for Racial Equality*, May: 8–10.

Haldrup, Michael, Lasse Koefoed and Kirsten Simonsen (2006) 'Practical Orientalism – Bodies, Everyday Life and the Construction of Otherness', *Geografiska Annaler: Series B, Human Geography* 88(2): 173–84.

Hall, Stuart (1992) 'The Question of Cultural Identity', in Stuart Hall and David Held (eds), *Modernity and its Futures*, Cambridge: Polity Press and Open University.

Hansen, Per (2006) 'Networks, Narratives, and New Markets: The Rise and Decline of Danish Modern Furniture Design, 1930–1970', *Business History Review* 80(3): 449–83.

Herder, Johann Gottfried (1800) *Outlines of a Philosophy of the History of Man*, trans. T.O. Churchill, London: Bergman.

Herder, Johann Gottfried (2004a) *Johann Gottfried von Herder. Philosophical Writings*, trans. and ed. Michael N. Forster, Cambridge: Cambridge University Press.

Herder, Johann Gottfried (2004b) *Another Philosophy of History and Selected Political Writings*, trans. Ioannis D. Evrigenis and Daniel Pellerin, Indianapolis/Cambridge: Hackett.

Herten, Lieve (1993) 'Ann Demeulemeester houdt Belgische eer hoog in Parijs', *De Standaard*, 12 October.

Hilton, Alison (1995) *Russian Folk Art*, Bloomington: Indiana University Press.

Hobsbawm, Eric J. (1991) *Nations and Nationalism since 1780: Programme, Myth, Reality*. Cambridge: Cambridge University Press.

Hobsbawm, Eric and Terence Ranger (eds) (1983) *The Invention of Tradition*, Cambridge: Cambridge University Press.

Hooper, John (1995) *The New Spaniards*, London: Penguin Books.

Huppatz, D.J. (2015) 'Globalizing Design History and Global Design History', *Journal of Design History* 28(2): 182–202.

Hutchinson, John (2006) 'Hot and Banal Nationalism: The Nationalization of "the Masses"', in Gerard Delanty and Kumar Krishan (eds), *The SAGE Handbook of Nations and Nationalism*, London: Sage.

Jasanoff, Sheila (2014) 'Imagined and Invented Worlds: The Three Symmetries of STS', available at https://vimeo.com/100715359 [accessed 17 April 2015].

Jerlei, Triin (2014) 'Socialist Elements in Soviet Design Ideology', in Helena Barbosa and Anna Calvera (eds), *Tradition, Transition, Trajectories: Major or Minor Influences? Proceedings*, Aveiro: University of Aveiro.

Jones, Michelle (2003) 'Design and the Domestic Persuader. Television and the British Broadcasting', *Journal of Design History* 16(4): 307–18.

Jones, Rhys and L. Desforges (2003) 'Localities and the Reproduction of Welsh Nationalism', *Political Geography* 22(3): 271–92.

Jones, Rhys and Peter Merriman (2009) 'Hot, Banal and Everyday Nationalism: Bilingual Road Signs in Wales', *Political Geography* 28: 164–73.

Juliá, Santos and José-Carlos Mainer (2000) *El aprendizaje de la Libertad 1973–1986. La cultura de la Transición*, Madrid: Alianza.

Julier, Guy (1993) *The Thames and Hudson Dictionary of 20th-century Design and Designers*, London: Thames and Hudson.

Kikuchi, Yuko (2004) *Japanese Modernisation and* Mingei *Theory. Cultural Nationalism and Oriental Orientalism*, London/New York: Routledge.

Kikuchi, Yuko and Yunah Lee (2014) 'Transnational Modern Design Histories in East Asia: An Introduction', *Journal of Design History* 27(4): 323–34.

Kirkham, Pat and Susan Weber (eds) (2013) *History of Design. Decorative Arts and Material Culture, 1400–2000*, New York/New Haven: Bard Graduate Center/Yale University Press.

Kristoffersson, Sara (2014) *Design by IKEA. A Cultural History*, New York/London: Bloomsbury Academic.

Kopytoff, Igor (1986) 'The Cultural Biography of Things: Commoditization as Process', in Arjun Appadurai (ed.), *The Social Life of Things. Commodities in Cultural Perspective*, Cambridge: Cambridge University Press.

Kukathas, Chandran (2003) *The Liberal Archipelago: A Theory of Diversity and Freedom,* Oxford: Oxford University Press.

Kymlicka, Will (1989) *Liberalism, Community, and Culture,* Oxford: Oxford University Press.

Kymlicka, Will (1995a) *Multicultural Citizenship,* Oxford: Clarendon Press.

Kymlicka, Will (ed.) (1995b) *The Rights of Minority Cultures,* Oxford: Oxford University Press.

Kymlicka, Will (2001) *Politics in the Vernacular: Nationalism, Multiculturalism and Citizenship,* Oxford: Oxford University Press.

Laclau, Ernesto and Chantal Mouffe (2001[1985]) *Hegemony and Socialist Strategy. Towards a Radical Democratic Politics*, London: Verso.

Lampaert, Herman (2005) interview with the author, 17 October.

Lane, Barbara Miller (2000) *National Romanticism and Modern Architecture in Germany and the Scandinavian Countries*, Cambridge: Cambridge University Press.

Large, Michael (1991) 'The Corporate Identity of the Canadian Government', *Journal of Design History* 4(1): 31–42.

Lash, Scott and John Urry (1994) *Economies of Signs and Space*, London: Sage.

Latour, Bruno (1996[1993]) *Aramis or the Love of Technology,* Cambridge and London: Harvard University Press.

Leblanc, Claire (ed.) (2005), *Art Nouveau & Design. Les arts décoratifs de 1830 à l'Expo 58*, Brussels: Racine.

Leerssen, Joep (2006) *National Thought in Europe. A Cultural History*, Amsterdam: Amsterdam University Press.

Leerssen, Joep (2013) 'Notes Towards a Definition of Romantic Nationalism', *Romantik: Journal for the Study of Romanticisms* 2: 9–35.

Leerssen, Joep (2014) *When Was Romantic Nationalism? The Onset, the Long Tail, the Banal*, NISE: Antwerp. Available at http://nise.eu/wp-content/uploads/2015/01/Nise-Essays-2_web.pdf [accessed 15 March 2015].

Livingstone, Karen (2008) 'Morris to Mingei: the Arts and Crafts Movement in Britain, Europe and Japan', in *Life and Art: Arts and Crafts from Morris to Mingei* [exhibition catalogue], Tokyo: Asahi Shinbunsha.

Livingstone, Karen and Linda Parry (eds) (2005) *International Arts and Crafts* [exhibition catalogue], London: V&A Publications.

Lovejoy, Arthur O. and George Boas (1997[1935]) *Primitivism and Related Ideas in Antiquity. A Documentary History of Primitivism and Related Ideas*, London/Baltimore: Johns Hopkins University Press.

Lynch, Richard (2011) 'Foucault's Theory of Power', in Dianna Taylor (ed.), *Michel Foucault. Key Concepts*, Durham: Acumen.

Mackrell, Alice (1998) 'Dress in *Le Style Troubadour*', *Costume* 32(1): 33–44.

Makovicki, Nicolette (2011) '"Erotic Needlework": Vernacular Designs on the 21st Century Market', in Alison Clarke (ed.), *Design Anthropology. Object Culture in the 21st Century*, Vienna/New York: Springer.

Margolin, Victor (2001) 'Can History Be Corrected. Needed: An Inclusive History for Chicago Graphic Design', *Inform* 13(3): 11–15.

Margolin, Victor (2015) *World History of Design*, London/New York: Bloomsbury Academic.

Marx, Karl (1963[1852]) *The Eighteenth Brumaire of Louis Bonaparte*, New York: International Publishers.

Massey, Doreen (1993) 'Power-geometry and a Progressive Sense of Place', in John Bird, Curtis Barry, Tim Putnam and Lisa Ticker (eds), *Mapping the Futures: Local Cultures, Global Change*, London/New York: Routledge.

Massey, Doreen (1994a) 'A Global Sense of Place', in Doreen Massey, *Space, Place and Gender*, Cambridge: Polity Press.

Massey, Doreen (1994b) 'A Place Called Home', in Doreen Massey, *Space, Place and Gender*, Cambridge: Polity Press.

McClellan, Andrew (1994) *Inventing the Louvre: Art, Politics, and the Origins of the Modern Museum in Eighteenth-Century Paris*, Berkeley/Los Angeles: University of California Press.

McDonald, Gay (2008) 'The "Advance" of American Postwar Design in Europe: MoMA and the Design for Use, USA Exhibition 1951–1953', *Design Issues* 24(2): 15–27.

McDonald, Gay (2010) 'The Modern American Home as Soft Power: Finland, Moma and the "American Home 1953" Exhibition', *Journal of Design History* 23(4): 387–408.

McGovern, Charles (2009) *Sold American: Consumption and Citizenship*. Chapel Hill: University of North Carolina Press.

Memmi, Albert (1957) *Portrait du colonisé; suivi de portrait du colonisateur*, Paris: Buchet.

Middendorp, Jan (2004) *Dutch Type*, Rotterdam: 010.

Miller, Daniel (1998) 'Coca-Cola. A Black Sweet Drink from Trinidad', in Daniel Miller (ed.), *Material Cultures. Why Some Things Matter*, London: University College London.

Miller, Daniel and Sophie Woodward (2012) *Blue Jeans. The Art of the Ordinary,* Berkeley: University of California Press.

Miller, David (1995) *On Nationality*, Oxford: Oxford University Press.

Ministerie van de Vlaamse Gemeenschap (1989) *Embleem en Huisstijl van de Vlaamse Gemeenschap*, Brussels: Ministerie van de Vlaamse Gemeenschap.

Ministerie van de Vlaamse Gemeenschap (2000) *Huisstijl herstijld van A tot Z*, Brussels: Ministerie van de Vlaamse Gemeenschap.

Ministry of Education, Culture and Science (2013) *The Dutch Cultural System*. Available at http://www.government.nl/files/documents-and-publications/leaflets/2013/06/17/the-dutch-cultural-system/exposition-of-the-dutch-cultural-system-def.pdf [accessed 19 March 2015].

Mitchell, Timothy (2006[1999]) 'Society, Economy, and the State Effect', in Aradhana Sharma and Akhil Gupta (eds), *The Anthropology of the State. A Reader*, Oxford: Blackwell Publishing.

Modood, Tariq (2013[2007]) *Multiculturalism*, Cambridge/Malden: Polity Press.

Morris, William (1888) 'The Revival of Handicraft', in Glenn Adamson (ed.) (2010) *The Craft Reader*, Oxford/New York: Berg.

Morris, William (1908[1890]) *News from Nowhere*, London: Longmans.

Narotzky, Viviana (2007) *La Barcelona del diseño*, Barcelona: Ediciones del Belloch.

National Olympic Committee for Germany (NOC Germany) (1972) *Die Spiele. The Official Report of the Organizing Committee for the Games of the 20th Olympiad Munich 1972*, vol. 1. *The Organization*, Munich: Pro Sport München.

Nkrumah, Kwame (1964) *Le Consciencisme: philosophie et idéologie pour la Décolonisation et le Développement, avec un référence particulière à la Révolution Africaine*, Paris: Payot.

Okin, Susan Moller (1999) 'Is Multiculturalism Bad For Women?', in Joshua Cohen, Matthew Howard and Martha C. Nussbaum (eds), *Is Multiculturalism Bad For Women?*, Princeton/Chichester: Princeton University Press.

Olaya, V.G. (1997) '*No nos sentimos madrileños*. El municipio de Garganta lleva 14 años sin izar la bandera regional porque no se identifica con la Comunidad de Madrid', *El País*, 10 April.

Olins, Wally (2002) 'Branding the Nation – the Historical Context', *Journal of Brand Management. Special Issue: Nation Branding* 9(4–5): 241–9.

Oring, Elliott (1994) 'The Arts, Artifacts and Artifices of Identity', *The Journal of American Folklore* 107(424): 211–33.

Özkirimli, Umut (2000) *Theories of Nationalism: A Critical Introduction*, Basingstoke/New York: Palgrave.

Palmer, Catherine (1998) 'From Theory to Practice. Experiencing the Nation in Everyday Life', *Journal of Material Culture* 3(2): 175–99.

Parekh, Bhikhu (1998) 'Equality in a Multicultural Society', *Citizenship Studies* 2(3): 397–411.

Parekh, Bhikhu (2000) *Rethinking Multiculturalism*, London: Palgrave Macmillan.

Patten, Alan (2010) '"The Most Natural State": Herder and Nationalism', *History of Political Thought* 31(4): 657–89.

Paulicelli, Eugenia (2004) *Fashion under Fascism: Beyond the Black Shirt*, Oxford/New York: Berg.

Pelta, Raquel (2010) 'Handicraft during Franco's dictatorship in Spain', in Javier Gimeno-Martínez and Fredie Floré (eds), *Design and Craft: A History of Convergences and Divergences*, Brussels: Koninklijke Vlaamse Academie van België voor Wetenschappen en Kunsten.

Penrose, Jan (1995) 'Essential Constructions? The "Cultural Bases" of Nationalist Movements', *Nations and Nationalism*, 1(3): 391–417.

Penrose, Jan (2002) 'Nations, States and Homelands: Territory and Territoriality in Nationalist Thought', *Nations and Nationalism*, 8(3): 277–97.

Penrose, Jan (2011) 'Designing the Nation. Banknotes, Banal Nationalism and Alternative Conceptions of the State', *Political Geography* 30: 429–40.

Penrose, Jan and Richard C.M. Mole (2008) 'Nation-States and National Identity', in Kevin Cox, Murray Low and Jenny Robinson (eds), *The SAGE Handbook of Political Geography*, London: Sage.

Pevsner, Nikolaus (1956) *The Englishness of English Art*, New York: Frederick A. Praeger.

Phillips, Anne (2007) *Multiculturalism without Culture*, New Jersey: Princeton University Press.

Powell, Charles (2001) *España en Democracia, 1975–2000*, Barcelona: Plaza & Janés.

Prades, Joaquina (1987) 'María Jesús Escribano. Todo "Made in Spain"', *El País*, 6 March.

Prideaux, Jillian (2009) 'Consuming Icons: Nationalism and Advertising in Australia', *Nations and Nationalism*, 15(4): 616–35.

Quito, Anne (2014) 'Branding the World's Newest Country', *Works that Work* 4: 58–62.

Raento, Pauliina and Stanley Brunn (2005) 'Visualizing Finland: Postage Stamps as Political Messengers', *Geografiska Annaler* 87B(2): 145–63.

Raento, Pauliina, Anna Hämäläinen, Hanna Ikonen and Nella Mikkonen (2004) 'Striking Stories: a Political Geography of Euro Coinage', *Political Geography* 23: 929–56.

Raizman, David (2010) *History of Modern Design*, London: Laurence King.

Ramakers, Renny (2002) *Less + More: Droog Design in Context*, Rotterdam: 010.

Ramakers, Renny and Gijs Bakker (eds.) (1998) *Droog Design: Spirit of the Nineties*, Rotterdam: 010.

Rapport, Nigel (2007) '"Je suis peut-être un salaud d'anglais, mais pas un feignant!" Être brancardier dans un hôpital Écossais', *Journal Ethnologie Francaise* 37(2): 255–64.

Reed, Eugene E. (1965) 'Herder, Primitivism and the Age of Poetry', *The Modern Language Review* 60(4): 553–67.

Reilly, Paul (1956) 'The Influence of National Character on Design', *Journal of the Royal Society of Arts*, 104(4989): 919–39.

Reynolds, Helen (1999) 'The Utility Garment: Its Design and Effect on the Mass Market', in Judith Attfield (ed.), *Utility Reassessed: The Role of Ethics in the Practice of Design*, Manchester: Manchester University Press.

Ribbens, Kees (2007) 'A Narrative that Encompasses Our History: Historical Culture and History Teaching', in Maria Grever and Siep Stuurman (eds), *Beyond the Canon. History for the Twenty-First Century*, Basingstoke: Palgrave Macmillan.

Ribeiro, Aileen (1986) *Dress and Morality*, London: Batsford.

Ribeiro, Aileen (1995) *The Art of Dress. Fashion in England and France 1750–1820*, New Haven/London: Yale University Press.

Ribeiro, Aileen (1999) *Ingres in Fashion. Representations of Dress and Appearance in Ingres's Images of Women*, New Haven/London: Yale University Press.

Ricard, André (1985) 'El Diseño mira a Europa', *El País*, 4 October.

Rock, Michael (2004) 'Mad Dutch Disease: The Strange Case of Dutch Design and other Contemporary Contagions', in Aad Krol and Timo De Rijk (eds), *Yearbook Dutch Design 03/04*, Rotterdam: Episode.

Said, Edward W. (1978) *Orientalism*, New York: Pantheon Books.

Salinas Flores, Oscar (2006) *Clara Porset's Design. Creating a Modern Mexico*, Mexico DF: Franz Mayer Museum/UNAM/Turne.

Salmond, Wendy (2000) 'Moscow Modern', in Paul Greenhalgh (ed.), *Art Nouveau 1890–1914*, London: V&A Publications.

Satué, Enric (1997) *El Diseño Gráfico en España. Historia de una Forma Comunicativa Nueva*, Madrid: Alianza.

Schnapp, Jeffrey T. (2001) 'The Romance of Caffeine and Aluminum', *Critical Inquiry* 28(1): 244–69.

Schütze, Martin (1921) 'The Fundamental Ideas in Herder's Thought III', *Modern Philology* 19(2): 113–30.

Schwarz, Angela (2012) 'The Regional and the Global. Folk Culture at World's Fairs and the Reinvention of the Nation', in Timothy Baycroft and David Hopkin (eds), *Folklore and Nationalism in Europe during the Long Nineteenth Century*, Leiden: Brill.

Sepúlveda, Isidro (1996) 'La eclosión nacionalista: regionalismos, nacionalidades y autonomies', in Javier Tusell and Álvaro Soto (eds), *Historia de la Transición 1975–1986,* Madrid: Alianza.

Sharma, Aradhana, and Akhil Gupta (2006) *The Anthropology of the State. A Reader,* Oxford: Blackwell Publishing.

Simon-Thomas, Mienke (2008) *Dutch Design: A History,* London: Reaktion.

Singh, Gurharpal (2005) 'British Multiculturalism and Sikhs', *Sikh Formations: Religion, Culture, Theory* 1(2): 157–73.

Skey, Michael (2009) 'The National in Everyday Life: A Critical Engagement with Michael Billig's Thesis of Banal Nationalism', *The Sociological Review* 57(2): 331–46.

Skey, Michael (2011) *National Belonging and Everyday Life: the Significance of Nationhood in an Uncertain World,* Basingstoke: Palgrave Macmillan.

Smith, Anthony D. (1988[1986]) *The Ethnic Origins of Nations,* Malden/Oxford: Blackwell.

Smith, Anthony D. (1991) *National Identity,* Reno: University of Nevada Press.

Smith, Anthony D. (1993) 'Art and Nationalism in Europe', in J.C.H. Blom, J.Th. Leerssen and P. de Rooy (eds), *De onmacht van het grote: Cultuur in Europa,* Amsterdam: Amsterdam University Press.

Smith, Anthony D. (1995) *Nations and Nationalism in a Global Era,* Cambridge: Polity Press.

Smith, Anthony D. (2001) *Nationalism: Theory, Ideology, History,* Cambridge: Polity Press.

Sparke, Penny (2013) *An Introduction to Design and Culture. 1900 to the Present. Third Edition,* London/New York: Routledge.

Spencer, Vicki (1993) 'Herder and Nationalism: Reclaiming the Principle of Cultural Respect', *Australian Journal of Politics and History* 43(1): 1–13.

Stuurman, Siep and Maria Grever (2007) 'Introduction: Old Canons and New Histories', in Maria Grever and Siep Stuurman (eds), *Beyond the Canon. History for the Twenty-First Century,* Basingstoke: Palgrave Macmillan.

Taylor, Charles (1994[1992]) 'The Politics of Recognition', in Amy Gutmann (ed.), *Multiculturalism. Examining the Politics of Recognition,* Princeton: Princeton University Press.

Taylor, Damon (2010) 'Mountain Climbing in Holland: Writing Dutchness into the Discourse', in Javier Gimeno-Martínez and Fredie Floré (eds), *Design and Craft: A History of Convergences and Divergences,* Brussels: Koninklijke Vlaamse Academie van België voor Wetenschappen en Kunsten.

Taylor, Dianna (2011) *Michel Foucault. Key Concepts,* Durham: Acumen.

Thiesse, Anne-Marie (1999) *La création des identités nationales. Europe XVIIIe–XXe siècle,* Paris: Éditions du Seuil.

Thiesse, Anne-Marie (2000) 'Des fictions créatrices: les identités nationales', *Romantisme* 30(110): 51–62.

Thiesse, Anne-Marie (2007) 'The Formation of National Identities', in Marion Demosssier (ed.), *The European Puzzle. The Political Structuring of National Identities at a Time of Transition,* New York/Oxford: Berghahn.

Thiesse, Anne-Marie (2013) *The Transnational Creation of National Arts and Crafts in 19th-century Europe,* NISE: Antwerp. Available at http://nise.eu/wp-content/uploads/2015/01/Nise-Monographs-1_web.pdf [accessed 13 March 2015].

Thompson, Christopher (2011) 'Modernizing for Trade: Institutionalizing Design Promotion in New Zealand', *Journal of Design History* 24(3): 223–39.

Tortora, Phyllis G. and Keith Eubank (2005) *Survey of Historic Costume. A History of Western Dress,* New York: Fairchild.

Traganou, Jilly (2011a) 'Tokyo's 1964 Olympic Design as a "Realm of [design] Memory"', *Sport in Society: Cultures, Commerce, Media, Politics* 14(4): 466–81.

Traganou, Jilly (2011b) 'From Nation-Bound Histories to Global Narratives of Architecture', in Glenn Adamson, Giorgio Riello and Sarah Teasley (eds), *Global Design History*, New York/London: Routledge.

Tully, James (1995) *Strange Multiplicity: Constitutionalism in an Age of Diversity*, Cambridge: Cambridge University Press.

Unwin, T. and V. Hewitt (2001) 'Banknotes and National Identity in Central and Eastern Europe', *Political Geography*, 20: 1005–28.

Valcke, Johan (2001) 'Het verhaal van de Dienst Vormgeving van het VIZO', *Vlaanderen*, January–February.

Van Ginderachter, Maarten and Marnix Beyen (eds) (2011) *Nationhood from Below. Europe in the Long Nineteenth Century*, Basingstoke: Palgrave Macmillan.

Vlaamse Raad (1989) *Handelingen Nr. 32*, Brussels, Vlaamse Raad, 2 May.

Vlemmings, Marc (2008) 'Het mooiste ontwerp van de (overheid-)wereld', *Items* 2: 28–33.

Votolato, Gregory (1998) *American Design in the Twentieth Century*, Manchester: Manchester University Press.

Vukić, Fedja (2015) *The Other Design History*, Zagreb: Upi2M.

Waithe, Marcus (2006) *William Morris's Utopia of Strangers. Victorian Medievalism and the Ideal of Hospitality*, Cambridge: D.S. Brewer.

Waldron, Jeremy (1995) 'Minority Cultures and Cosmopolitan Alternatives', in Will Kymlicka (ed.), *The Rights of Minority Cultures*, Oxford: Oxford University Press.

Walker, John A. (1989) *Design History and the History of Design*, London: Pluto.

Weber, Max (1946) 'Bureaucracy', in Hans H. Gerth and Charles Wright Mills (eds), *From Max Weber: Essays in Sociology*, New York: Oxford University Press.

Wichmann, Hans (1987) *System-Design, Bahnbrecher: Hans Gugelot 1920–1965* [exhibition catalogues], Basel: Springer.

Wilson, William A. (1973) 'Herder, Folklore and Romantic Nationalism', *The Journal of Popular Culture* 6(4): 819–35.

Winner, Langdon (1986) *The Whale and the Reactor. A Search for Limits in an Age of High Technology*, Chicago: University of Chicago Press.

Witte, Els, Jan Craeybeckx and Alain Meynen (1997) *Politieke Geschiedenis van België*, Antwerp: Standaard.

Woodham, Jonathan M. (1997) *Twentieth-Century Design*, Oxford/New York: Oxford University Press.

Woodham, Jonathan (1999) 'Design and the State: Post-War Horizons and Pre-Millenial Aspirations', in Judith Attfield (ed.), *Utility Reassessed: The Role of Ethics in the Practice of Design*, Manchester: Manchester University Press.

Woodham, Jonathan (2005) 'Local, National and Global. Redrawing the Design Historical Map', *Journal of Design History* 18(3): 257–67.

Woodham, Jonathan (2010) 'Formulating National Design Policies in the United States: Recycling the "Emperor's New Clothes"?', *Design issues* 26(2): 27–46.

Yagou, Artemis (2005) 'Unwanted Innovation. The Athens Design Centre (1961–1963)', *Journal of Design History* 18(3): 269–83.

Yagou, Artemis (2007) 'Metamorphoses of Formalism: National Identity as a Recurrent Theme of Design in Greece', *Journal of Design History* 20(2): 145–59.

Yagou, Artemis (2012) 'Narratives of Heritage and Modernity: National Production and Consumption in Greek Advertising', in: Oliver Kühschelm, Franz X. Eder and Hannes Siegrist (eds), *Konsum und Nation, Zur Geschichte nationalisierender Inszenierungen in der Produktkommunikation*, Bielefeld: Transcript.

Young, Iris Marion (1990) *Justice and the Politics of Difference*, Princeton: Princeton University Press.

Zanin, Éva (2014) *The Politics of Fashion. A Study of the Hungarian Fashion Design Contest Gombold Újra! Between 2011 and 2012*. Available at: https://www.academia.edu/8179748/The_Politics_Of_Fashion._A_Study_Of_The_Hungarian_Fashion_Design_Contest_Gombold_%C3%9Ajra_Between_2011_And_2012 [accessed October 2014].

# Index

Illustrations are denoted by the use of *italics* and major discussion by the use of **bold**.